にょ。nyo

Other titles available from Broccoli Books

Di Gi Charat Theater: Piyoko is Number One! (December 2003)
Watch out Di Gi Charat! The Black Gema Gema Gang, lead by Piyoko, has landed in Akihabara. And their mission is to raise money to save the poor Planet Analogue. Even if that means kidnapping Dejiko for ransom!
Story & Art by Koge-Donbo and others
Suggested Retail Price: $9.99

Di Gi Charat Theater: Dejiko's Adventure (Spring 2004)
Dejiko's done it again. With her Laser Eye Beam, Dejiko destroys the Gamers store! Now it's up to Dejiko, Puchiko and Rabi-en-Rose to find the "secret treasure" that will bring prosperity to Gamers and rebuild the store.
Story & Art by Yuki Kiriga
Suggested Retail Price: $9.99
Volumes 1 - 3 Coming Soon!

Di Gi Charat Theater: Leave it to Piyoko! (Summer 2004)
Follow the daily adventures of the Black Gema Gema Gang, as they continue their road to evil.
Story & Art by Hina.
Suggested Retail Price: $9.99
Volumes 1 - 2 Coming Soon!

Galaxy Angel vol. 1 (Spring 2004)
It's up to five female pilots, each possessing a unique talent, to protect young Prince Shiva and to save the universe!
Story & Art by Kanan
Suggested Retail Price: $9.99

Aquarian Age - Juvenile Orion vol. 1 (January 2004)
In a world of chaos, five guardians unite to protect a girl who holds the key to the future.
Story & Art by Sakurako Gokurakuin
Suggested Retail Price: $9.99

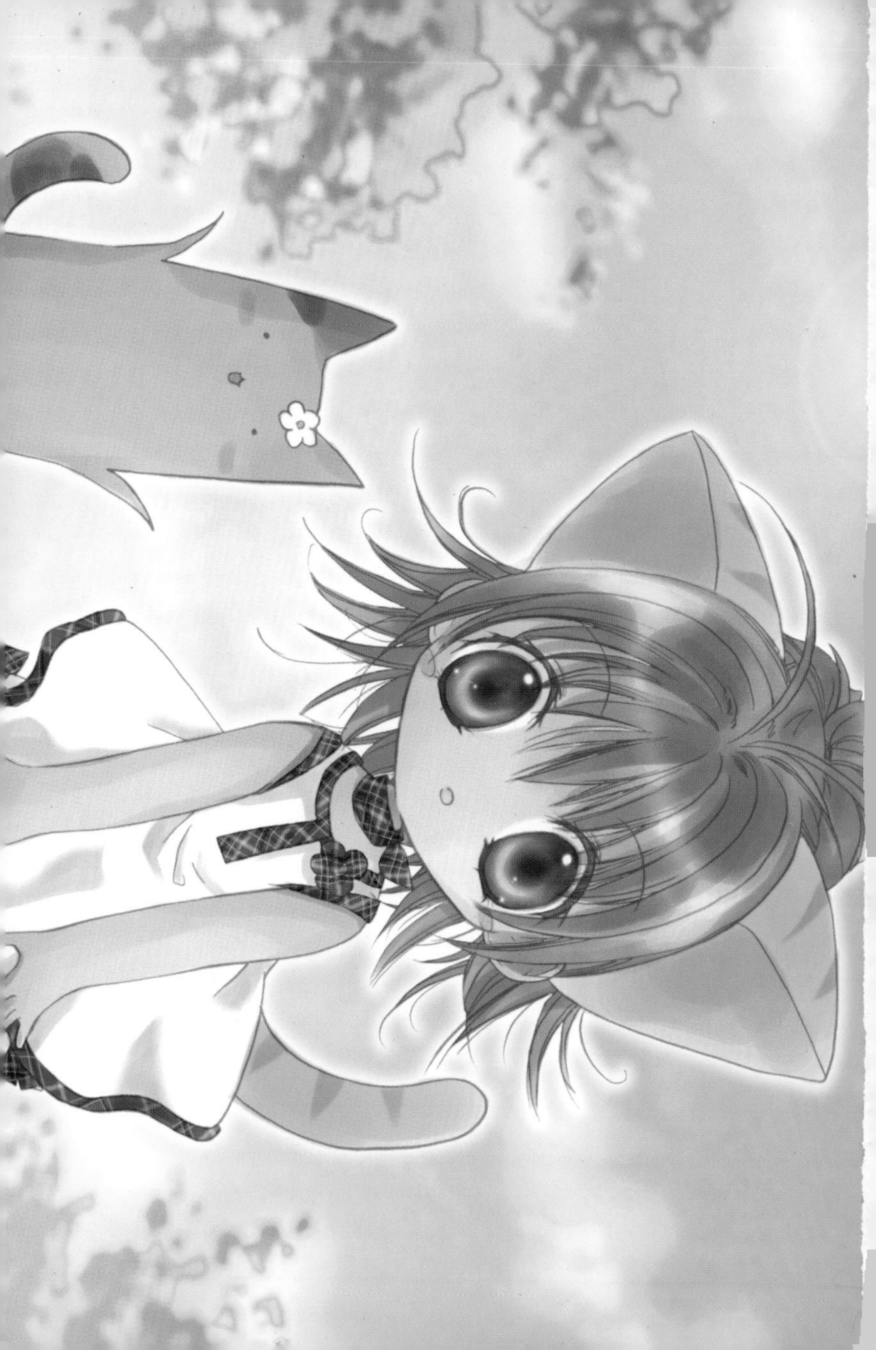

DI GI CHARAT

THEATER

Dejiko's Summer Vacation

by Koge-Donbo and others

brought to you by
BROCCOLI BOOKS
A DIVISION OF BROCCOLI INTERNATIONAL USA

Di Gi Charat™ Theater - Dejiko's Summer Vacation

English Adaptation Staff
Translation: Ken "KJ1980" Wakita
English Adaptation: Stephanie Sheh
Touch-Up & Lettering: Fawn "tails" Lau
Cover & Graphic Design: Chris McDougall

Editor: Satsuki Yamashita
Sales Manager: Ardith D. Santiago
Managing Editor: Shizuki Yamashita
Publisher: Hideki Uchino

Email: editor@broccolibooks.com
Website: www.broccolibooks.com

All illustrations by Koge-Donbo with the exception of:
pg. 11, 107 Majin Gappa by Clim; pg. 109 Takaaki Kidani by Miki Yokoyama;
pg. 152 Sasa Dango by Miki Yokoyama; pg. 157 Hokke Mirin by Miki Yokoyama

A (B) BROCCOLI BOOKS Manga
Broccoli Books is a division of Broccoli International USA, Inc.
12211 W. Washington Blvd, Suite 110, Los Angeles CA 90066

Japanese Edition Staff
Editor: Hitomi Koshiki, Iwao Yanagisawa, Yuki Mikawa, Takuto Hanai
Publisher: Takaaki Kidani

© 2000-2003 BROCCOLI
First published by Broccoli Co, Ltd., Tokyo, Japan.
Di Gi Charat is a trademark of Broccoli Co, Ltd.

ISBN: 1-932480-07-2
Published by Broccoli International USA, Inc.
First printing, September 2003

www.animegamers.com

10 9 8 7 6 5 4 3 2 1
Printed in the United States

Table of Contents

Dejiko's Summer Vacation

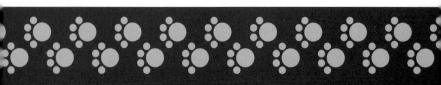

Table of Contents

Synopsis

Di Gi Charat, or Dejiko for short, is an alien hybrid-cat-eared girl with the ambition of becoming a super star on planet Earth. However, once she arrives at Akihabara (the Electric District of Tokyo), she discovers that the living expenses are too high and she needs to get a job to support herself along with her buddy Petit Charat (Puchiko for short). Luckily, she finds a job and housing at an anime chain store called Gamers, and quickly becomes popular with the customers who shop there. With Rabi~en~Rose competing for the popularity and Pyocola (Piyoko for short) coming to kidnap her, Dejiko's adventures are endless!

About Di Gi Charat

Dejiko was created in 1998 as the official mascot character for the popular anime/game store Gamers in Japan. When Gamers decided to create a commercial featuring Dejiko and her friends, a television network producer saw it and suggested that they make an anime. And thus, the TV anime series *Di Gi Charat* was born. Di Gi Charat was already featured on CDs and other merchandise, but it is the television series where she gained popularity nationwide, and eventually worldwide.

Di Gi Charat (Dejiko)

Dejiko is the princess of Planet Di Gi Charat, and comes to Earth to study and become a star. Contrary to her cute appearance, she is self-centered and evil, and often plots against Rabi~en~Rose and Piyoko. Her dialect back at home makes her sentences end with a "nyo."

Real name: Chocola
Alias: Dejiko
Hometown: Planet Di Gi Charat
Height: 4' 10" (Including cat ears)
Weight: 84 lbs.
Birthday: February 8 (Aquarius)
Age: 10
Blood type: O
Favorite food: Broccoli
Special move: Laser Eye Beam
Remarks: First Princess of Planet Di Gi Charat

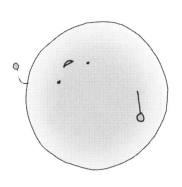

Gema

Gema is Dejiko's unidentified flying caretaker. His duty is to stop Dejiko's reckless behavior, but for a lack of any special moves, he gets beaten up in return. He has a habit of adding "gema" to the end of his sentences.

Hometown: Planet Di Gi Charat
Birthday: July 13 (Cancer)
Age: ?
Blood type: O
Favorite food: Broccoli
Special move: Blowgun
Remarks: Always has something extra to say

Petit Charat (Puchiko)

Puchiko has been with Dejiko ever since Dejiko saved her when she was stuck down a hole. Although she is quiet for most of the time, when she speaks she is really sharp-tongued. She ends her sentences with a "nyu."

Real name: Capetieno
Alias: Puchiko
Hometown: Planet Di Gi Charat
Height: 3' 4" (Including cat ears)
Weight: 39 lbs.
Birthday: January 21 (Aquarius)
Age: 5
Blood type: B
Favorite food: Steak (cooked rare)
Special move: Laser Eye Beam (in training)
Remarks: Hobby is putting curses on others

Hokke Mirin

Hokke Mirin has been with Puchiko ever since she was found abandoned on a rainy day. She is very good at walking sideways. She recently gave birth to five kittens "Sa," "Shi," "Su," "Se," and "So."

Birthday: ?
Age: ?
Blood type: ?
Favorite food: ?
Special move: Walking sideways

Rabi~en~Rose (Usada)

Rabi~en~Rose is a normal human being, and has been working for Gamers before Dejiko joined. She often competes with Dejiko for the number one clerk position. Her real name is Hikaru Usada, but hates it when people refer to her as Usada.

Real name: Hikaru Usada
Alias: Usada
Hometown: Planet Earth
Height: 5' 4" (including heels)
Weight: Secret
Birthday: August 30 (Virgo)
Age: 14
Blood type: A
Favorite food: Sasa Dango (rice patty wrapped in bamboo leaf), Kaki no Tane (spicy rice cracker)
Special move: Bunny ear-copter
Remarks: Very poor

Majin Gappa

Majin Gappa is Rabi~en~Rose's secret weapon against Dejiko. But actually, he is just a kappa. Sometimes appears in multiple quantities to support Usada.

Birthday: October 25 (Scorpio)
Age: ?
Blood type: A
Favorite food: Cucumber
Special move: Water tricks

Pyocola (Piyoko)

Piyoko is the head of the Evil
Organization, the Black Gema
Gema Gang. She came after Dejiko
to kidnap and hold her ransom to
raise money for planet Analogue.
Piyoko pursues a road of evil, but
she is actually kind-hearted and lov-
ing toward her subjects. Her dialect
back at home makes her end her
sentences with a "pyo."

Real name: Pyocola Analogue III
Alias: Piyoko
Hometown: Planet Analogue
Height: 4' 6"
Weight: Secret
Birthday: October 23 (Libra)
Age: 8
Blood type: AB
Favorite food: Crème-filled cookies
Special move: Upchuck Bazooka
Remarks: Calls Dejiko "Oneechan,"
which means "big sister," but no
relation

Coo Erhard

Coo is the Major of the Black
Gema Gema Gang. He is part of
the Pyocola Keeping Operations,
also known as PKO. He knows
Piyoko from childhood, and thinks
of her like a little sister. Thus, he is
closest to Piyoko among the PKO.
He is Piyoko's personal doctor.

Real Name: Coo Erhard
Height: 5' 1"
Weight: 110 lbs.
Birthday: May 5 (Taurus)
Age: 13
Blood type: O
Favorite food: Mochi (rice cake),
Natto (fermented soy beans)
Remarks: Physician

Ky Schweitzer

Ky is the Lieutenant General of the Black Gema Gema Gang, and also part of PKO. He has a strong sense of responsibility. He is Piyoko's personal dentist, and is in charge of checking Piyoko's dental hygiene everyday.

Real name: Ky Schweitzer
Height: 5' 6"
Weight: 123 lbs.
Birthday: March 3 (Pisces)
Age: 13
Blood type: A
Favorite food: Mild curry rice
Remarks: Dentist

Rik Heisenberg

Rik is the General of the Black Gema Gema Gang, and also part of PKO. He is calm and blunt; he easily comes up with cruel things to say. He is a Veterinarian, and thus loves animals of all kinds.

Real Name: Rik Heisenberg
Height: 6' 3"
Weight: 187 lbs.
Birthday: April 4 (Aries)
Age: 26
Blood type: AB
Favorite food: Sushi, fried noodles
Remarks: Veterinarian

13

ビーチだよ！全員集合
Hit the Beach!
Koge-Donbo

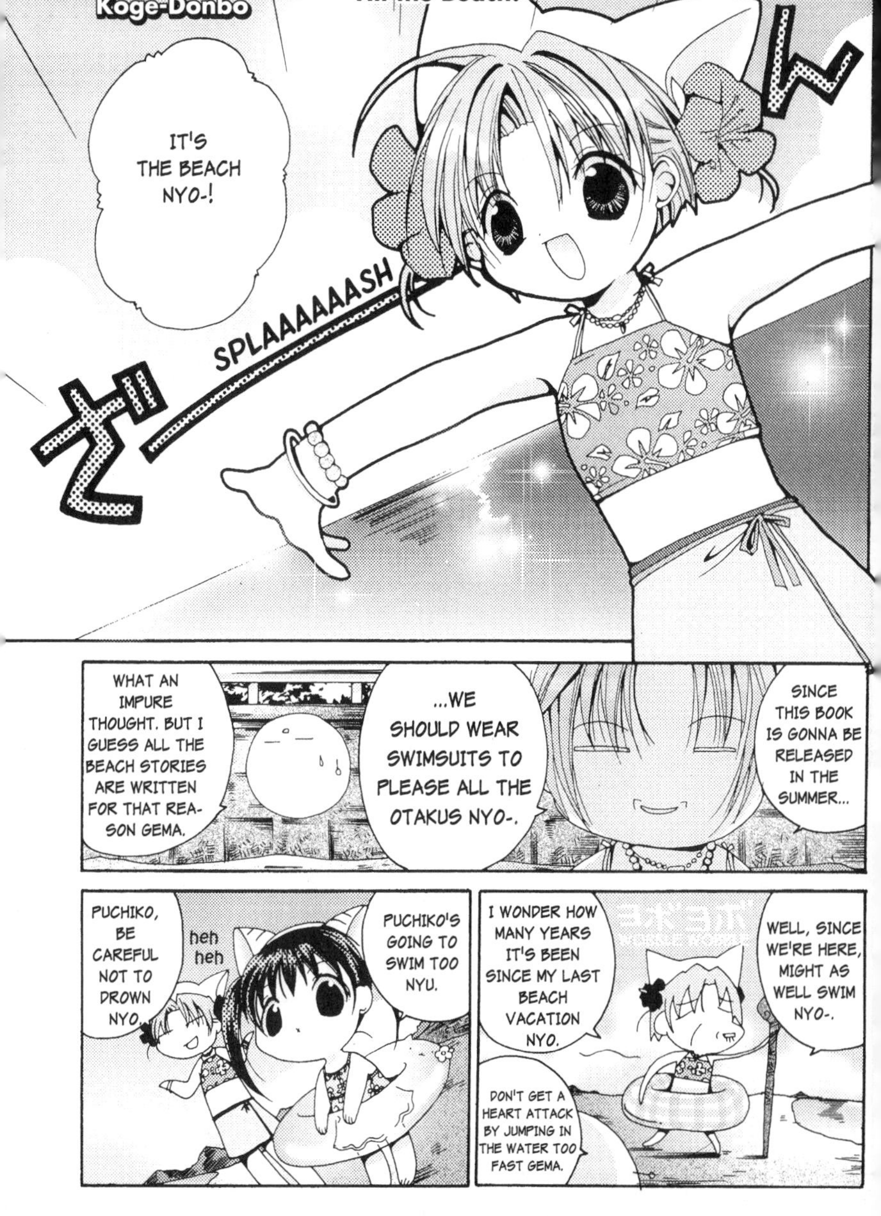
ざ
SPLAAAAAASH
ん
IT'S THE BEACH NYO-!
SINCE THIS BOOK IS GONNA BE RELEASED IN THE SUMMER...
...WE SHOULD WEAR SWIMSUITS TO PLEASE ALL THE OTAKUS NYO-.
WHAT AN IMPURE THOUGHT. BUT I GUESS ALL THE BEACH STORIES ARE WRITTEN FOR THAT REA-SON GEMA.
WELL, SINCE WE'RE HERE, MIGHT AS WELL SWIM NYO-.
I WONDER HOW MANY YEARS IT'S BEEN SINCE MY LAST BEACH VACATION NYO.
DON'T GET A HEART ATTACK BY JUMPING IN THE WATER TOO FAST GEMA.
PUCHIKO'S GOING TO SWIM TOO NYU.
heh heh
PUCHIKO, BE CAREFUL NOT TO DROWN NYO.

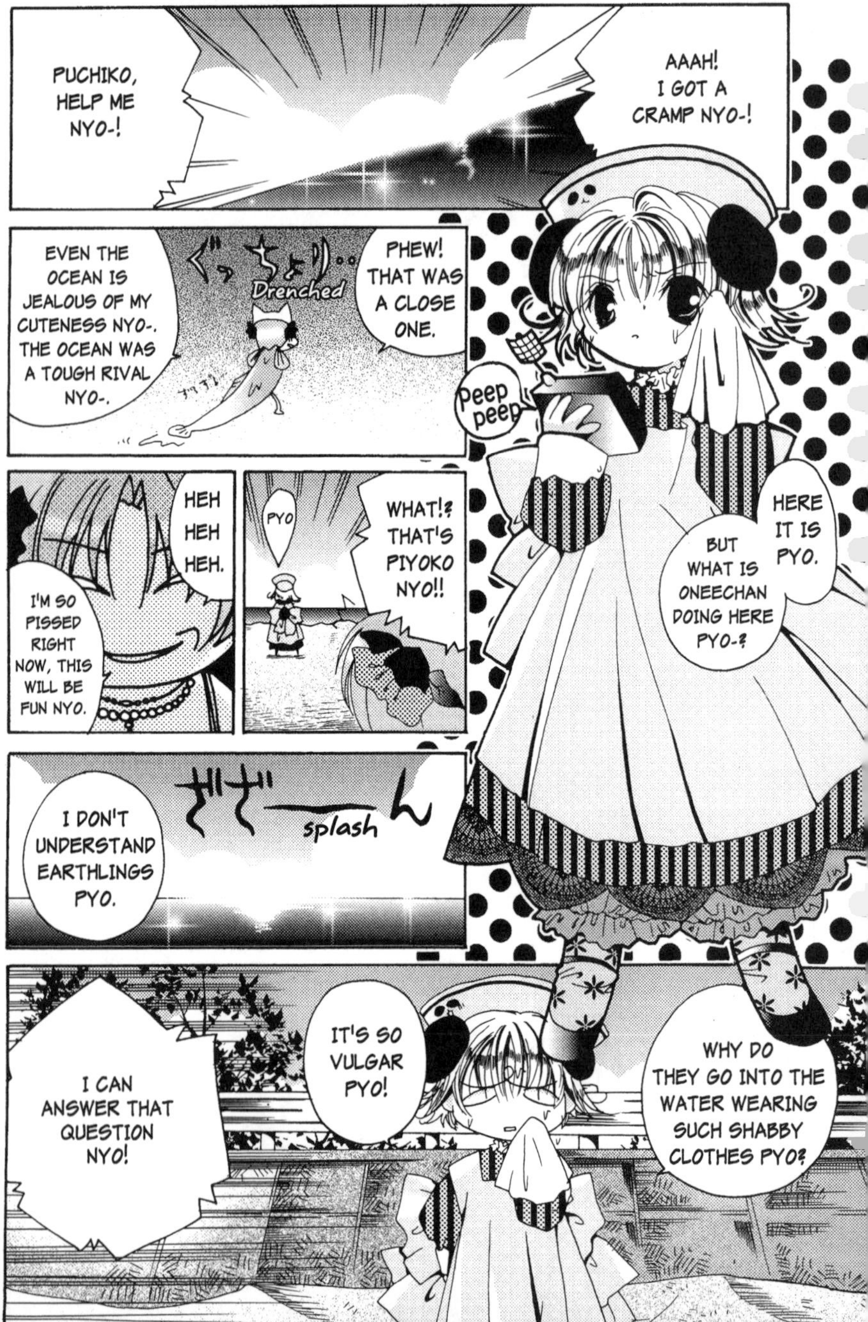

AAAH! I GOT A CRAMP NYO-!
PUCHIKO, HELP ME NYO-!
Peep peep
HERE IT IS PYO.
BUT WHAT IS ONEECHAN DOING HERE PYO-?
PHEW! THAT WAS A CLOSE ONE.
Drenched
EVEN THE OCEAN IS JEALOUS OF MY CUTENESS NYO-. THE OCEAN WAS A TOUGH RIVAL NYO-.
WHAT!? THAT'S PIYOKO NYO!!
PYO
HEH HEH HEH.
I'M SO PISSED RIGHT NOW, THIS WILL BE FUN NYO.
splash
I DON'T UNDERSTAND EARTHLINGS PYO.
WHY DO THEY GO INTO THE WATER WEARING SUCH SHABBY CLOTHES PYO?
IT'S SO VULGAR PYO!
I CAN ANSWER THAT QUESTION NYO!

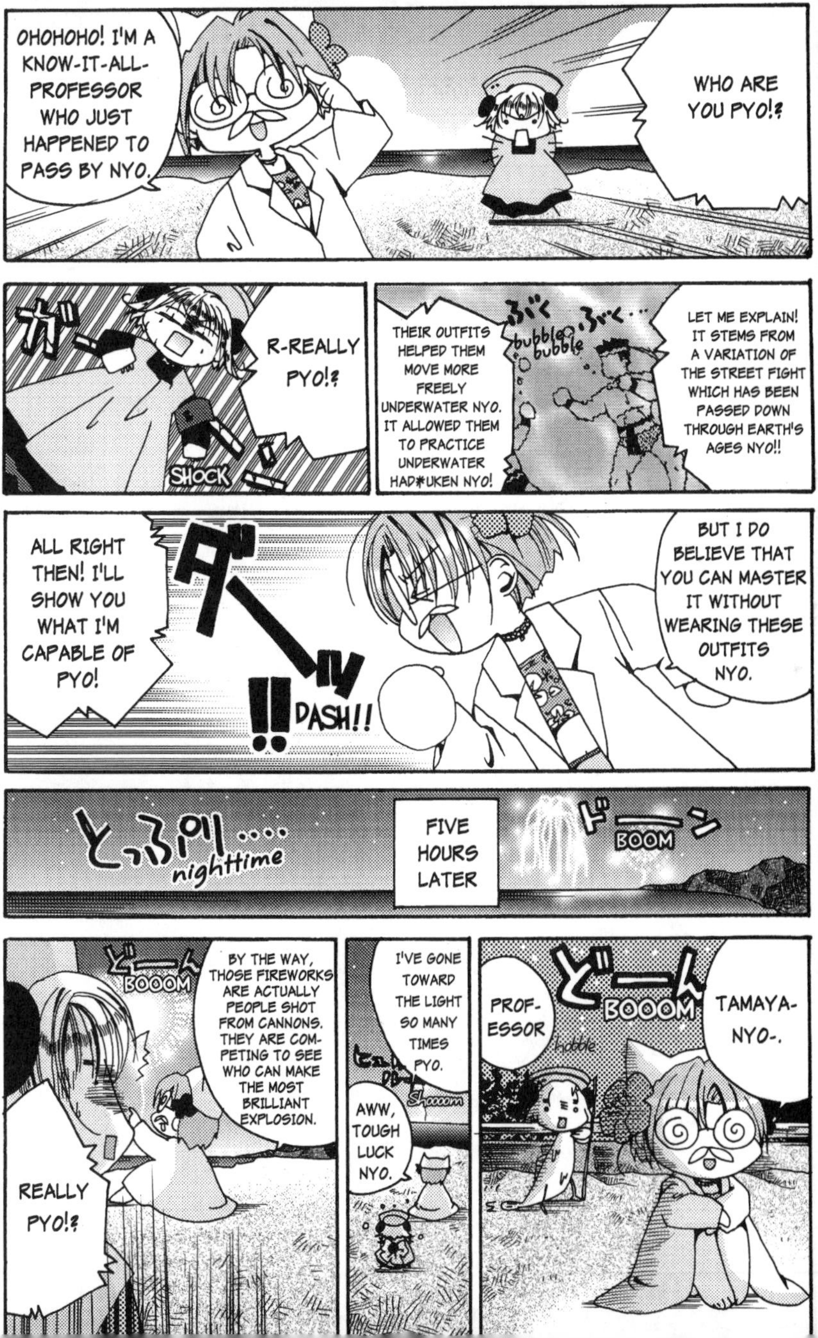

WHO ARE YOU PYO!?
OHOHOHO! I'M A KNOW-IT-ALL-PROFESSOR WHO JUST HAPPENED TO PASS BY NYO.
LET ME EXPLAIN! IT STEMS FROM A VARIATION OF THE STREET FIGHT WHICH HAS BEEN PASSED DOWN THROUGH EARTH'S AGES NYO!!
ぶく bubble ぶく… bubble
THEIR OUTFITS HELPED THEM MOVE MORE FREELY UNDERWATER NYO. IT ALLOWED THEM TO PRACTICE UNDERWATER HAD*UKEN NYO!
R-REALLY PYO!?
ガー
SHOCK
BUT I DO BELIEVE THAT YOU CAN MASTER IT WITHOUT WEARING THESE OUTFITS NYO.
ダーッ!! DASH!!
ALL RIGHT THEN! I'LL SHOW YOU WHAT I'M CAPABLE OF PYO!
ドーン BOOM
FIVE HOURS LATER
とっぷり…… nighttime
TAMAYA-NYO-.
どーん BOOOM
PROF-ESSOR
bubble
I'VE GONE TOWARD THE LIGHT SO MANY TIMES PYO.
Shoooom
AWW, TOUGH LUCK NYO.
BY THE WAY, THOSE FIREWORKS ARE ACTUALLY PEOPLE SHOT FROM CANNONS. THEY ARE COMPETING TO SEE WHO CAN MAKE THE MOST BRILLIANT EXPLOSION.
どーん BOOOM
REALLY PYO!?

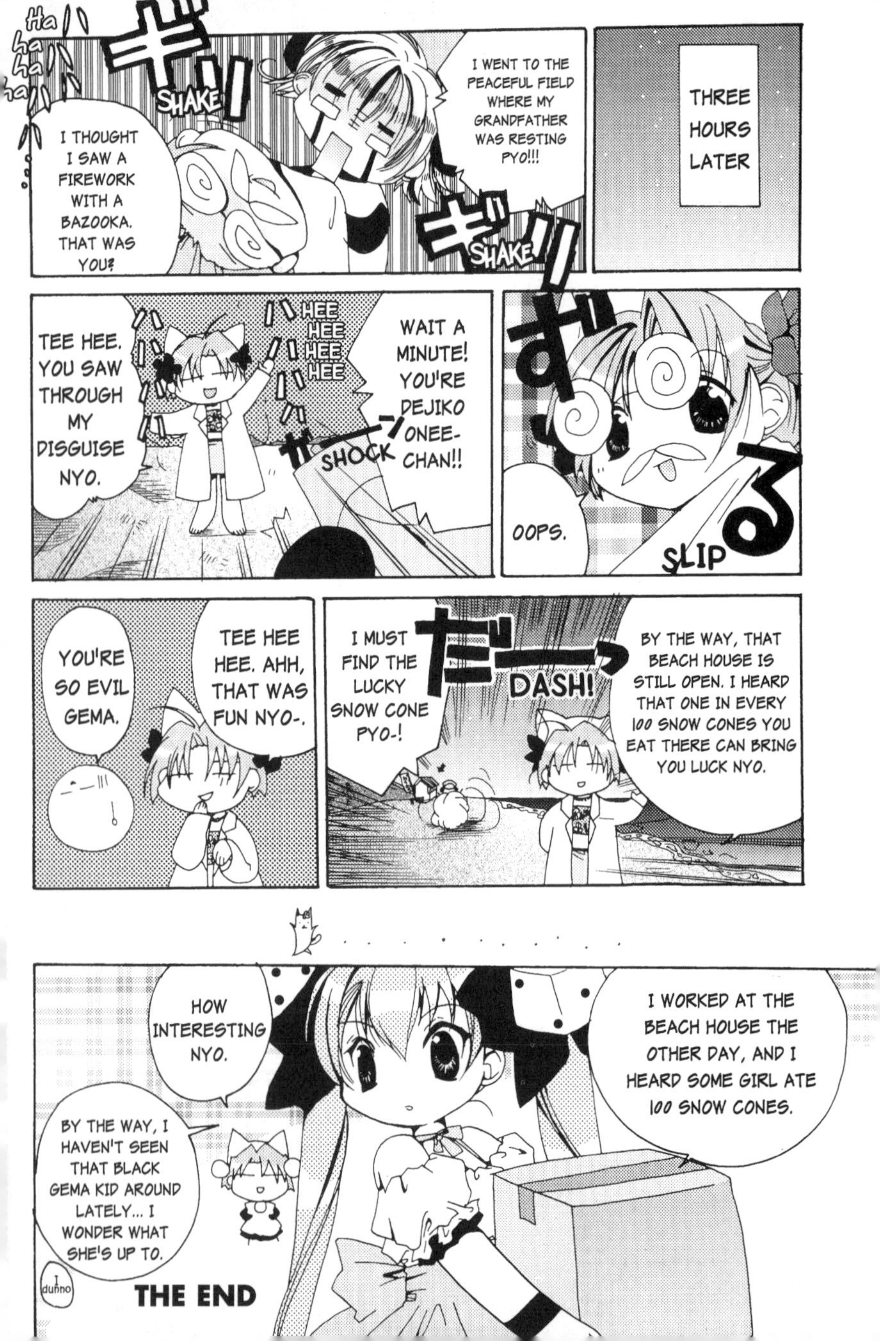
THREE HOURS LATER
I WENT TO THE PEACEFUL FIELD WHERE MY GRANDFATHER WAS RESTING PYO!!!
SHAKE
SHAKE
I THOUGHT I SAW A FIREWORK WITH A BAZOOKA. THAT WAS YOU?
Ha ha ha ha
OOPS.
SLIP
WAIT A MINUTE! YOU'RE DEJIKO ONEE-CHAN!!
HEE HEE HEE HEE
SHOCK
TEE HEE. YOU SAW THROUGH MY DISGUISE NYO.
BY THE WAY, THAT BEACH HOUSE IS STILL OPEN. I HEARD THAT ONE IN EVERY 100 SNOW CONES YOU EAT THERE CAN BRING YOU LUCK NYO.
DASH!
I MUST FIND THE LUCKY SNOW CONE PYO-!
TEE HEE HEE. AHH, THAT WAS FUN NYO-.
YOU'RE SO EVIL GEMA.
I WORKED AT THE BEACH HOUSE THE OTHER DAY, AND I HEARD SOME GIRL ATE 100 SNOW CONES.
HOW INTERESTING NYO.
BY THE WAY, I HAVEN'T SEEN THAT BLACK GEMA KID AROUND LATELY... I WONDER WHAT SHE'S UP TO.
I dunno
THE END

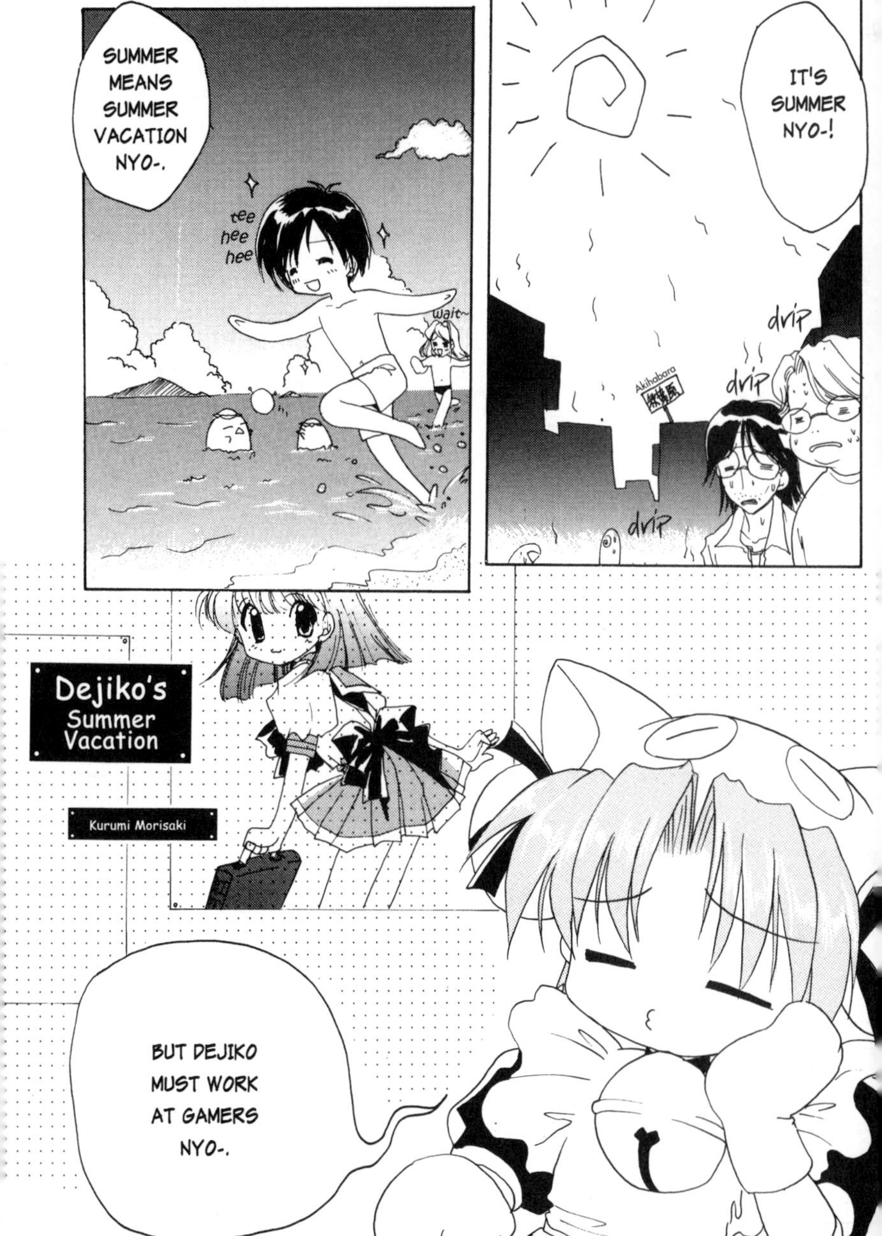
IT'S SUMMER NYO-!
drip
drip
Akihabara
drip
SUMMER MEANS SUMMER VACATION NYO-.
tee hee hee
wait~
Dejiko's Summer Vacation
Kurumi Morisaki
BUT DEJIKO MUST WORK AT GAMERS NYO-.

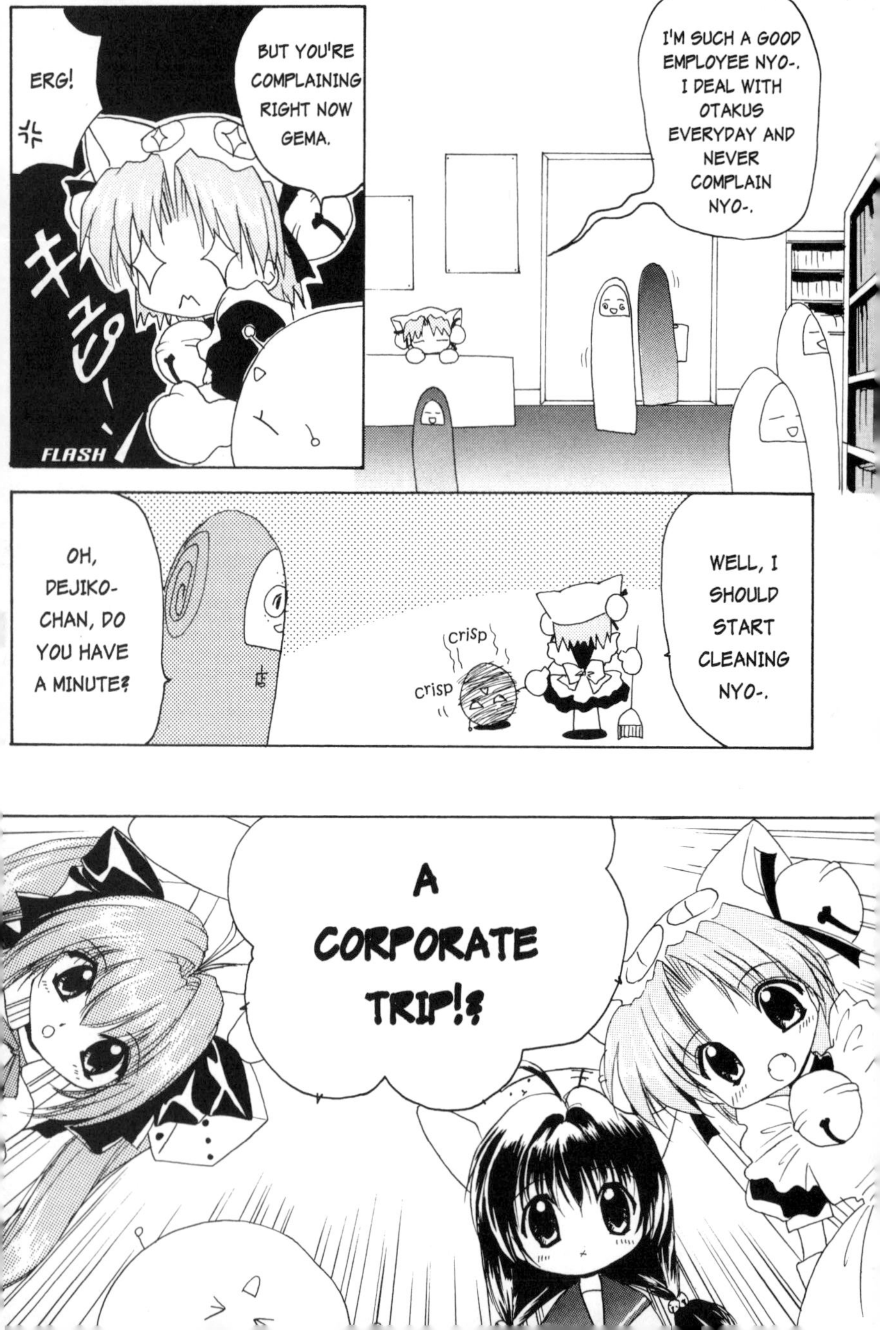
I'M SUCH A GOOD EMPLOYEE NYO-. I DEAL WITH OTAKUS EVERYDAY AND NEVER COMPLAIN NYO-.
BUT YOU'RE COMPLAINING RIGHT NOW GEMA.
ERG!
FLASH
WELL, I SHOULD START CLEANING NYO-.
crisp
crisp
OH, DEJIKO-CHAN, DO YOU HAVE A MINUTE?
A CORPORATE TRIP!?

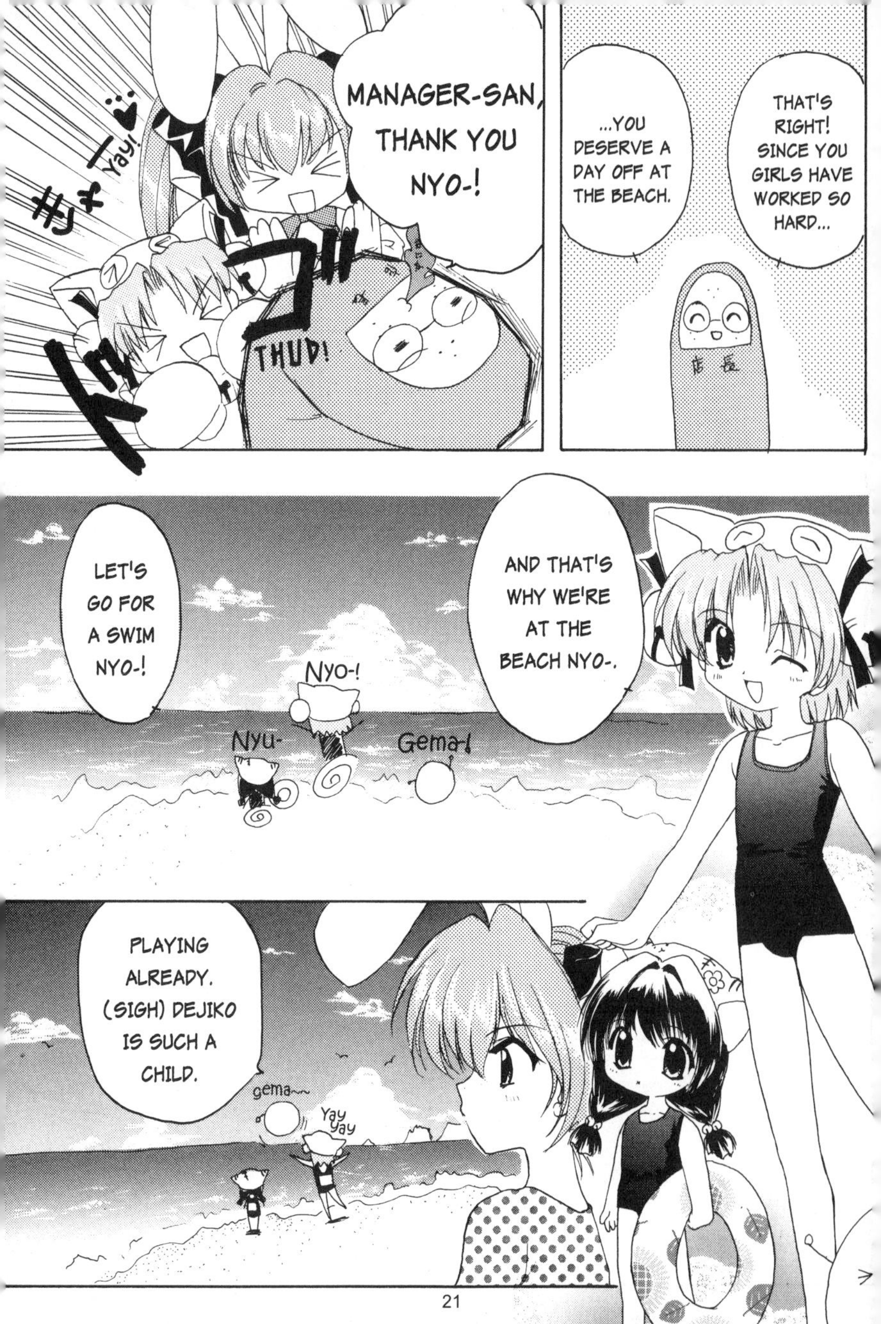
THAT'S RIGHT! SINCE YOU GIRLS HAVE WORKED SO HARD...
...YOU DESERVE A DAY OFF AT THE BEACH.
MANAGER-SAN, THANK YOU NYO-!
Yay!
THUD!
AND THAT'S WHY WE'RE AT THE BEACH NYO-.
LET'S GO FOR A SWIM NYO-!
Nyo-!
Gema-!
Nyu-
PLAYING ALREADY. (SIGH) DEJIKO IS SUCH A CHILD.
Yay yay
gema~~

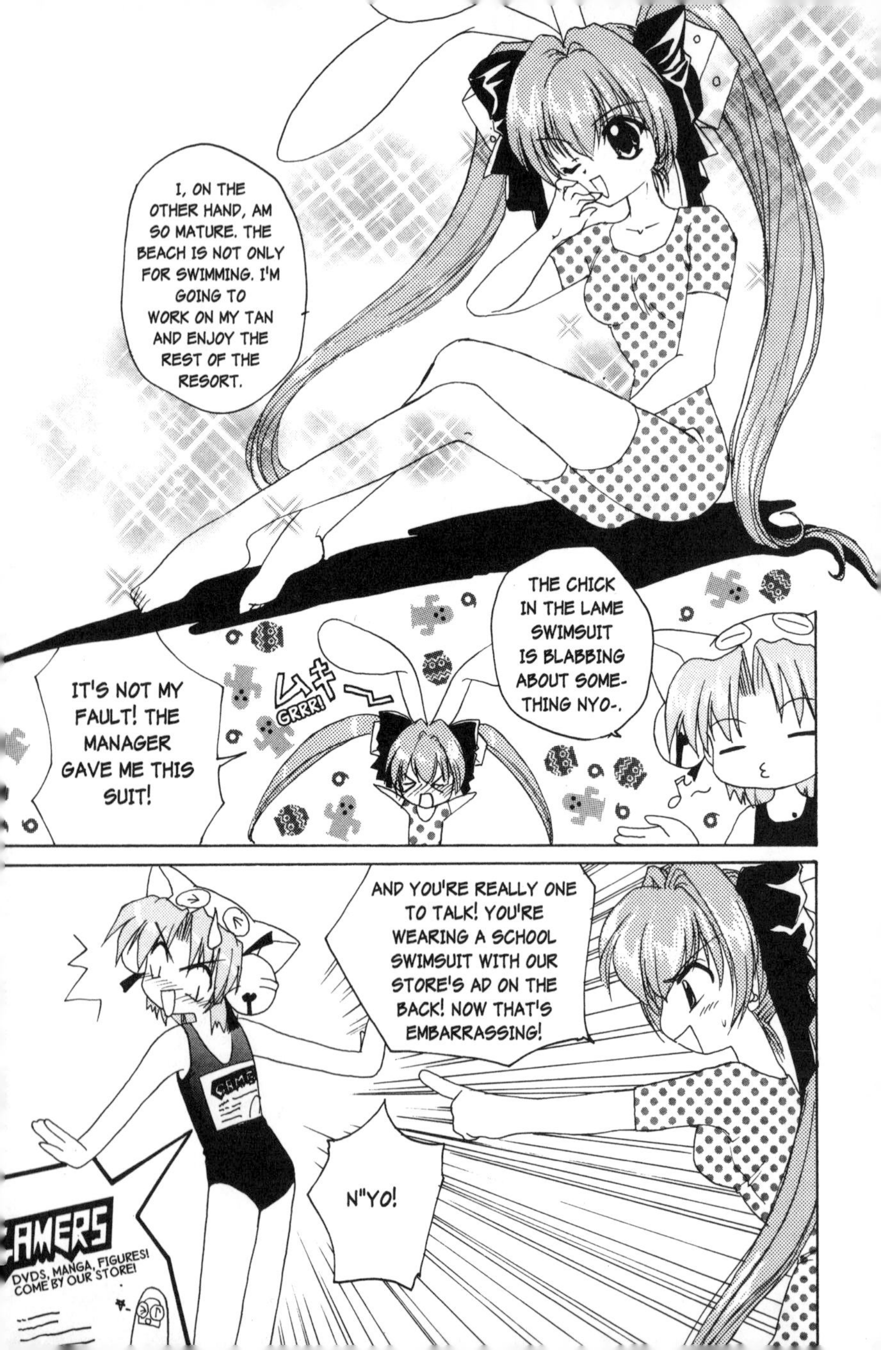
I, ON THE OTHER HAND, AM SO MATURE. THE BEACH IS NOT ONLY FOR SWIMMING. I'M GOING TO WORK ON MY TAN AND ENJOY THE REST OF THE RESORT.
THE CHICK IN THE LAME SWIMSUIT IS BLABBING ABOUT SOME-THING NYO-.
ムキー
GRRR!
IT'S NOT MY FAULT! THE MANAGER GAVE ME THIS SUIT!
AND YOU'RE REALLY ONE TO TALK! YOU'RE WEARING A SCHOOL SWIMSUIT WITH OUR STORE'S AD ON THE BACK! NOW THAT'S EMBARRASSING!
N"YO!
AMERS
DVDS, MANGA, FIGURES! COME BY OUR STORE!

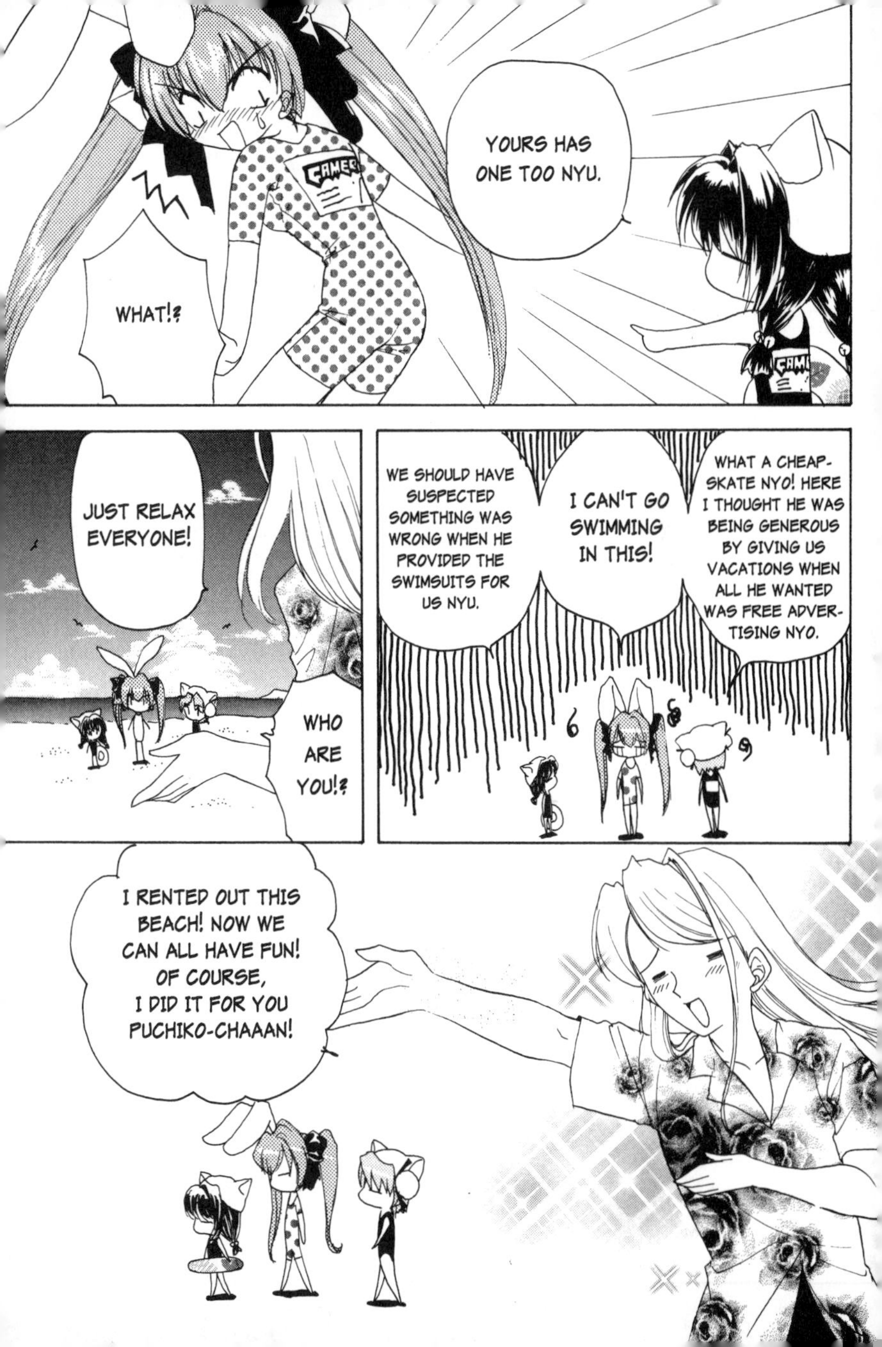
YOURS HAS ONE TOO NYU.
WHAT!?
WHAT A CHEAP-SKATE NYO! HERE I THOUGHT HE WAS BEING GENEROUS BY GIVING US VACATIONS WHEN ALL HE WANTED WAS FREE ADVERTISING NYO.
I CAN'T GO SWIMMING IN THIS!
WE SHOULD HAVE SUSPECTED SOMETHING WAS WRONG WHEN HE PROVIDED THE SWIMSUITS FOR US NYU.
JUST RELAX EVERYONE!
WHO ARE YOU!?
I RENTED OUT THIS BEACH! NOW WE CAN ALL HAVE FUN! OF COURSE, I DID IT FOR YOU PUCHIKO-CHAAAN!

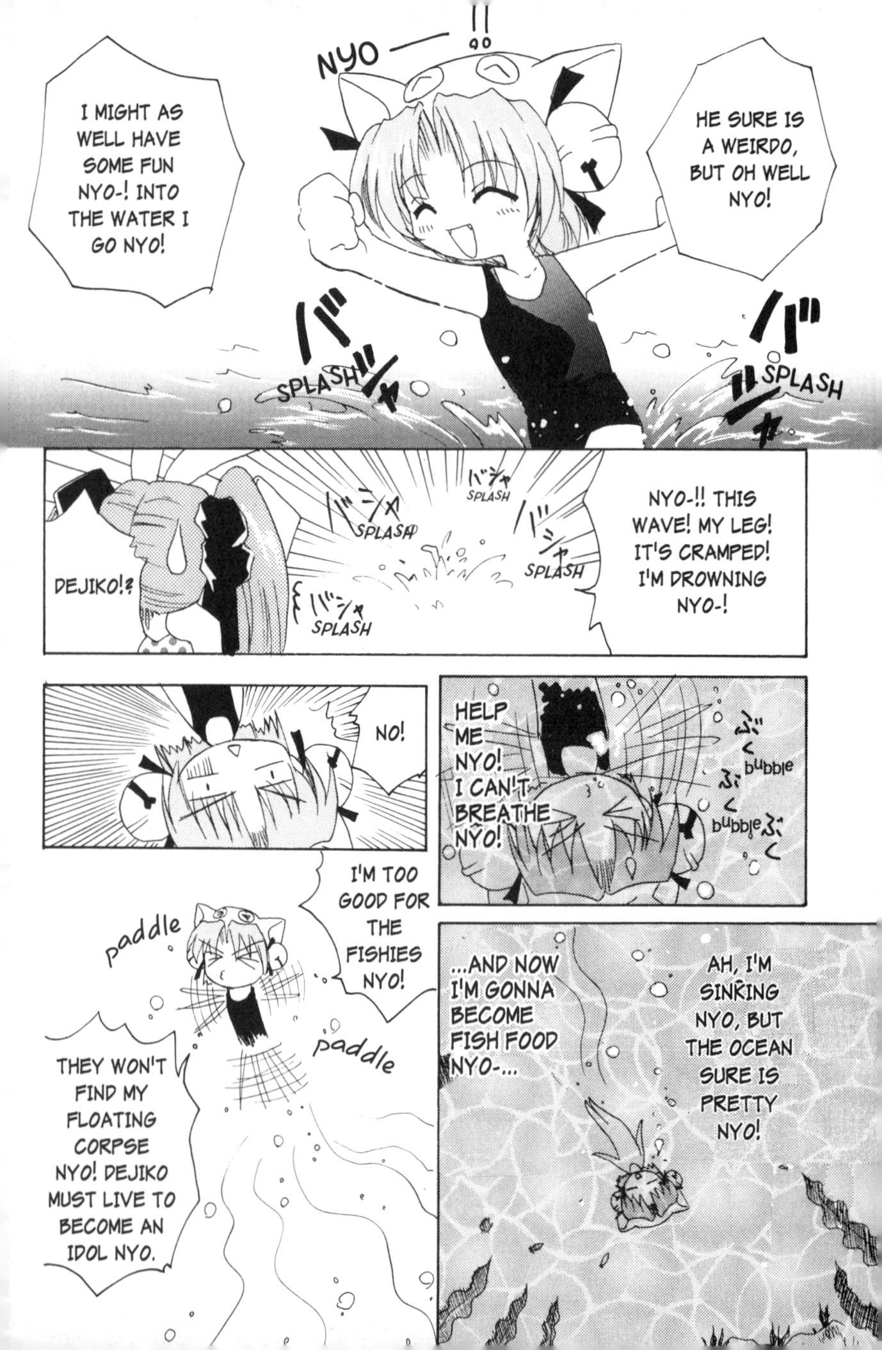
NYO—!!
HE SURE IS A WEIRDO, BUT OH WELL NYO!
I MIGHT AS WELL HAVE SOME FUN NYO-! INTO THE WATER I GO NYO!
SPLASH
SPLASH
NYO-!! THIS WAVE! MY LEG! IT'S CRAMPED! I'M DROWNING NYO-!
SPLASH
SPLASH
SPLASH
SPLASH
DEJIKO!?
HELP ME NYO! I CAN'T BREATHE NYO!
bubble
bubble
NO!
AH, I'M SINKING NYO, BUT THE OCEAN SURE IS PRETTY NYO!
...AND NOW I'M GONNA BECOME FISH FOOD NYO-...
I'M TOO GOOD FOR THE FISHIES NYO!
paddle
paddle
THEY WON'T FIND MY FLOATING CORPSE NYO! DEJIKO MUST LIVE TO BECOME AN IDOL NYO.

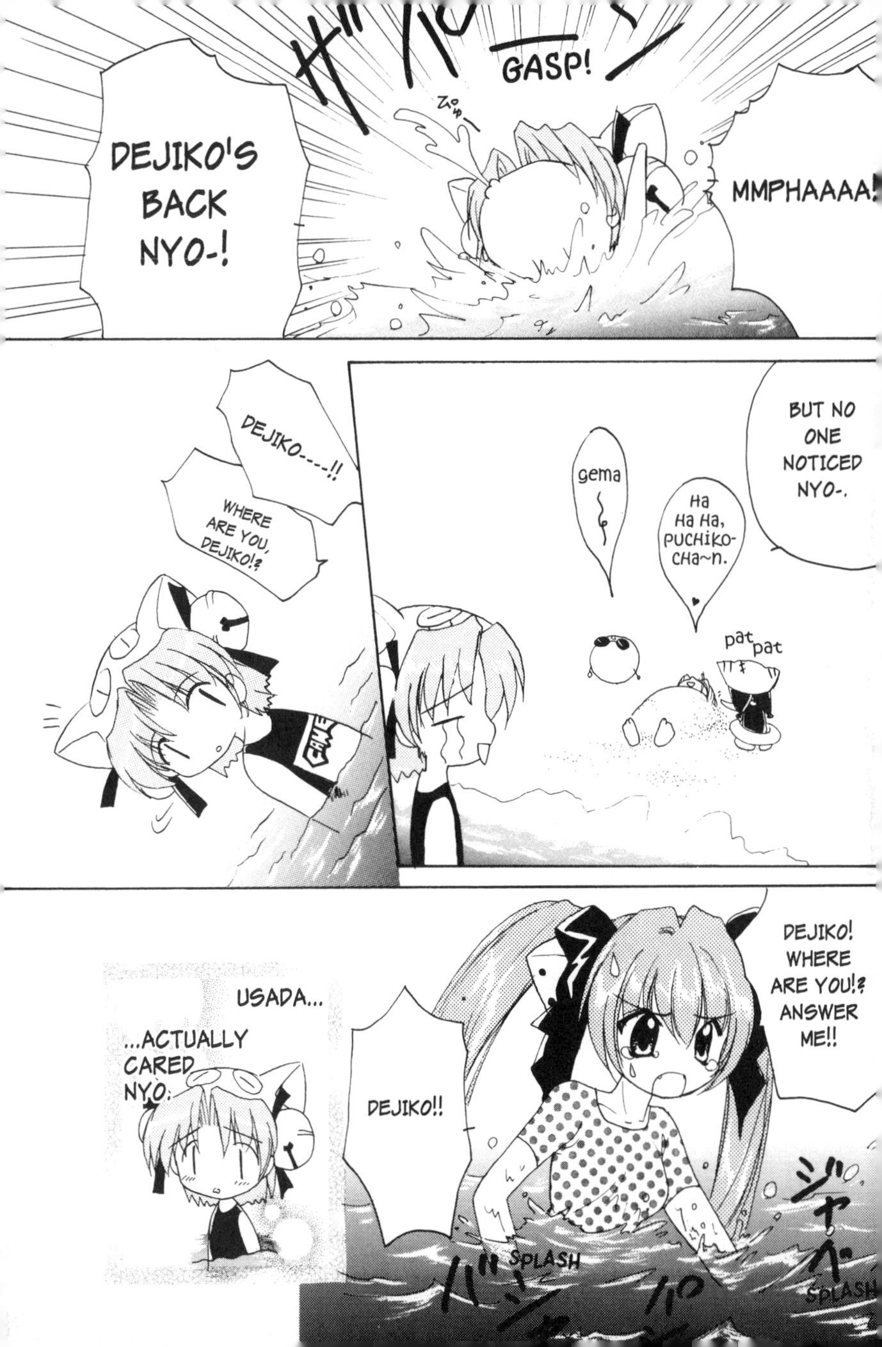
MMPHAAAA!
GASP!
DEJIKO'S BACK NYO-!
BUT NO ONE NOTICED NYO-.
Ha Ha Ha, PUCHIKO-CHa~n.
gema
pat pat
DEJIKO----!!
WHERE ARE YOU, DEJIKO!?
DEJIKO! WHERE ARE YOU!? ANSWER ME!!
SPLASH
DEJIKO!!
SPLASH
USADA...
...ACTUALLY CARED NYO.

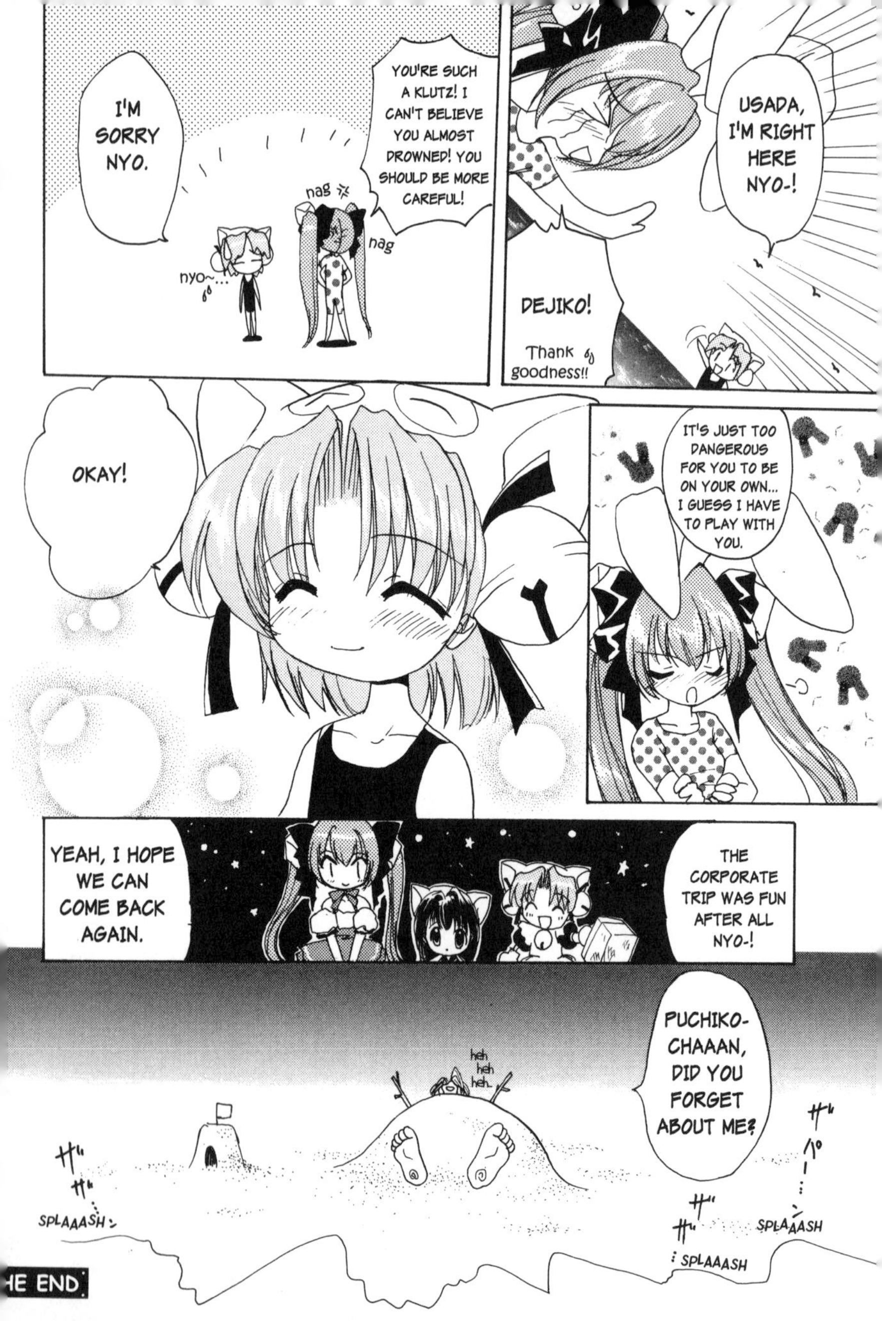
USADA, I'M RIGHT HERE NYO-!
DEJIKO!
Thank goodness!!
YOU'RE SUCH A KLUTZ! I CAN'T BELIEVE YOU ALMOST DROWNED! YOU SHOULD BE MORE CAREFUL!
nag
nag
I'M SORRY NYO.
nyo~...
IT'S JUST TOO DANGEROUS FOR YOU TO BE ON YOUR OWN... I GUESS I HAVE TO PLAY WITH YOU.
OKAY!
THE CORPORATE TRIP WAS FUN AFTER ALL NYO-!
YEAH, I HOPE WE CAN COME BACK AGAIN.
PUCHIKO-CHAAAN, DID YOU FORGET ABOUT ME?
heh heh heh...
SPLAAASH
SPLAAASH
SPLAAASH
HE END.

Who's your favorite character in Di Gi Charat?

I LIKE EVERYONE, BUT IN MY OPINION, A CHARACTER WITHOUT HUMAN FEATURES IS GREAT. IT'S GOTTA BE GEMA, BECAUSE ANYONE CAN DRAW HIM.

LAUGH

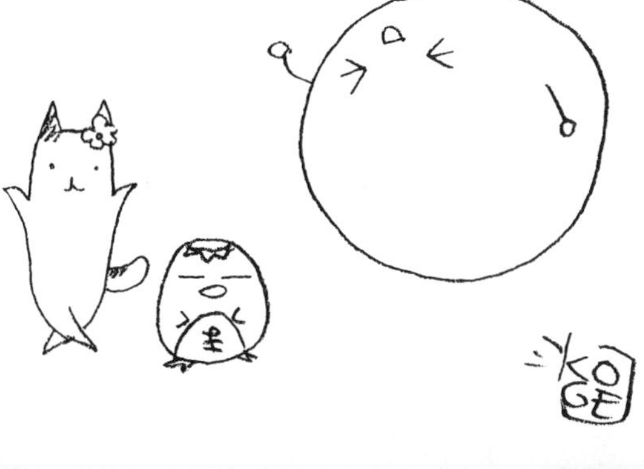
KOGE

Koge-Donbo

Who's your favorite character in Di Gi Charat?

PUCHIKO-CHAN. SHE'S SO CUTE! IN MY OPINION, DEJIKO IS NOTHING BUT A SMEAR IN FRONT OF PUCHIKO. I'M SORRY THAT I MADE DEJIKO'S FACE SO TWISTED THOUGH... IT'S PROBABLY BECAUSE I WATCHED THE ANIME OVER AND OVER AGAIN (FOR RESEARCH). 森崎くるみ

http://www.geocities.co.jp/
Playtown-Dice/5541/

Morisaki Kurumi

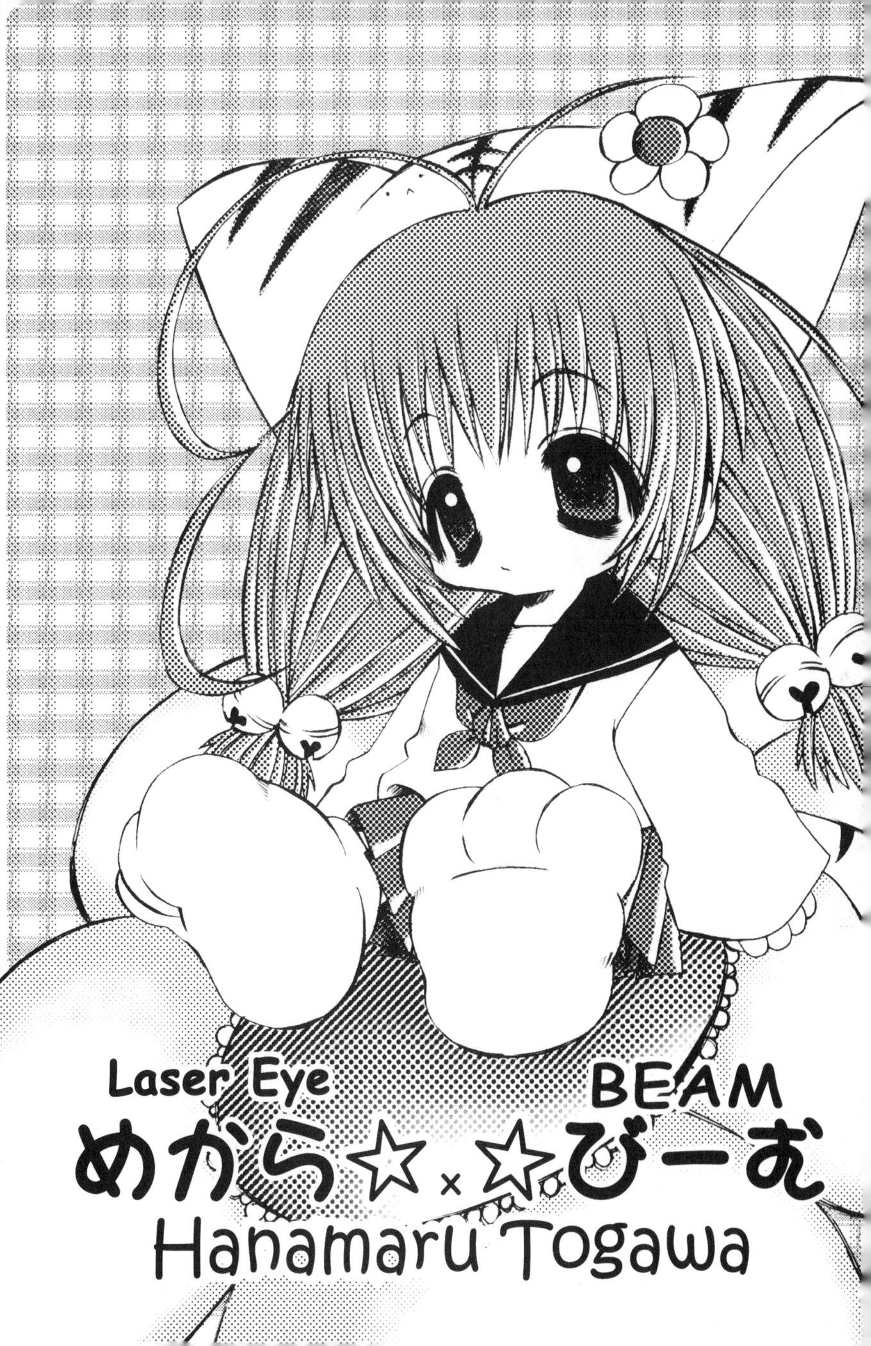
Laser Eye
BEAM
めがら☆×☆びーむ
Hanamaru Togawa

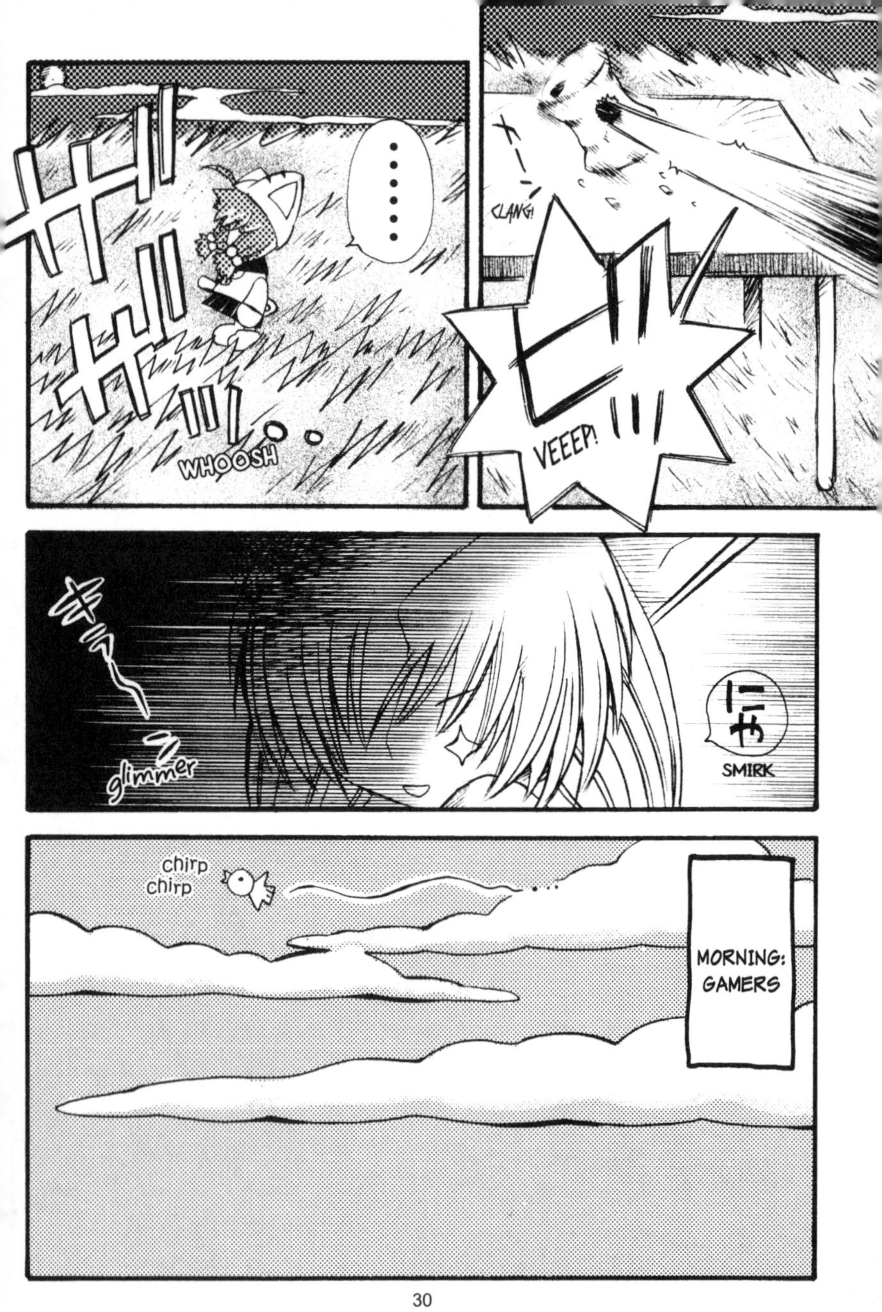
CLANG!
VEEEP!
......
WHOOSH
にや
SMIRK
glimmer
MORNING: GAMERS
chirp
chirp

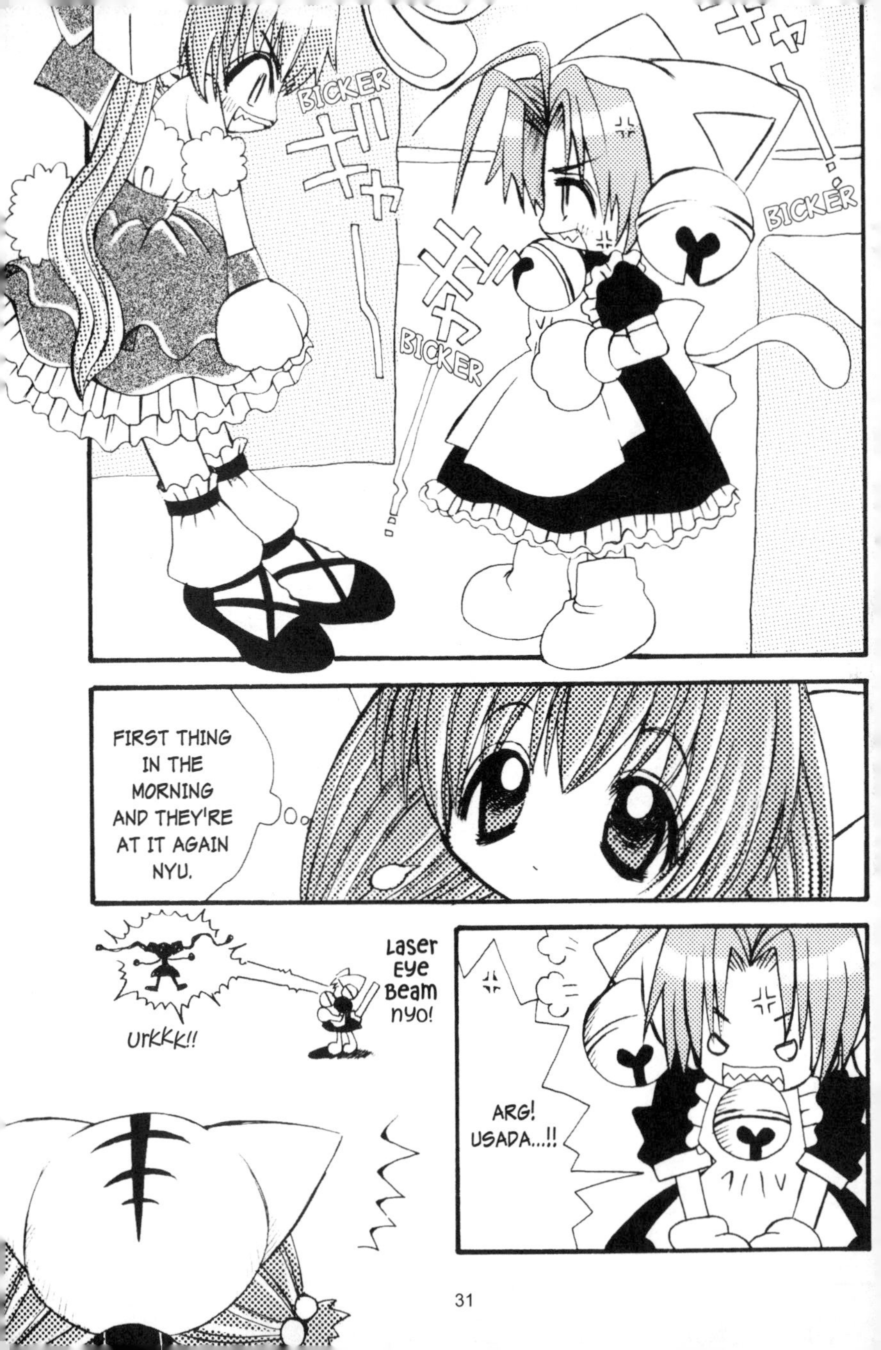

BICKER
BICKER
BICKER
FIRST THING IN THE MORNING AND THEY'RE AT IT AGAIN NYU.
ARG! USADA...!!
Laser Eye Beam nyo!
UrKKK!!

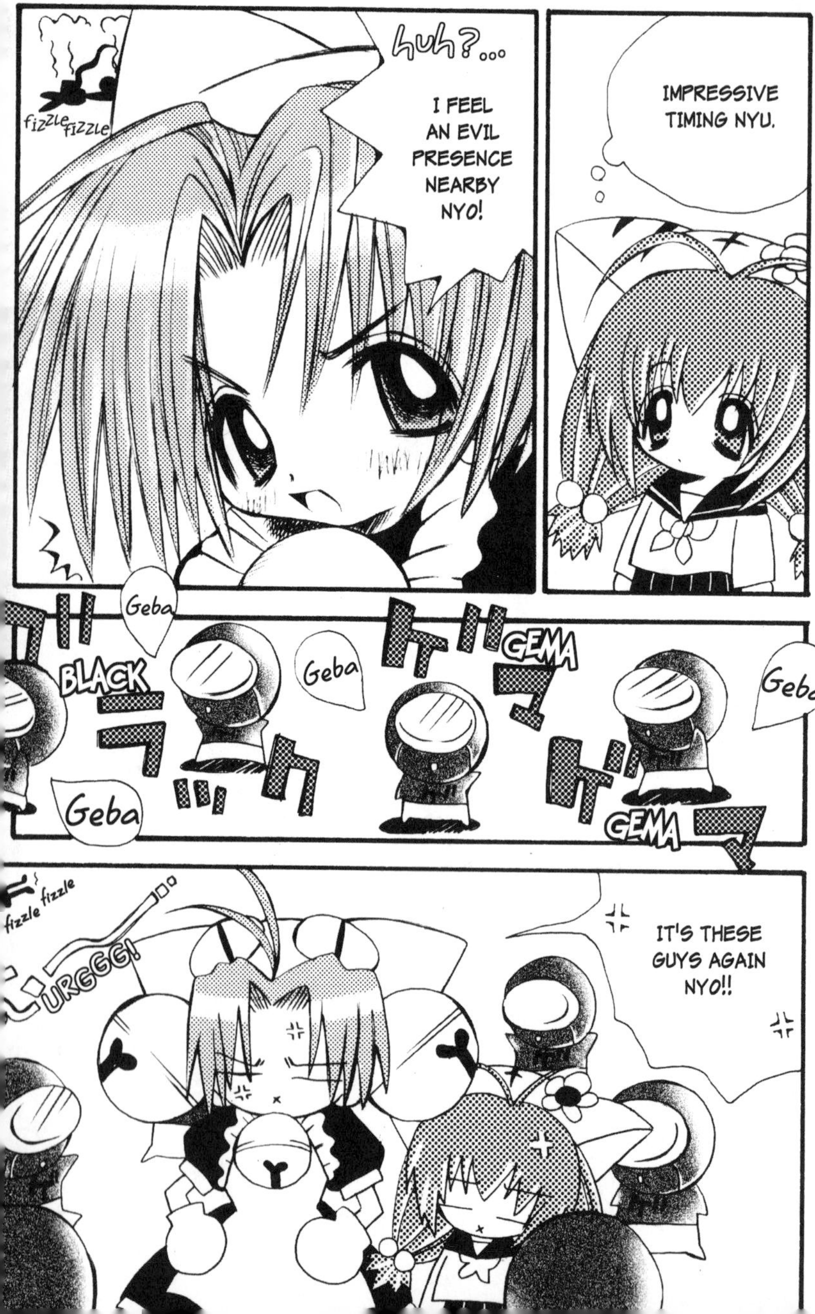

IMPRESSIVE TIMING NYU.
huh?...
I FEEL AN EVIL PRESENCE NEARBY NYO!
fizzle fizzle
Geba
GEMA
Geba
Geba
BLACK
Geba
GEMA
IT'S THESE GUYS AGAIN NYO!!
URGGG!
fizzle fizzle

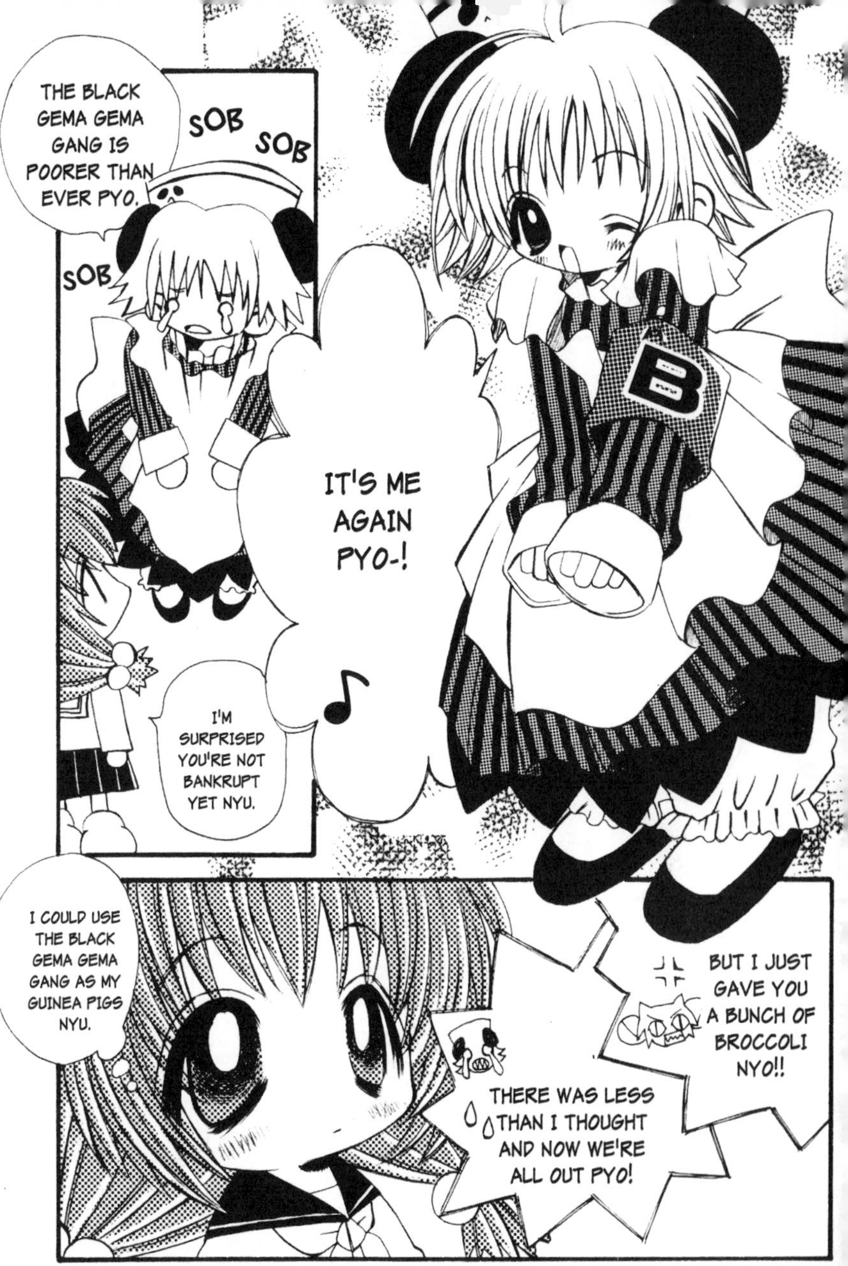
IT'S ME AGAIN PYO-!
THE BLACK GEMA GEMA GANG IS POORER THAN EVER PYO.
SOB
SOB
SOB
I'M SURPRISED YOU'RE NOT BANKRUPT YET NYU.
BUT I JUST GAVE YOU A BUNCH OF BROCCOLI NYO!!
THERE WAS LESS THAN I THOUGHT AND NOW WE'RE ALL OUT PYO!
I COULD USE THE BLACK GEMA GEMA GANG AS MY GUINEA PIGS NYU.

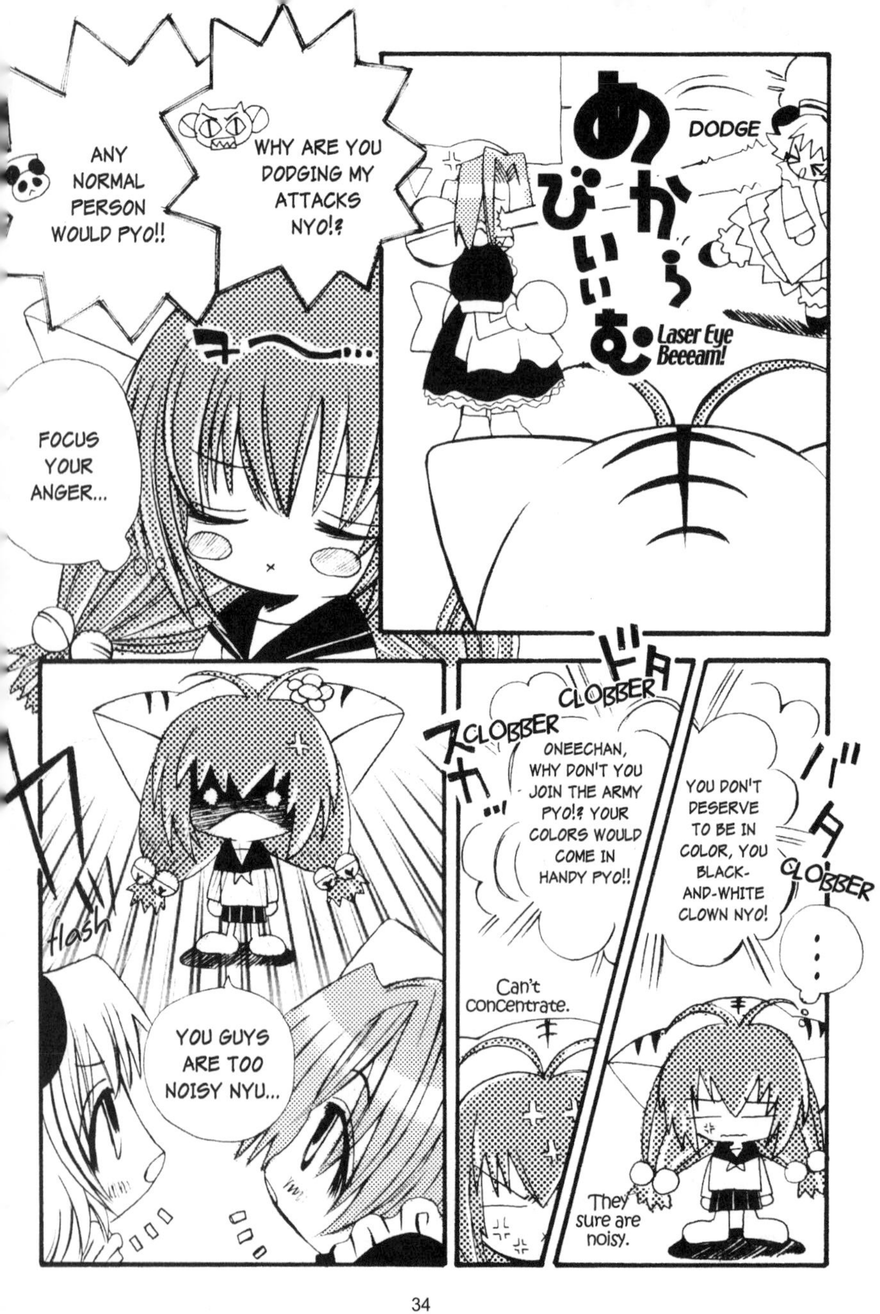
めからびいいむ
Laser Eye Beeeam!
DODGE
WHY ARE YOU DODGING MY ATTACKS NYO!?
ANY NORMAL PERSON WOULD PYO!!
FOCUS YOUR ANGER...
バタ
CLOBBER
YOU DON'T DESERVE TO BE IN COLOR, YOU BLACK-AND-WHITE CLOWN NYO!
...
They sure are noisy.
ドタ
CLOBBER
スカ
CLOBBER
ONEECHAN, WHY DON'T YOU JOIN THE ARMY PYO!? YOUR COLORS WOULD COME IN HANDY PYO!!
Can't concentrate.
flash
YOU GUYS ARE TOO NOISY NYU...

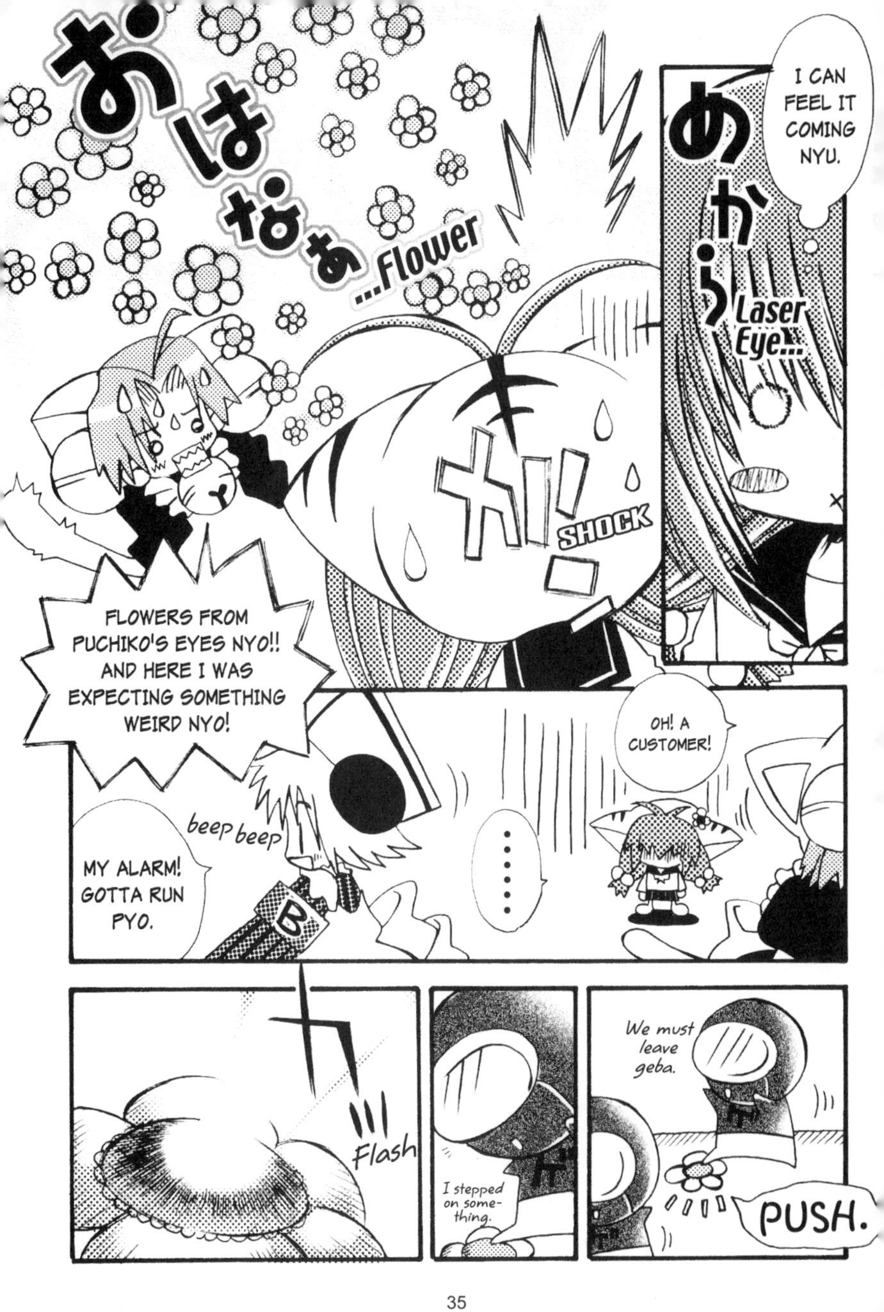
I CAN FEEL IT COMING NYU.
あから
Laser Eye...
おはなあ
...Flower
SHOCK
FLOWERS FROM PUCHIKO'S EYES NYO!! AND HERE I WAS EXPECTING SOMETHING WEIRD NYO!
OH! A CUSTOMER!
......
beep beep
MY ALARM! GOTTA RUN PYO.
We must leave geba.
PUSH.
I stepped on some-thing.
Flash

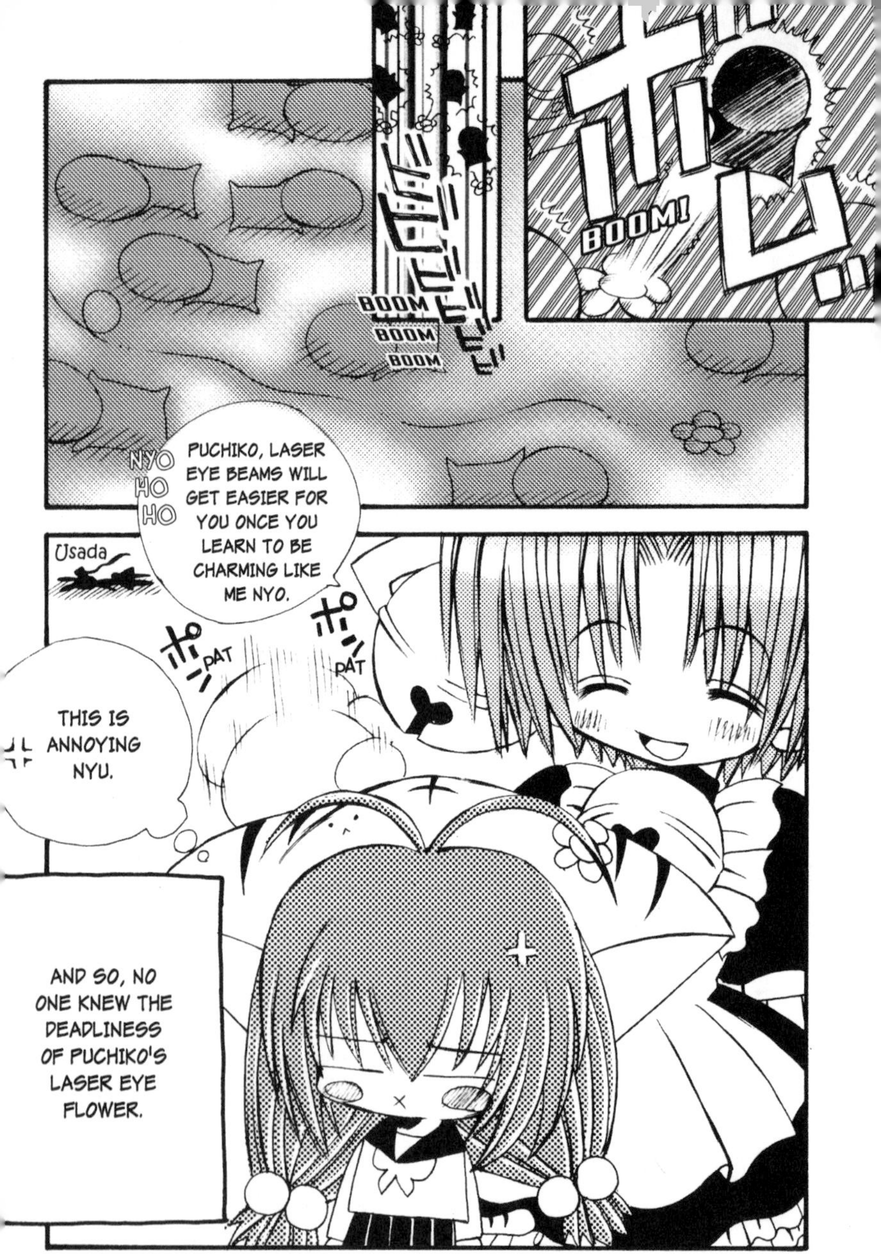
BOOM!
BOOM
BOOM
BOOM
PAT
PUCHIKO, LASER EYE BEAMS WILL GET EASIER FOR YOU ONCE YOU LEARN TO BE CHARMING LIKE ME NYO.
NYO HO HO
Usada
PAT
THIS IS ANNOYING NYU.
AND SO, NO ONE KNEW THE DEADLINESS OF PUCHIKO'S LASER EYE FLOWER.

THE END

Puchiko Catches a Cold

Towa Oozora

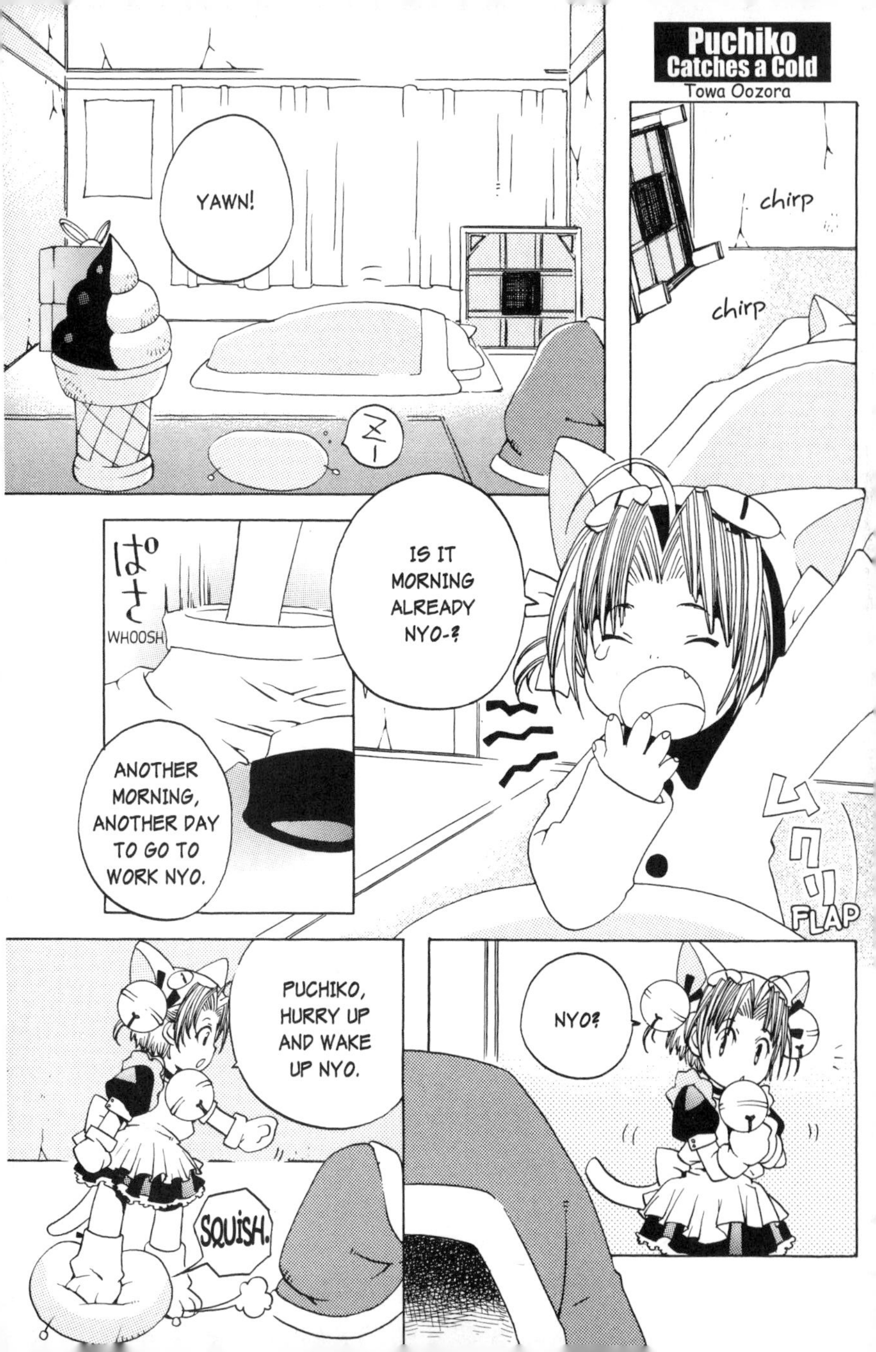
chirp
chirp
YAWN!
ズー
IS IT MORNING ALREADY NYO-?
ムクリ
FLAP
ぱさ
WHOOSH
ANOTHER MORNING, ANOTHER DAY TO GO TO WORK NYO.
NYO?
PUCHIKO, HURRY UP AND WAKE UP NYO.
SQUISH.

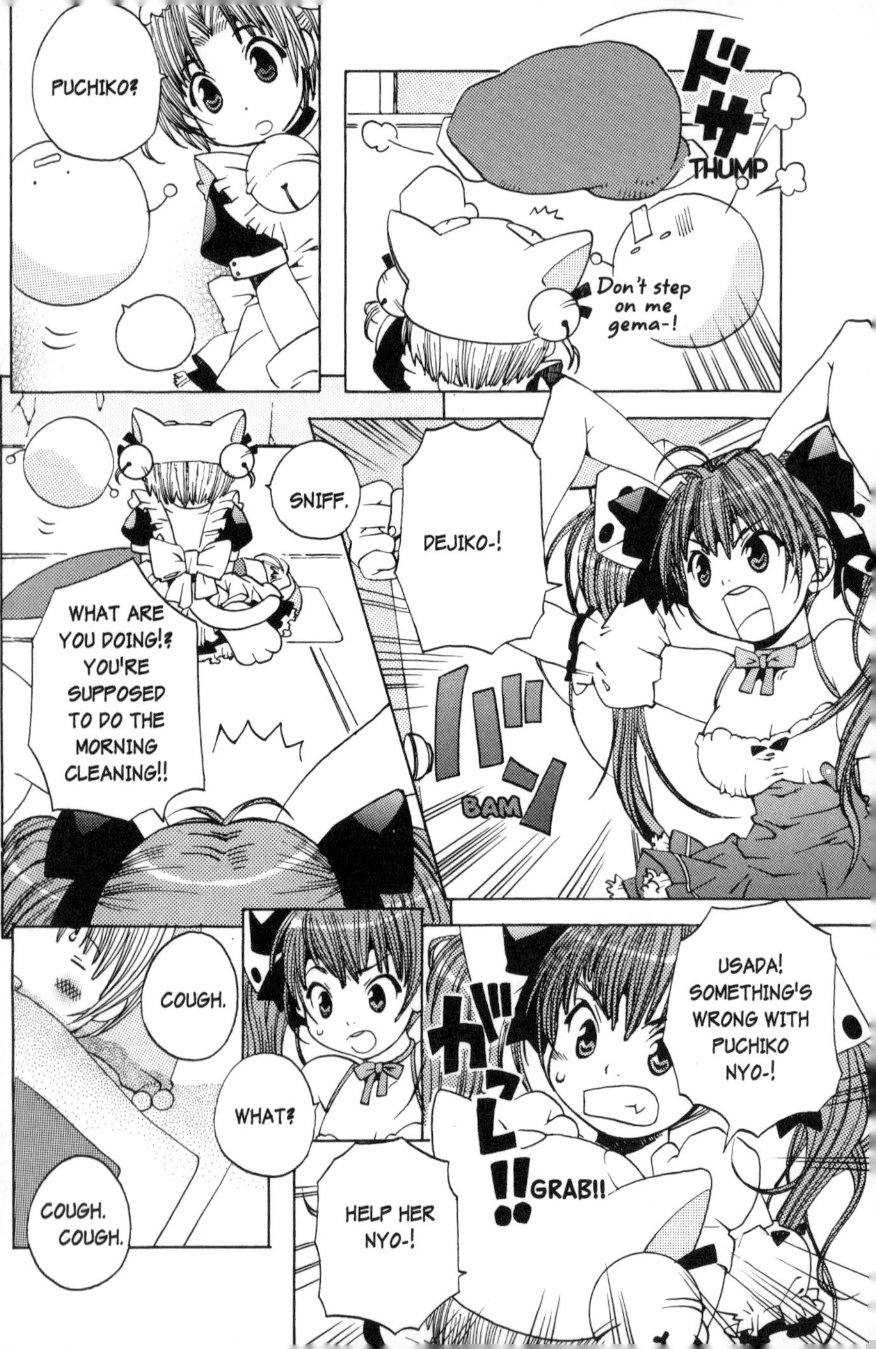
ドサ
THUMP
Don't step on me gema-!
PUCHIKO?
DEJIKO-!
バン
BAM
SNIFF.
WHAT ARE YOU DOING!? YOU'RE SUPPOSED TO DO THE MORNING CLEANING!!
USADA! SOMETHING'S WRONG WITH PUCHIKO NYO-!
ガっし!!
GRAB!!
HELP HER NYO-!
WHAT?
COUGH.
COUGH. COUGH.

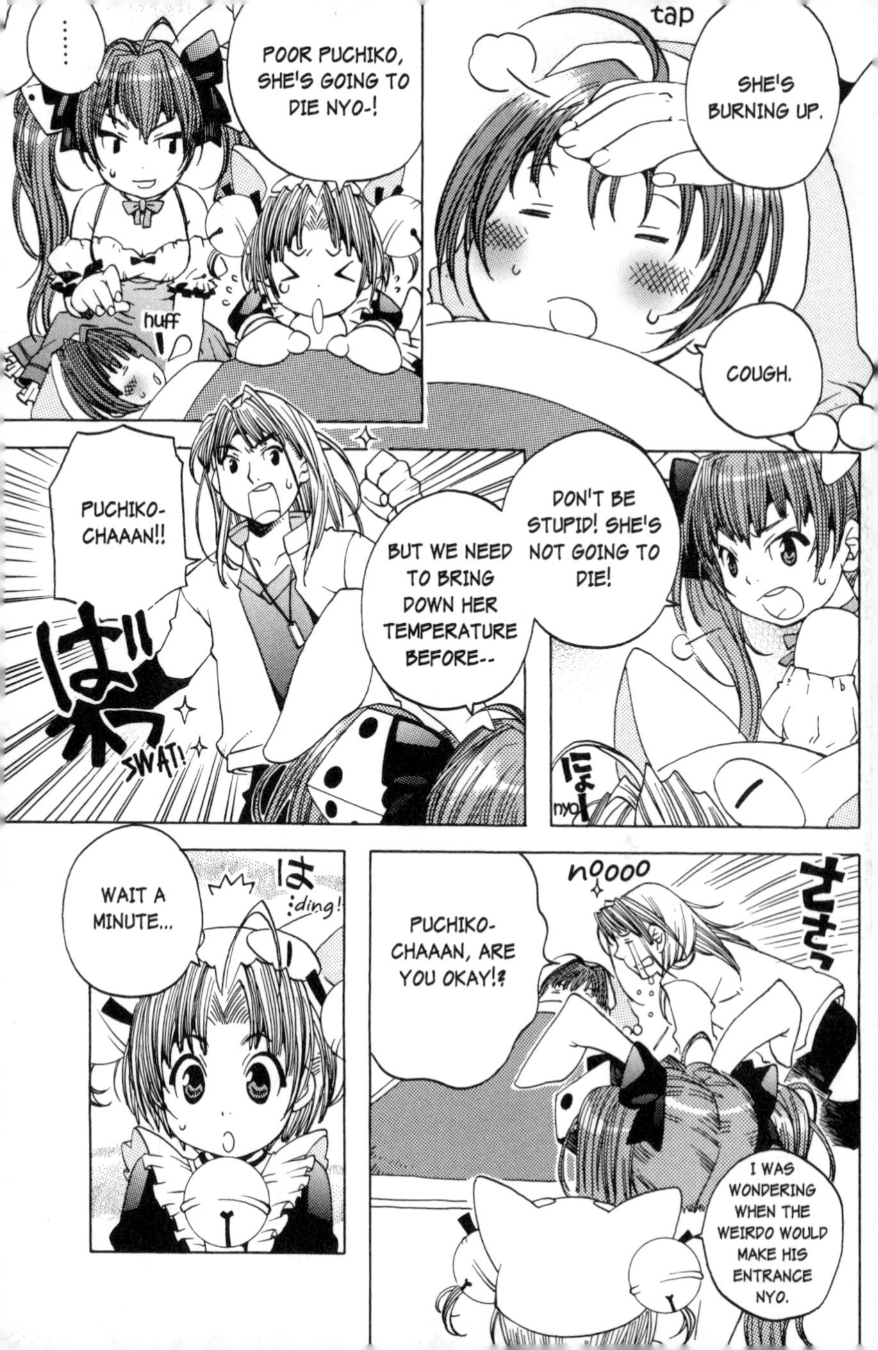
tap
SHE'S BURNING UP.
COUGH.
......
POOR PUCHIKO, SHE'S GOING TO DIE NYO-!
huff
DON'T BE STUPID! SHE'S NOT GOING TO DIE!
にょー
nyo
BUT WE NEED TO BRING DOWN HER TEMPERATURE BEFORE--
PUCHIKO-CHAAAN!!
ばっ
SWAT!
さっ
noooo
PUCHIKO-CHAAAN, ARE YOU OKAY!?
I WAS WONDERING WHEN THE WEIRDO WOULD MAKE HIS ENTRANCE NYO.
は
ding!
WAIT A MINUTE...

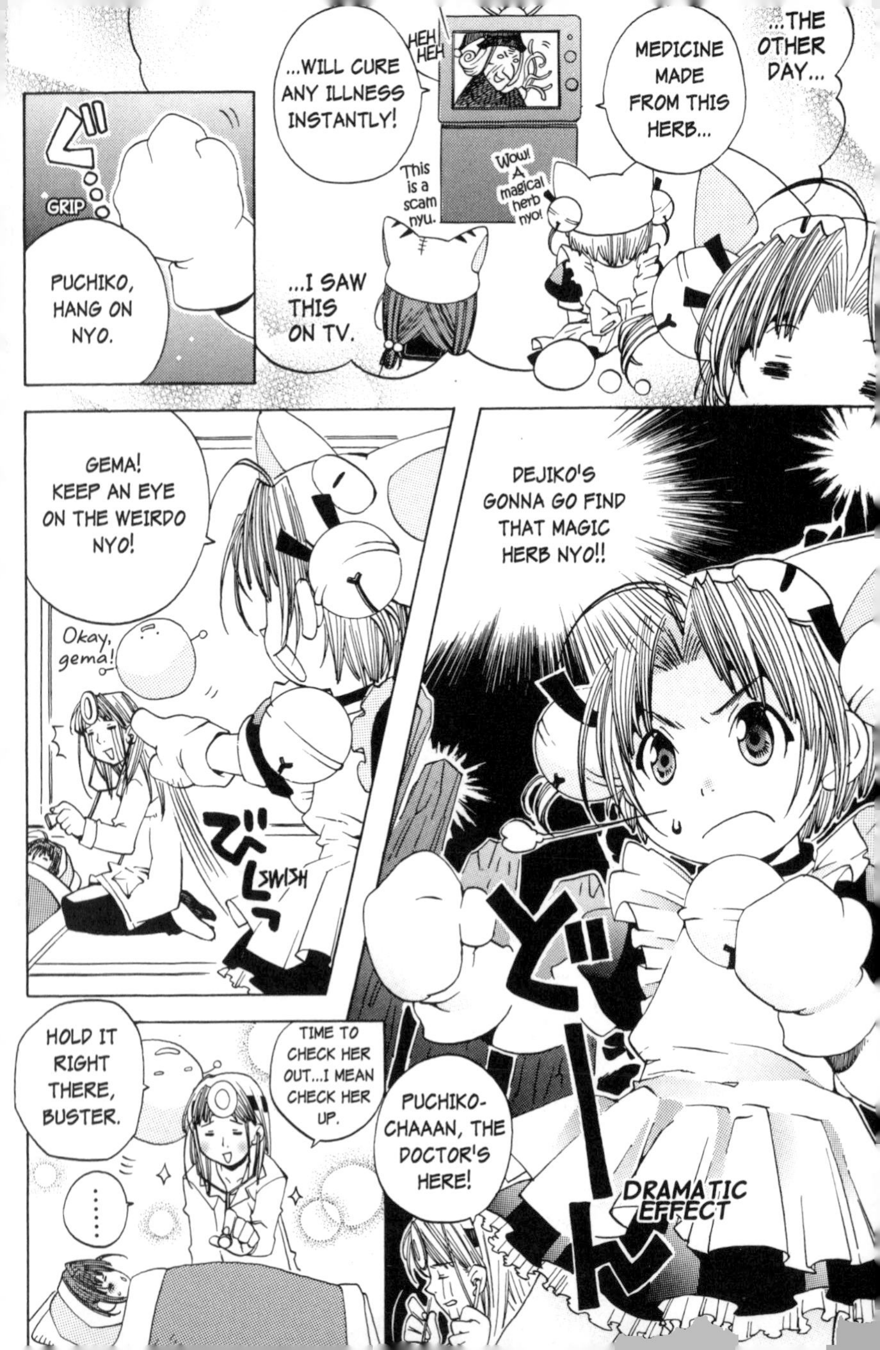
...THE OTHER DAY...
MEDICINE MADE FROM THIS HERB...
HEH HEH
...WILL CURE ANY ILLNESS INSTANTLY!
Wow! A magical herb nyo!
This is a scam nyu.
...I SAW THIS ON TV.
GRIP
PUCHIKO, HANG ON NYO.
DEJIKO'S GONNA GO FIND THAT MAGIC HERB NYO!!
DRAMATIC EFFECT
PUCHIKO-CHAAAN, THE DOCTOR'S HERE!
GEMA! KEEP AN EYE ON THE WEIRDO NYO!
Okay, gema!
SWISH
TIME TO CHECK HER OUT...I MEAN CHECK HER UP.
HOLD IT RIGHT THERE, BUSTER.
......

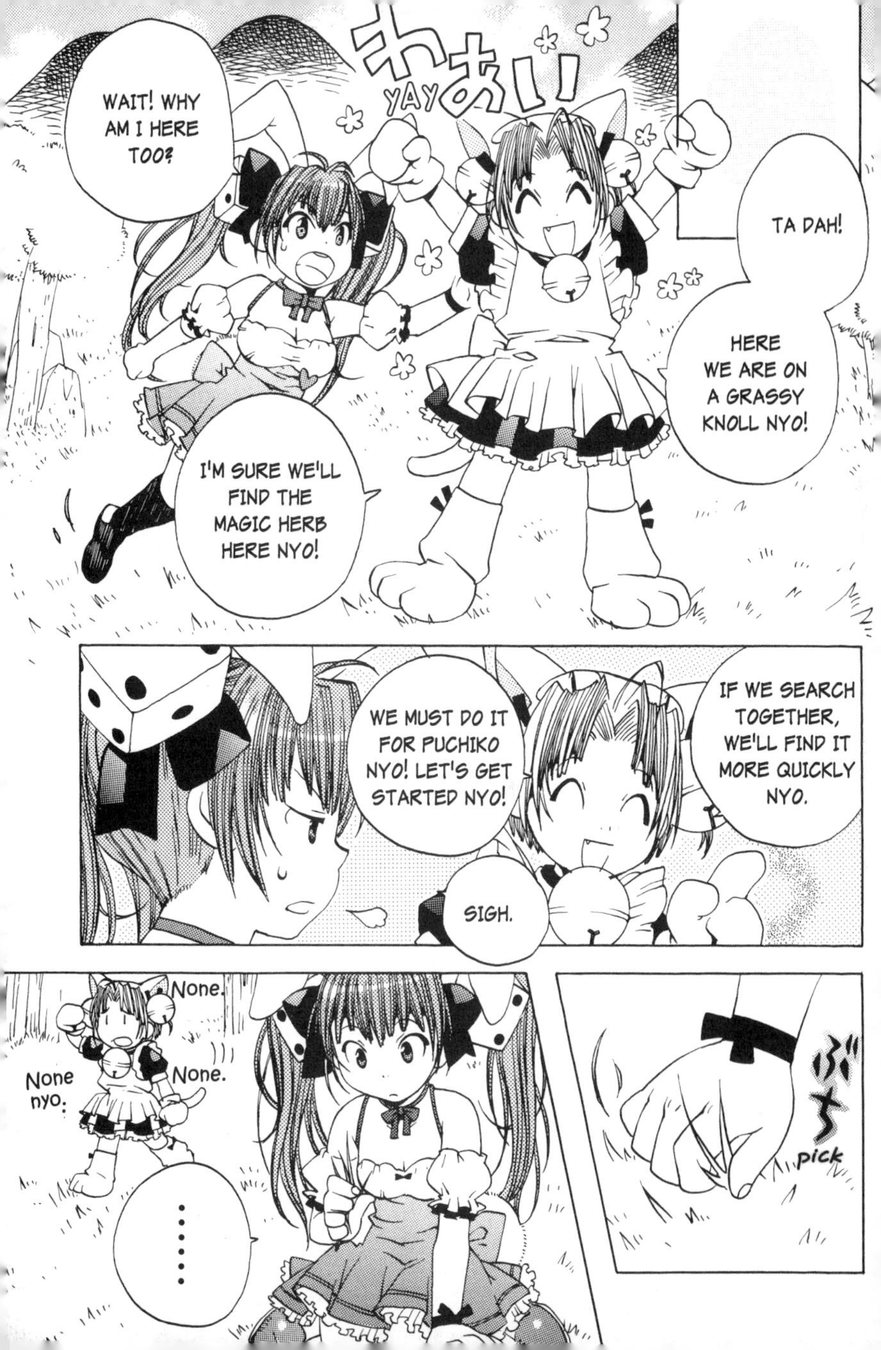

わあい
YAY
TA DAH!
HERE WE ARE ON A GRASSY KNOLL NYO!
WAIT! WHY AM I HERE TOO?
I'M SURE WE'LL FIND THE MAGIC HERB HERE NYO!
IF WE SEARCH TOGETHER, WE'LL FIND IT MORE QUICKLY NYO.
WE MUST DO IT FOR PUCHIKO NYO! LET'S GET STARTED NYO!
SIGH.
ぶち
pick
None.
None.
None nyo.
......

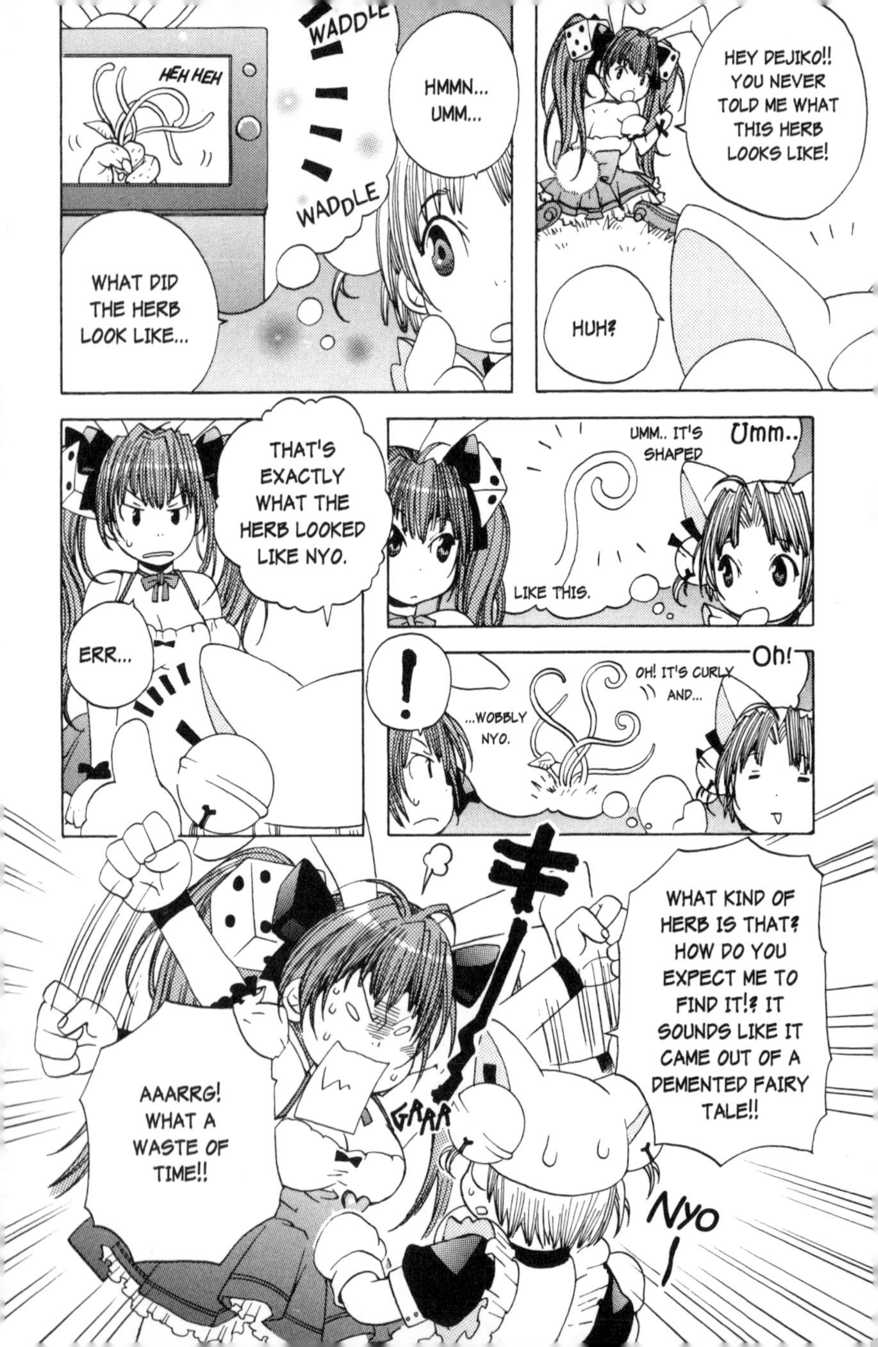
HEY DEJIKO!! YOU NEVER TOLD ME WHAT THIS HERB LOOKS LIKE!
HUH?
HMMN... UMM...
WADDLE
WADDLE
HEH HEH
WHAT DID THE HERB LOOK LIKE...
Umm..
UMM.. IT'S SHAPED
LIKE THIS.
Oh!
OH! IT'S CURLY AND...
...WOBBLY NYO.
!
THAT'S EXACTLY WHAT THE HERB LOOKED LIKE NYO.
ERR...
WHAT KIND OF HERB IS THAT? HOW DO YOU EXPECT ME TO FIND IT!? IT SOUNDS LIKE IT CAME OUT OF A DEMENTED FAIRY TALE!!
Nyo
GRRR
AAARRG! WHAT A WASTE OF TIME!!

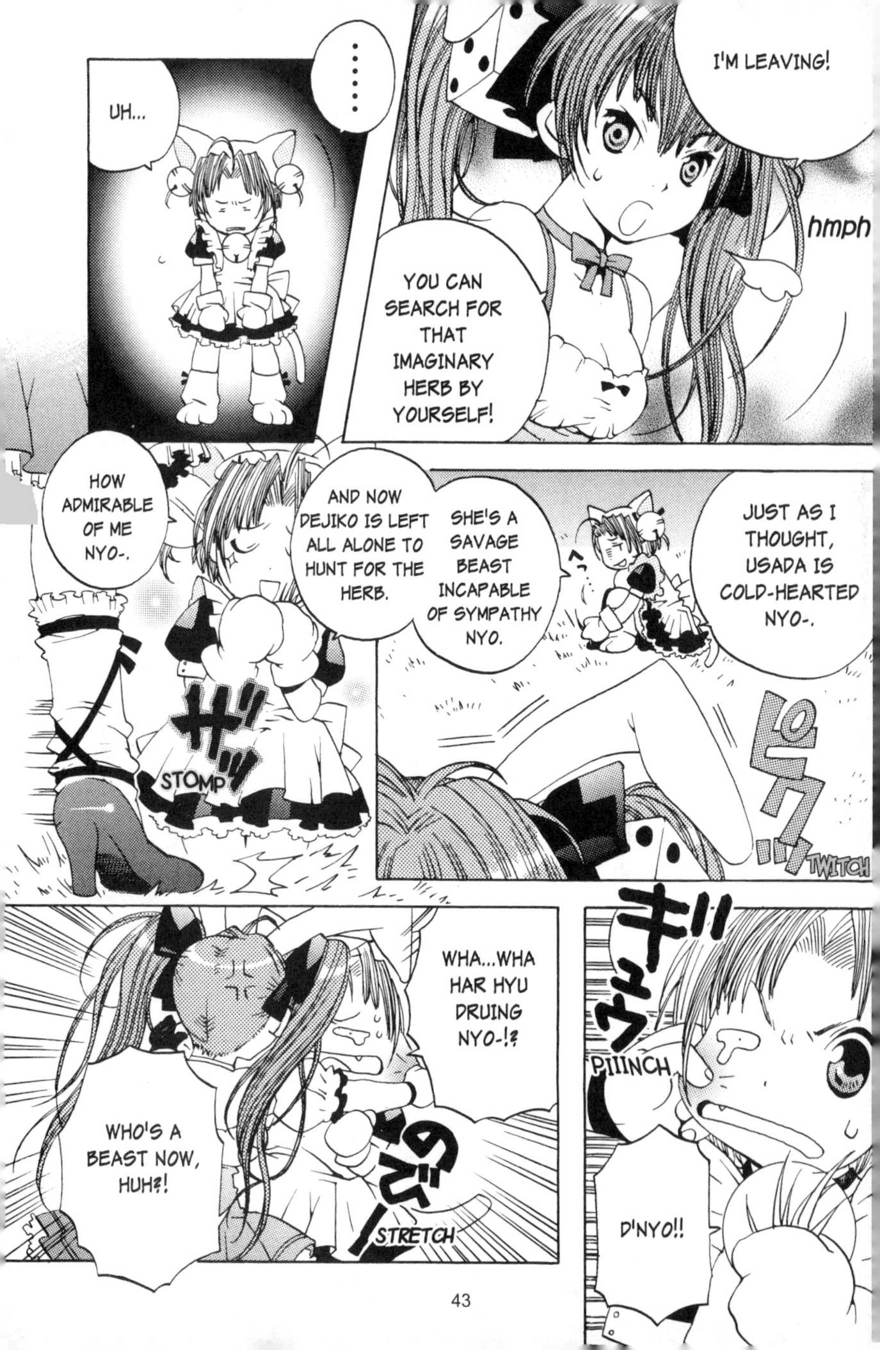
I'M LEAVING!
YOU CAN SEARCH FOR THAT IMAGINARY HERB BY YOURSELF!
hmph
......
UH...
JUST AS I THOUGHT, USADA IS COLD-HEARTED NYO-.
SHE'S A SAVAGE BEAST INCAPABLE OF SYMPATHY NYO.
TWITCH
AND NOW DEJIKO IS LEFT ALL ALONE TO HUNT FOR THE HERB.
HOW ADMIRABLE OF ME NYO-.
STOMP
PIIINCH
D'NYO!!
WHA...WHA HAR HYU DRUING NYO-!?
WHO'S A BEAST NOW, HUH?!
STRETCH

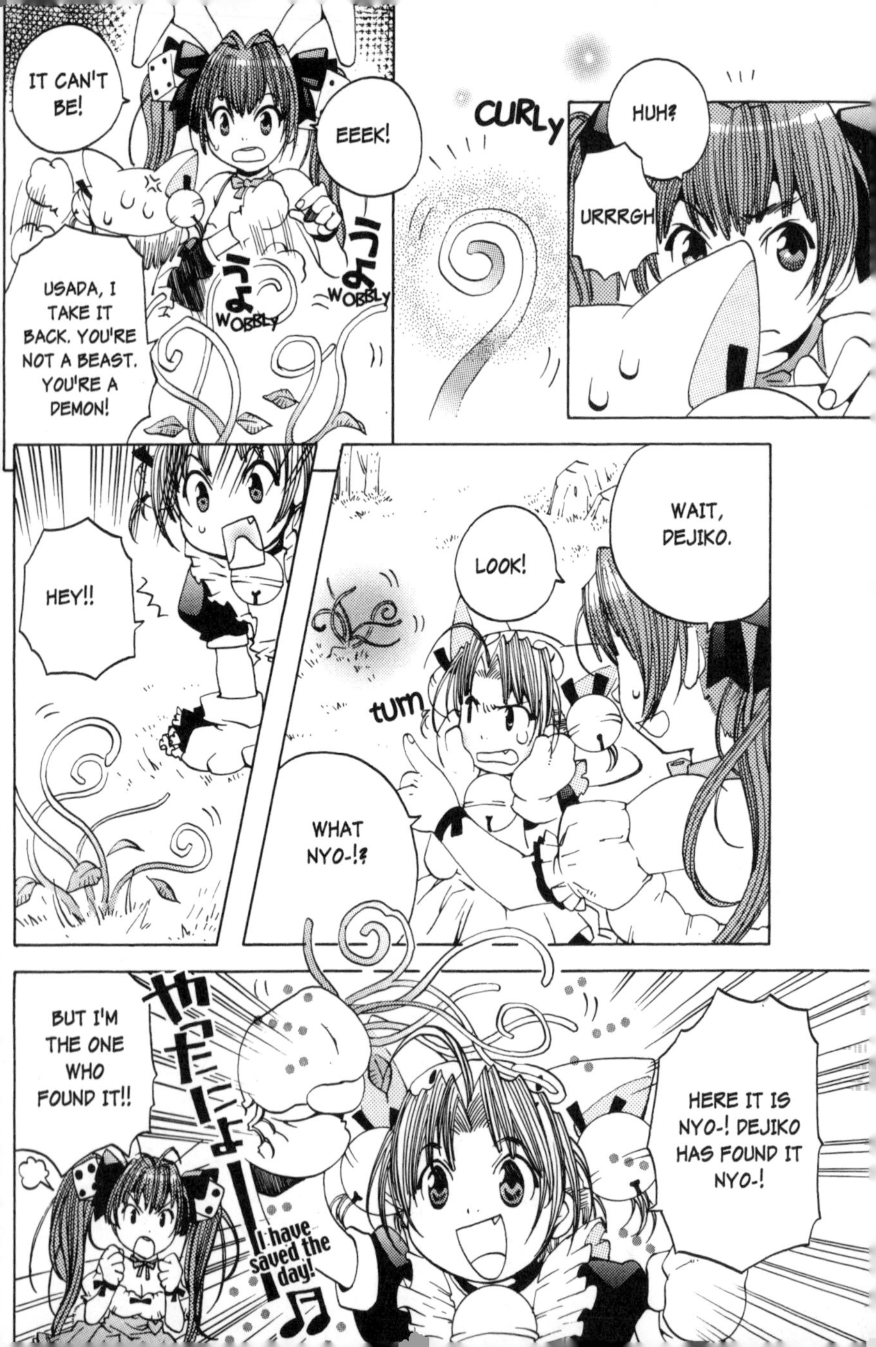
HUH?
URRRGH
CURLy
EEEK!
IT CAN'T BE!
うよ
WOBBLy
うよ
WOBBLy
USADA, I TAKE IT BACK. YOU'RE NOT A BEAST. YOU'RE A DEMON!
WAIT, DEJIKO.
LOOK!
turn
WHAT NYO-!?
HEY!!
HERE IT IS NYO-! DEJIKO HAS FOUND IT NYO-!
やったーにょー!
I have saved the day!
BUT I'M THE ONE WHO FOUND IT!!

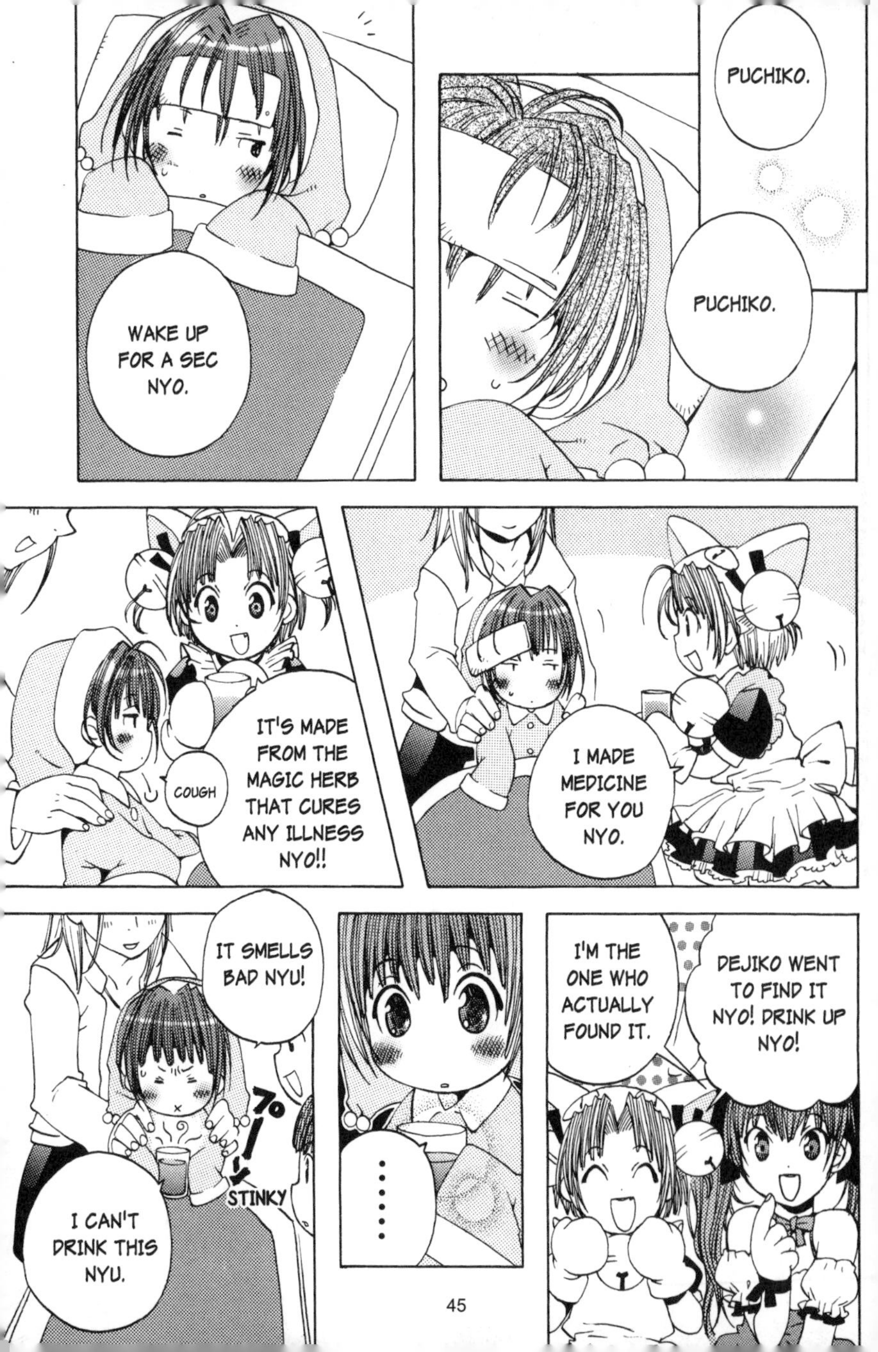

PUCHIKO.
PUCHIKO.
WAKE UP FOR A SEC NYO.
I MADE MEDICINE FOR YOU NYO.
IT'S MADE FROM THE MAGIC HERB THAT CURES ANY ILLNESS NYO!!
COUGH
DEJIKO WENT TO FIND IT NYO! DRINK UP NYO!
I'M THE ONE WHO ACTUALLY FOUND IT.
......
IT SMELLS BAD NYU!
STINKY
I CAN'T DRINK THIS NYU.

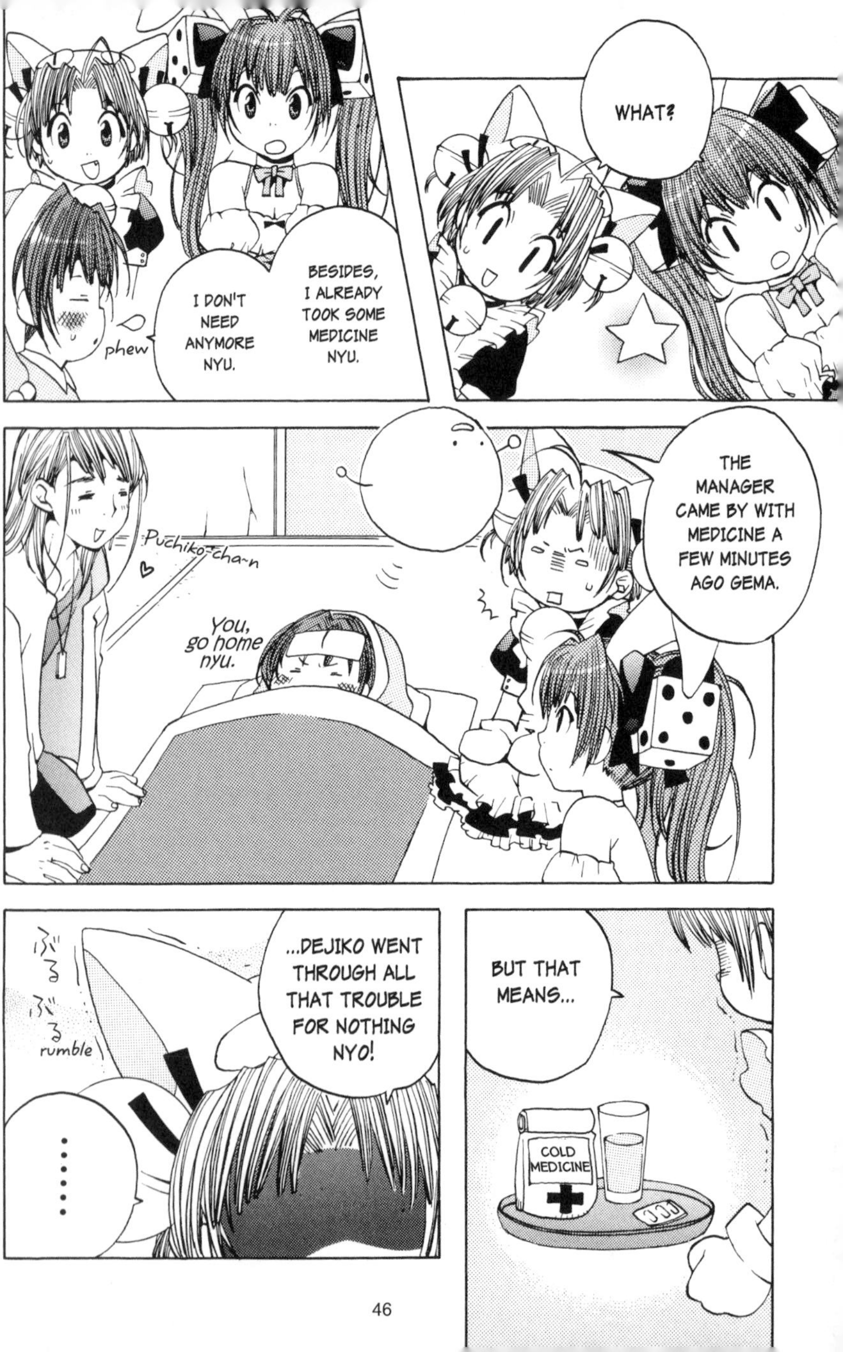
WHAT?
I DON'T NEED ANYMORE NYU.
BESIDES, I ALREADY TOOK SOME MEDICINE NYU.
phew
THE MANAGER CAME BY WITH MEDICINE A FEW MINUTES AGO GEMA.
Puchiko-cha~n
You, go home nyu.
BUT THAT MEANS...
COLD MEDICINE
...DEJIKO WENT THROUGH ALL THAT TROUBLE FOR NOTHING NYO!
ぶるぶる
rumble
......

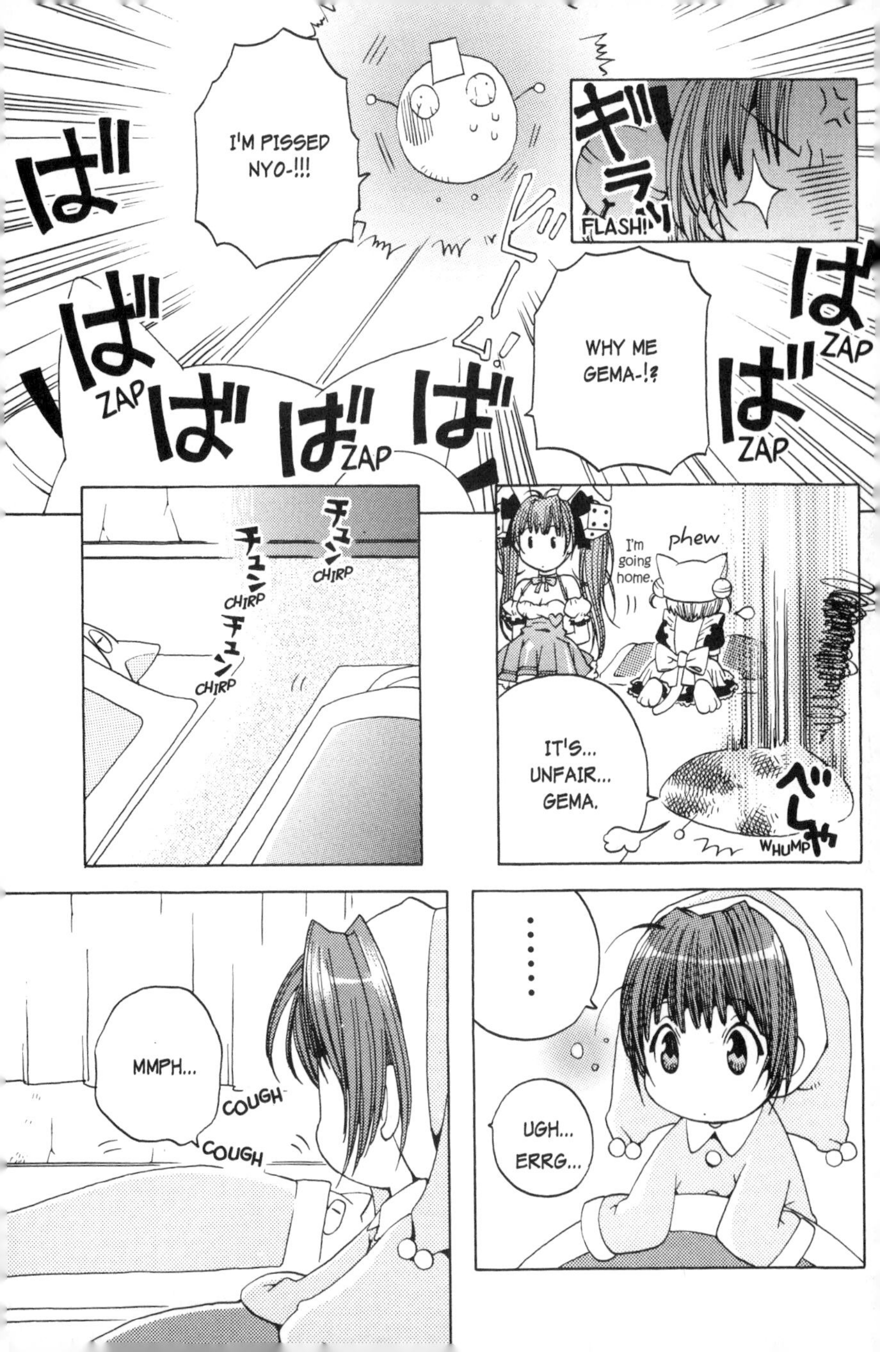
ギラッ
FLASH!
I'M PISSED NYO-!!!
WHY ME GEMA-!?
ば ZAP
ば ZAP
ばばばば ZAP
ZAP
phew
I'm going home.
IT'S... UNFAIR... GEMA.
べしゃ
WHUMP
チュン CHIRP
チュン CHIRP
チュン CHIRP
......
UGH... ERRG...
MMPH...
COUGH
COUGH

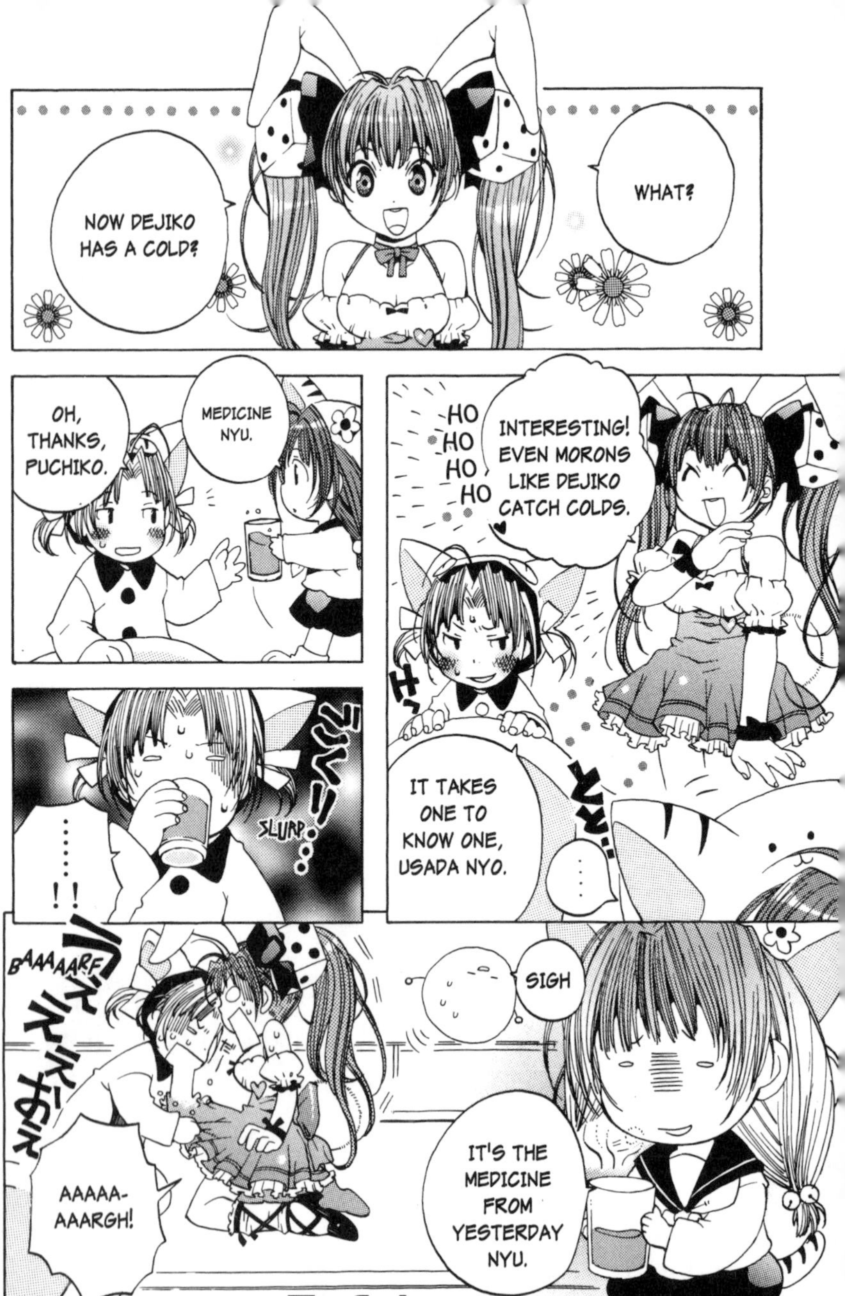
WHAT?
NOW DEJIKO HAS A COLD?
HO HO HO HO HO
INTERESTING! EVEN MORONS LIKE DEJIKO CATCH COLDS.
IT TAKES ONE TO KNOW ONE, USADA NYO.
...
MEDICINE NYU.
OH, THANKS, PUCHIKO.
SLURP
......
!!
SIGH
IT'S THE MEDICINE FROM YESTERDAY NYU.
BAAAAARF
AAAAA-AAARGH!

The End

Who's your favorite character in Di Gi Charat?

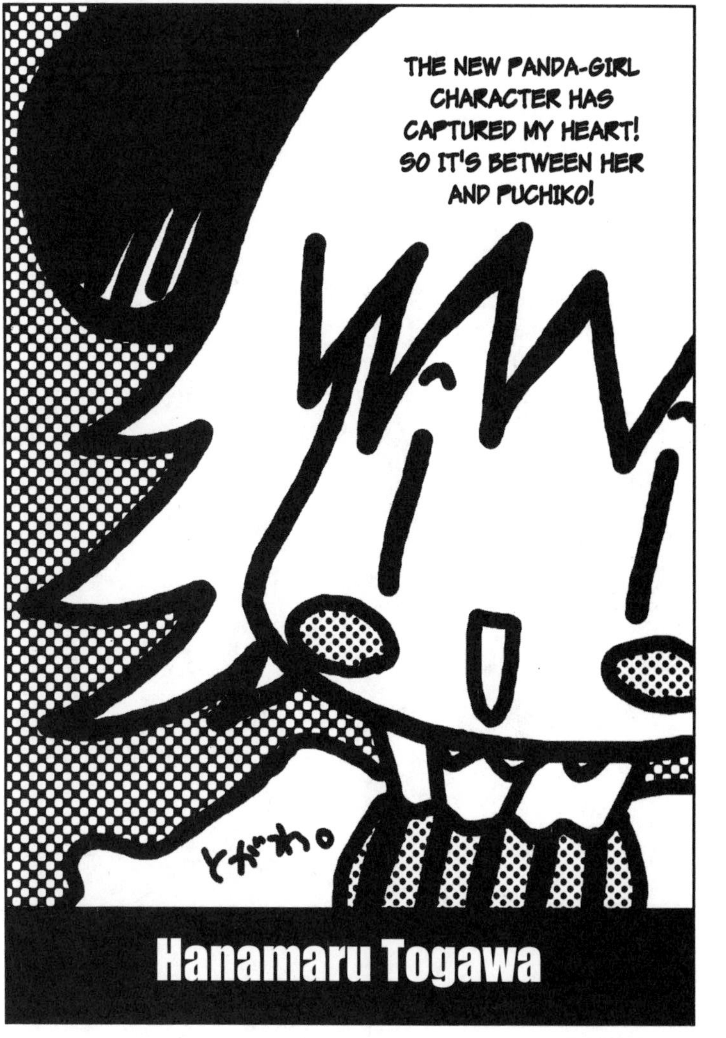
THE NEW PANDA-GIRL CHARACTER HAS CAPTURED MY HEART! SO IT'S BETWEEN HER AND PUCHIKO!
とがわ。
Hanamaru Togawa

Who's your favorite character in Di Gi Charat?

EVERYONE IS SO CUTE THAT I CAN'T TAKE MY EYES OFF OF THEM, BUT MY NUMBER ONE FAVORITE IS PUCHIKO-CHAN! I JUST WANT TO PICK HER UP.

に nyu ゅ

Oozora TOWA

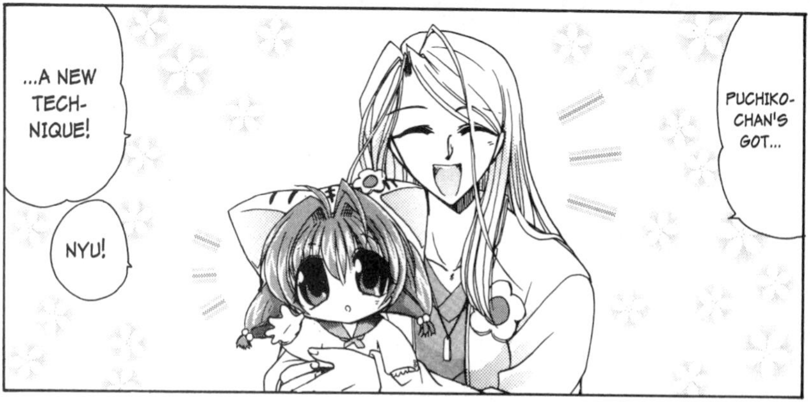
PUCHIKO-CHAN'S GOT...
...A NEW TECH-NIQUE!
NYU!

If Looks Could Kill
Hisaya Minamoto

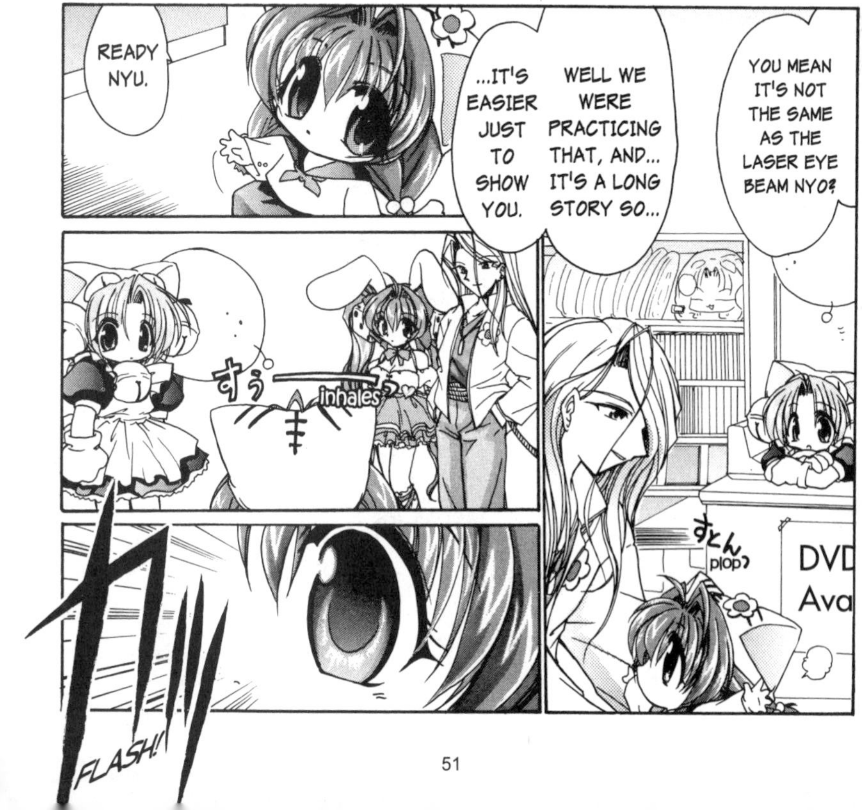
YOU MEAN IT'S NOT THE SAME AS THE LASER EYE BEAM NYO?
WELL WE WERE PRACTICING THAT, AND... IT'S A LONG STORY SO...
...IT'S EASIER JUST TO SHOW YOU.
すとん
plop
DVD
Ava
READY NYU.
すぅーっ
inhales
FLASH!

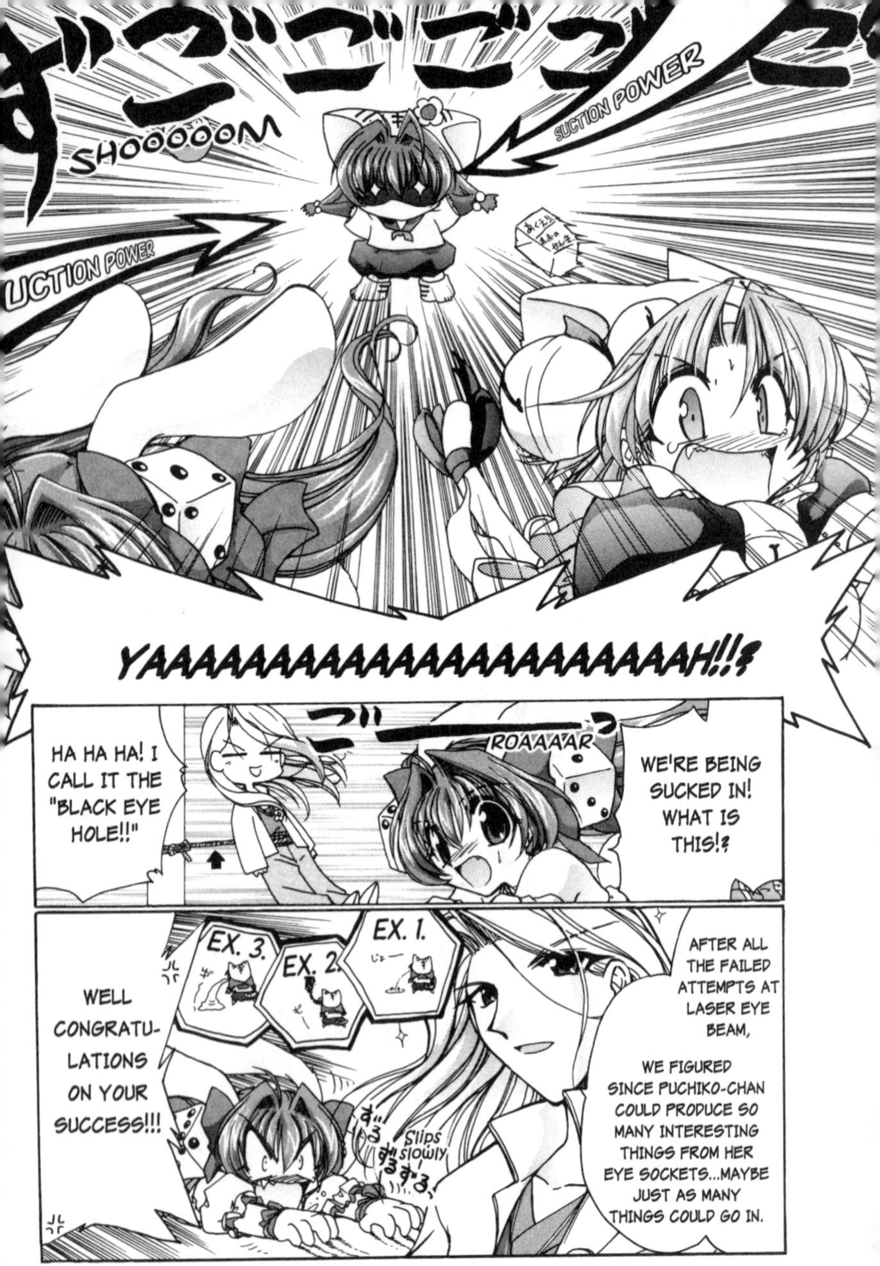
SUCTION POWER
SHOOOOOM
UCTION POWER
YAAAAAAAAAAAAAAAAAAAAAAH!!?
ROAAAAR
WE'RE BEING SUCKED IN! WHAT IS THIS!?
HA HA HA! I CALL IT THE "BLACK EYE HOLE!!"
AFTER ALL THE FAILED ATTEMPTS AT LASER EYE BEAM,
WE FIGURED SINCE PUCHIKO-CHAN COULD PRODUCE SO MANY INTERESTING THINGS FROM HER EYE SOCKETS...MAYBE JUST AS MANY THINGS COULD GO IN.
EX. 1.
EX. 2.
EX. 3.
Slips slowly
WELL CONGRATU-LATIONS ON YOUR SUCCESS!!!

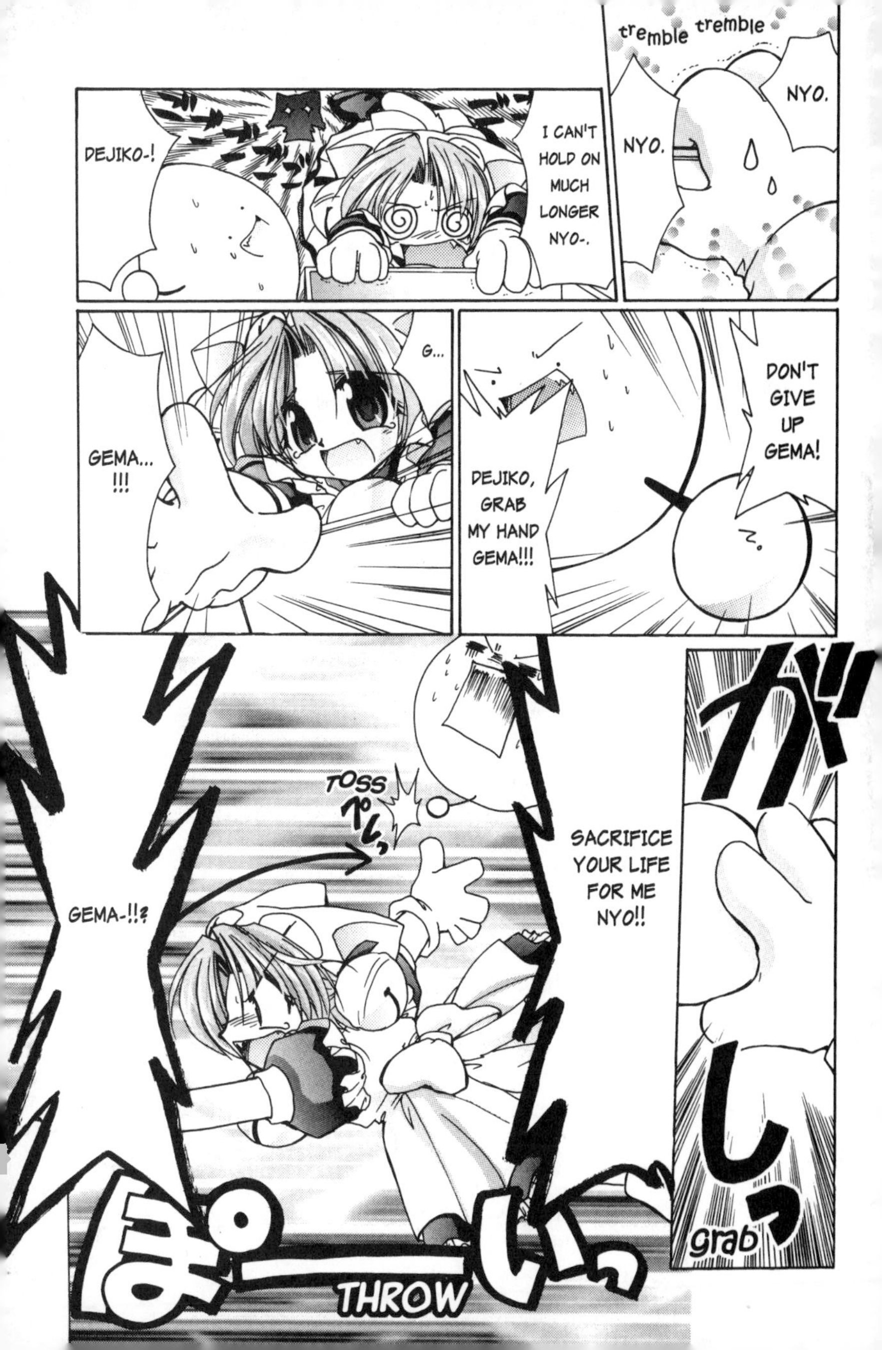

tremble tremble
NYO.
NYO.
I CAN'T HOLD ON MUCH LONGER NYO-.
DEJIKO-!
DON'T GIVE UP GEMA!
DEJIKO, GRAB MY HAND GEMA!!!
G...
GEMA... !!!
ガしっ
grab
SACRIFICE YOUR LIFE FOR ME NYO!!
ぺしっ
TOSS
GEMA-!!?
ぽーいっ
THROW

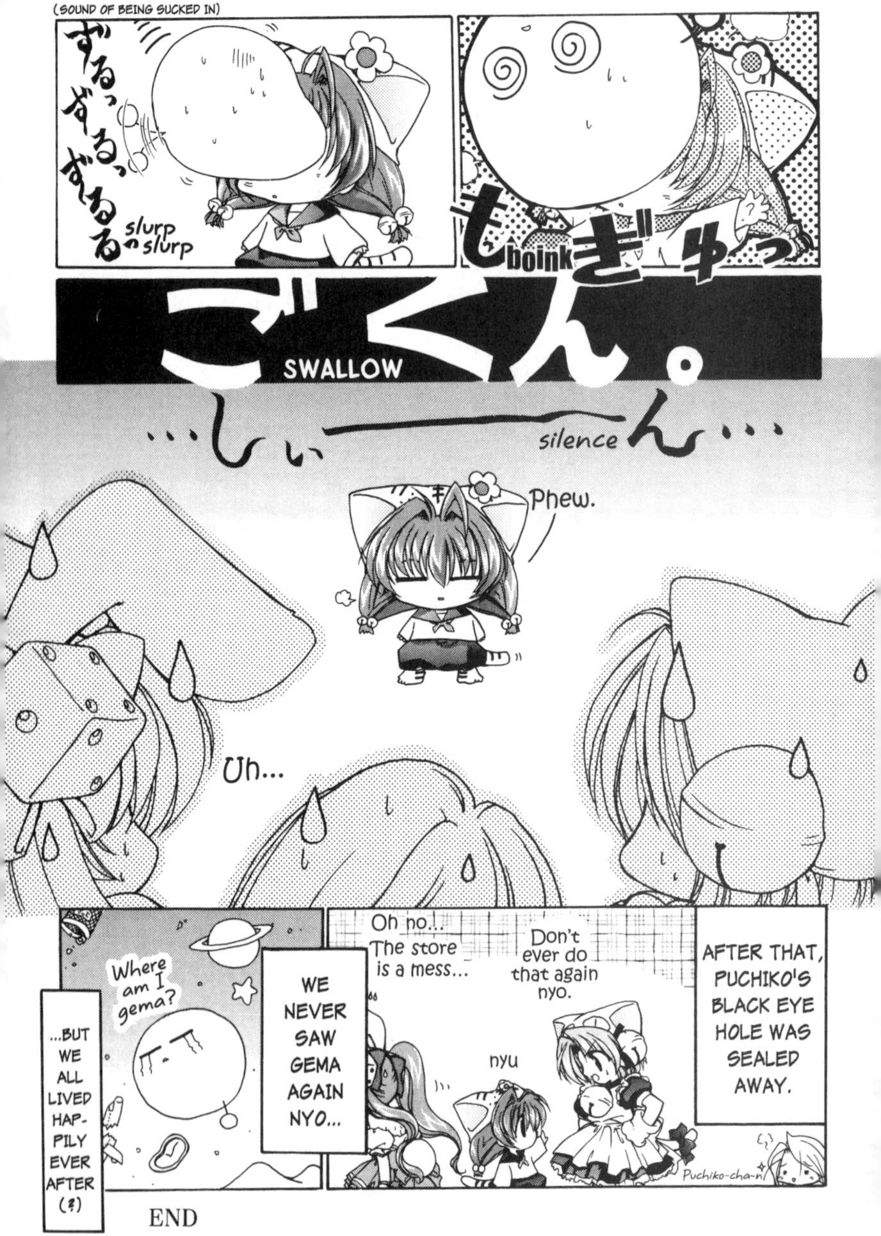
もぎゅっ
boink
(SOUND OF BEING SUCKED IN)
ずるっずるっずるる
slurp slurp
ごくん。
SWALLOW
…しぃーーーん…
silence
Phew.
Uh...
AFTER THAT, PUCHIKO'S BLACK EYE HOLE WAS SEALED AWAY.
Don't ever do that again nyo.
Oh no... The store is a mess...
nyu
Puchiko-cha-n
WE NEVER SAW GEMA AGAIN NYO...
Where am I gema?
...BUT WE ALL LIVED HAP-PILY EVER AFTER (?)
END

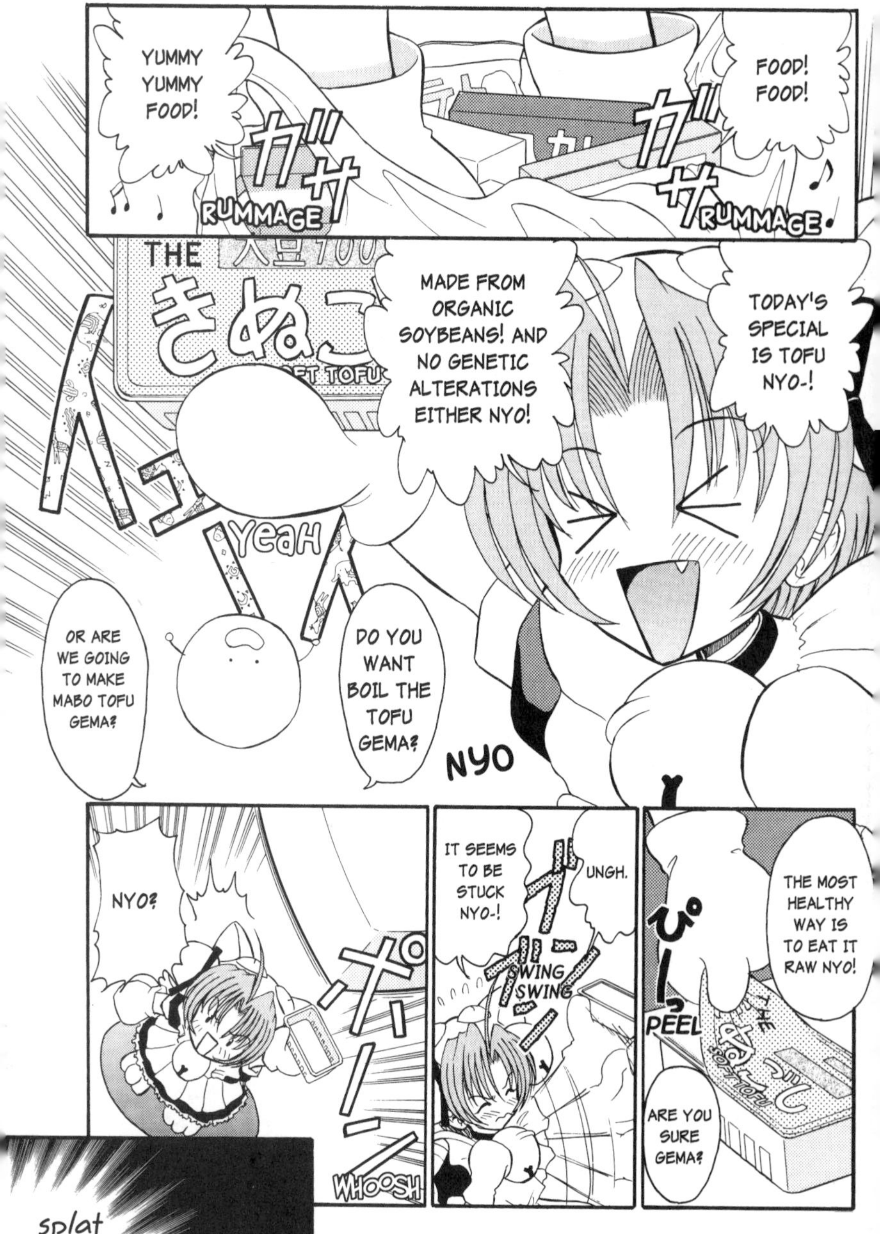
FOOD! FOOD!
RUMMAGE
YUMMY YUMMY FOOD!
RUMMAGE
TODAY'S SPECIAL IS TOFU NYO-!
MADE FROM ORGANIC SOYBEANS! AND NO GENETIC ALTERATIONS EITHER NYO!
SOFT TOFU
YEAH
NYO
DO YOU WANT BOIL THE TOFU GEMA?
OR ARE WE GOING TO MAKE MABO TOFU GEMA?
THE MOST HEALTHY WAY IS TO EAT IT RAW NYO!
PEEL
ARE YOU SURE GEMA?
UNGH.
IT SEEMS TO BE STUCK NYO-!
SWING SWING
WHOOSH
NYO?
splat

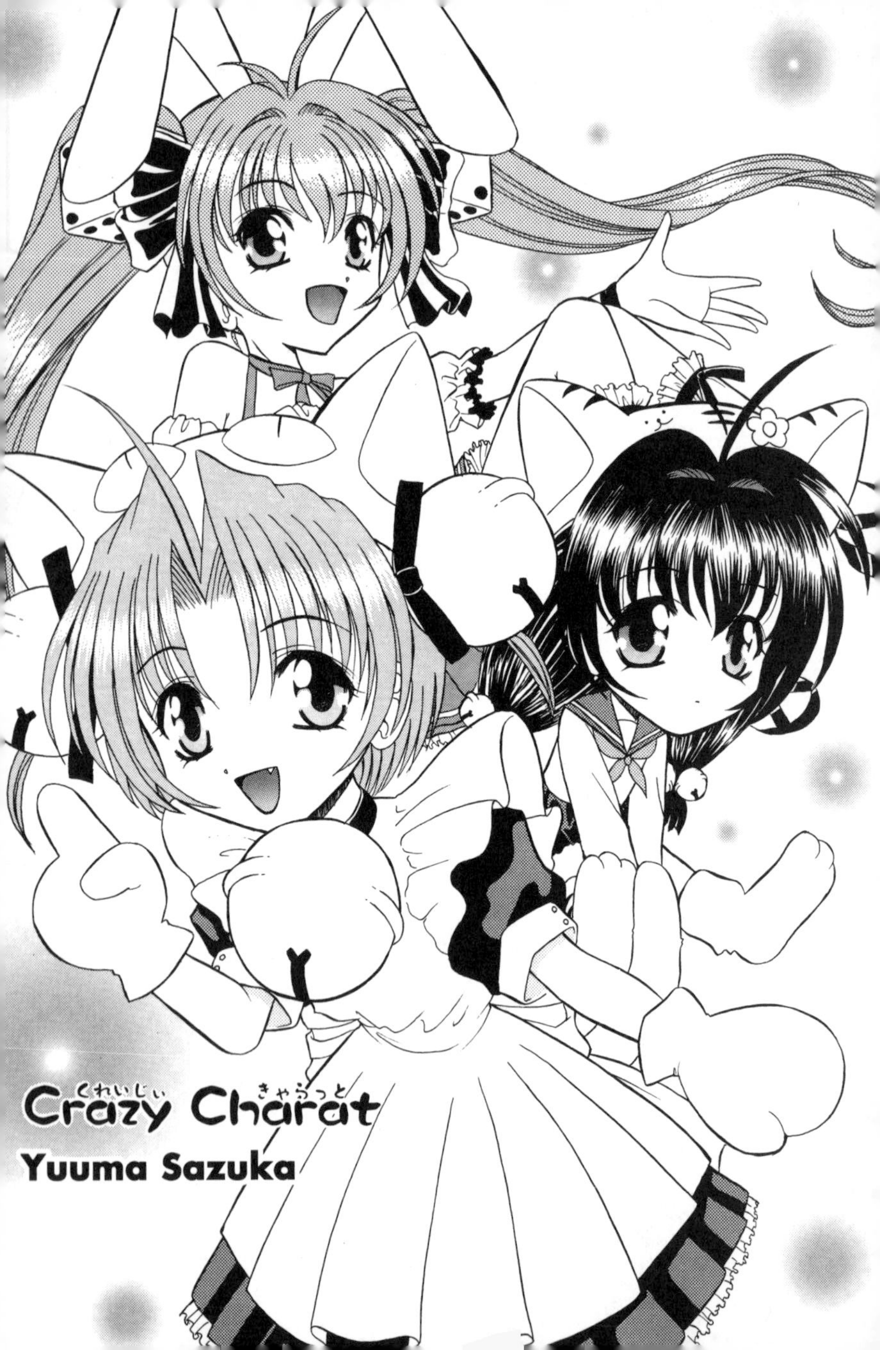

くれいじい
きゃらっと
Crazy Charat
Yuuma Sazuka

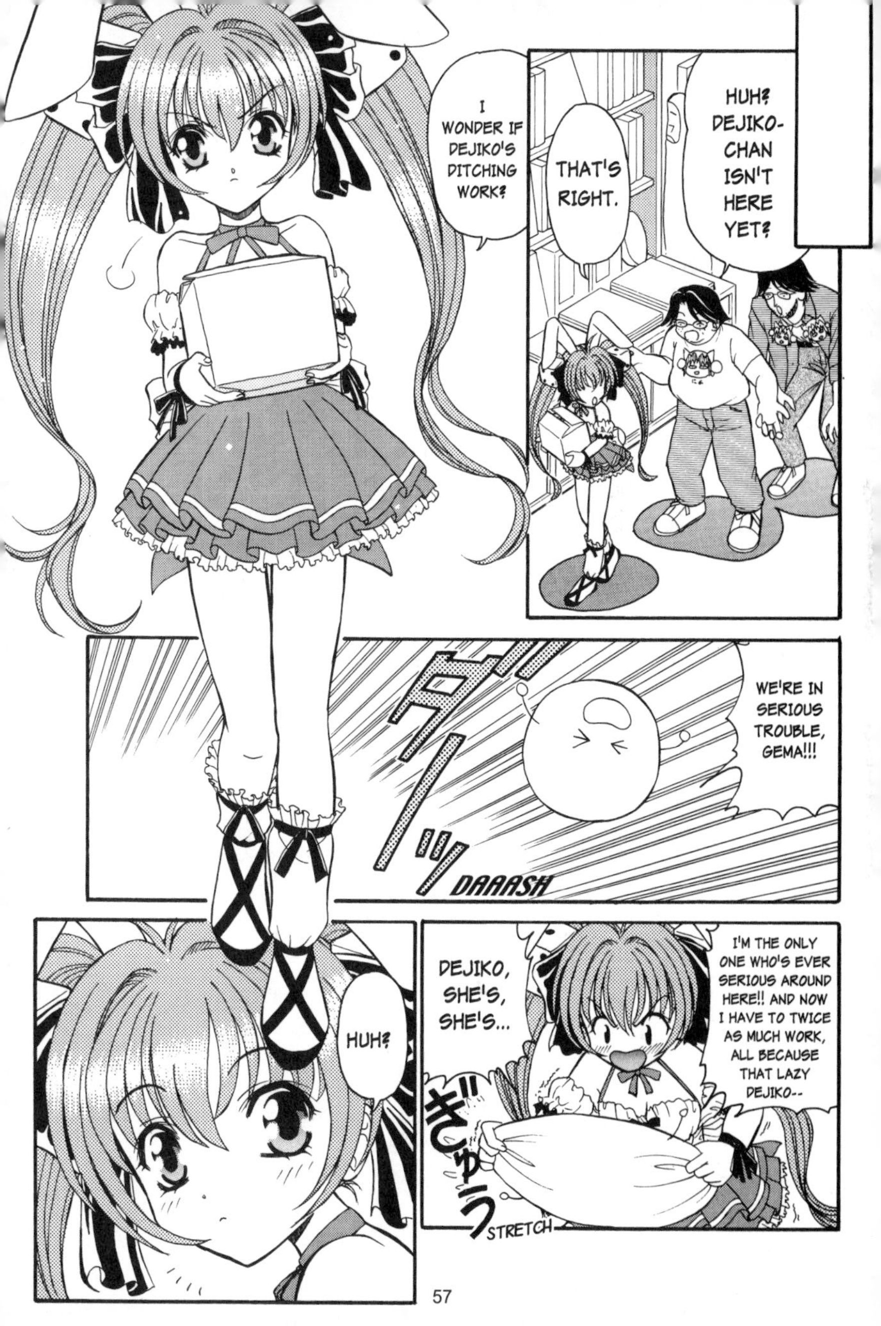
HUH? DEJIKO-CHAN ISN'T HERE YET?
THAT'S RIGHT.
I WONDER IF DEJIKO'S DITCHING WORK?
WE'RE IN SERIOUS TROUBLE, GEMA!!!
ダッ
DAAASH
I'M THE ONLY ONE WHO'S EVER SERIOUS AROUND HERE!! AND NOW I HAVE TO TWICE AS MUCH WORK, ALL BECAUSE THAT LAZY DEJIKO--
DEJIKO, SHE'S, SHE'S...
ぎゅう
STRETCH
HUH?

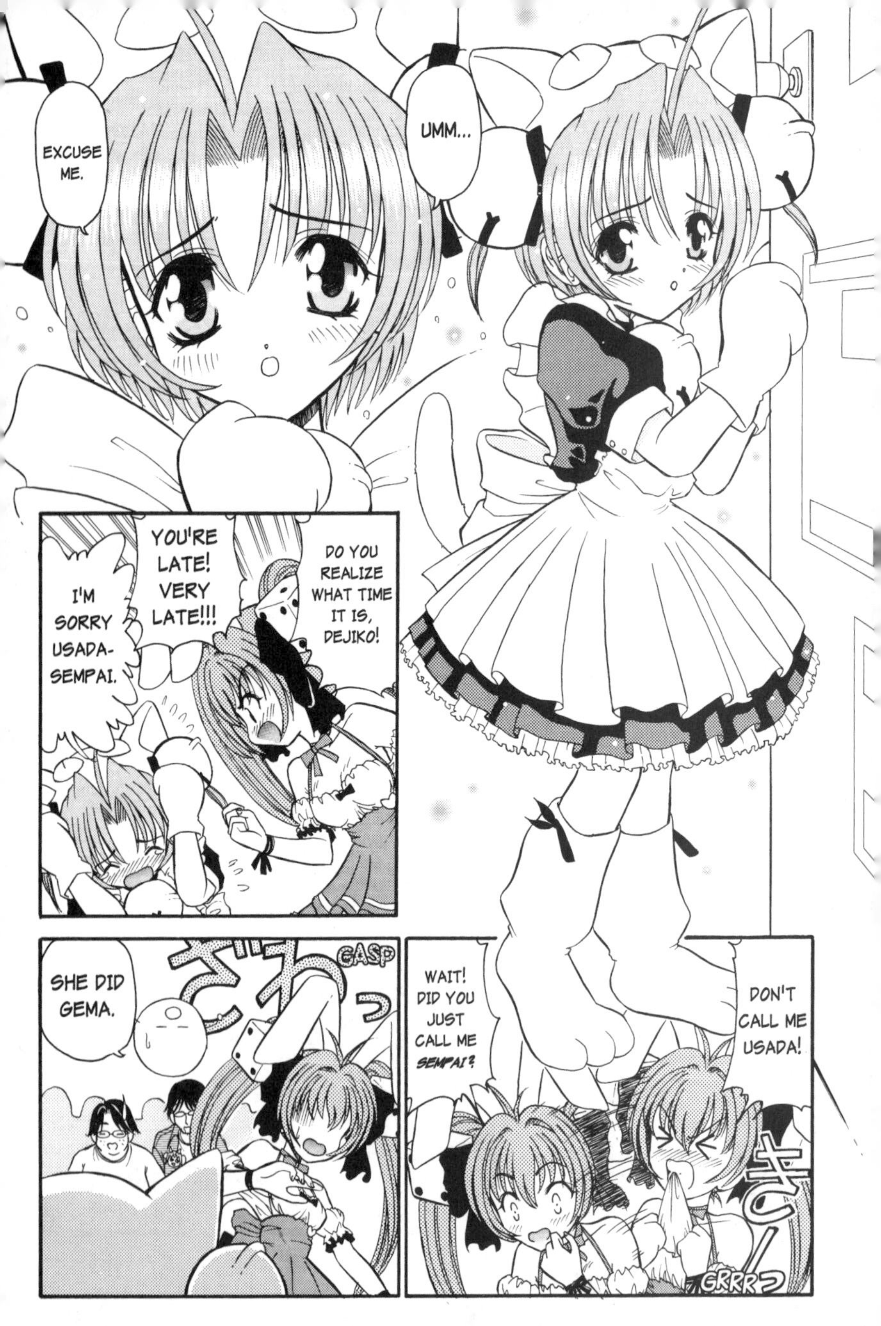
UMM...
EXCUSE ME.
DO YOU REALIZE WHAT TIME IT IS, DEJIKO!
YOU'RE LATE! VERY LATE!!!
I'M SORRY USADA-SEMPAI.
DON'T CALL ME USADA!
WAIT! DID YOU JUST CALL ME *SEMPAI*?
GRRR
GASP
SHE DID GEMA.

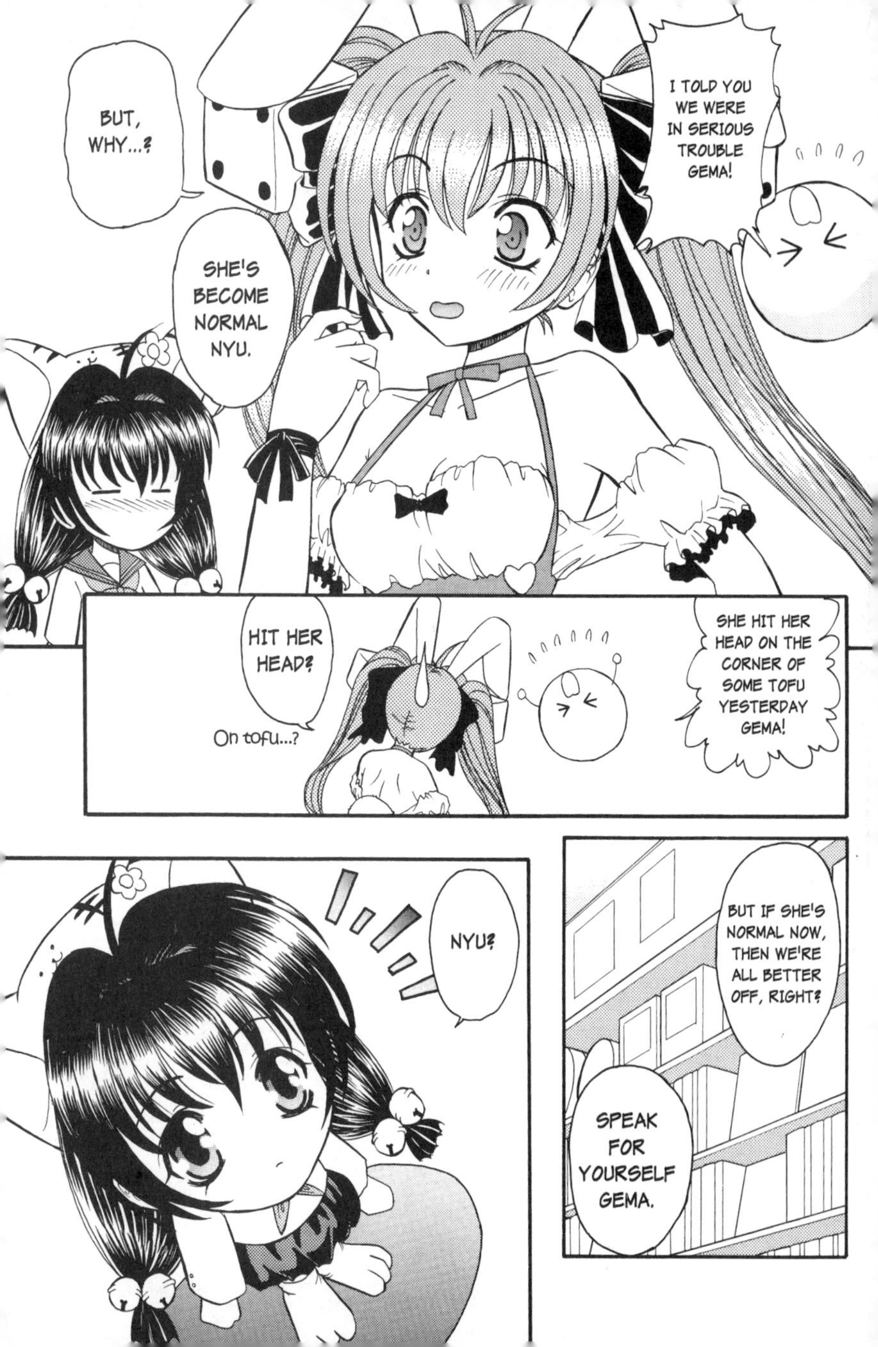
I TOLD YOU WE WERE IN SERIOUS TROUBLE GEMA!
BUT, WHY...?
SHE'S BECOME NORMAL NYU.
SHE HIT HER HEAD ON THE CORNER OF SOME TOFU YESTERDAY GEMA!
HIT HER HEAD?
On tofu...?
BUT IF SHE'S NORMAL NOW, THEN WE'RE ALL BETTER OFF, RIGHT?
SPEAK FOR YOURSELF GEMA.
NYU?

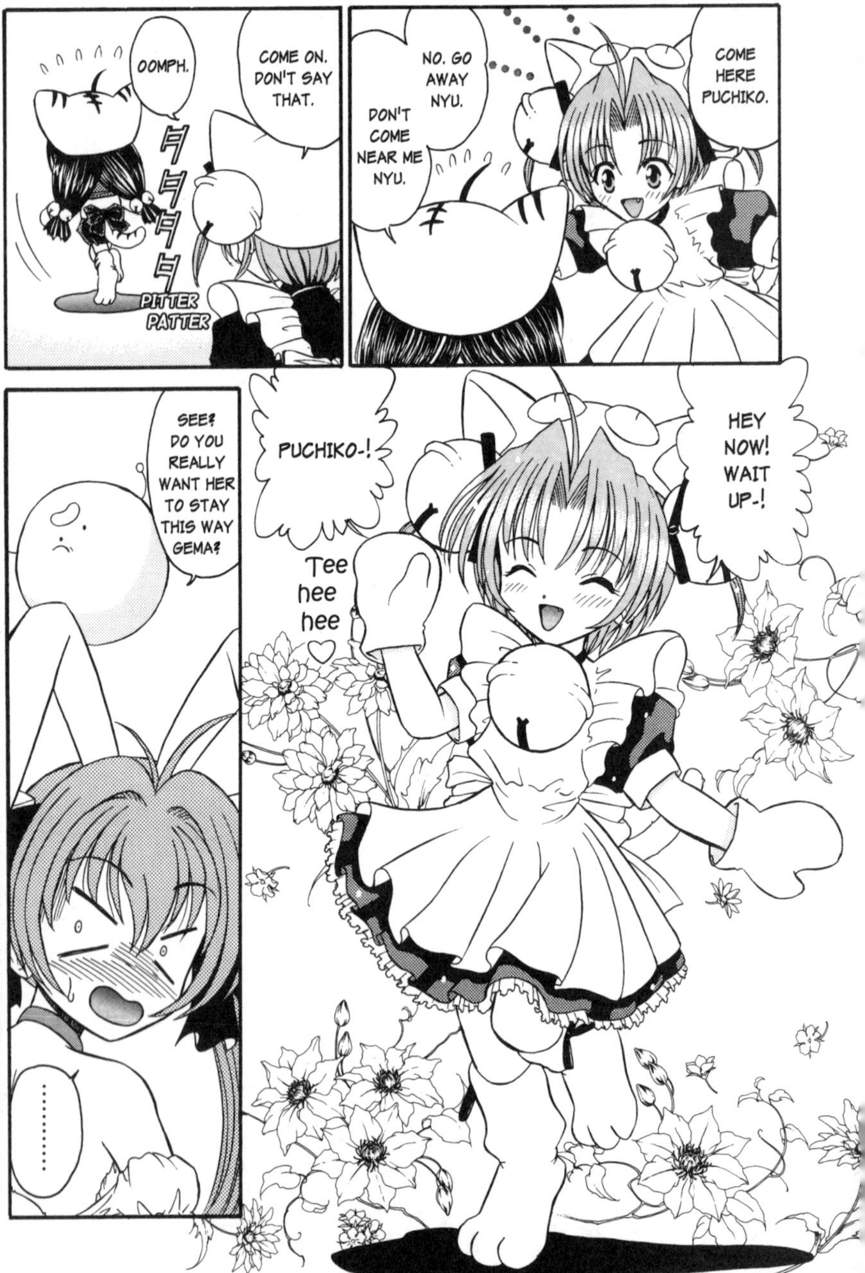
COME HERE PUCHIKO.
NO. GO AWAY NYU.
DON'T COME NEAR ME NYU.
COME ON. DON'T SAY THAT.
OOMPH.
PITTER PATTER
HEY NOW! WAIT UP-!
PUCHIKO-!
Tee hee hee
SEE? DO YOU REALLY WANT HER TO STAY THIS WAY GEMA?
....

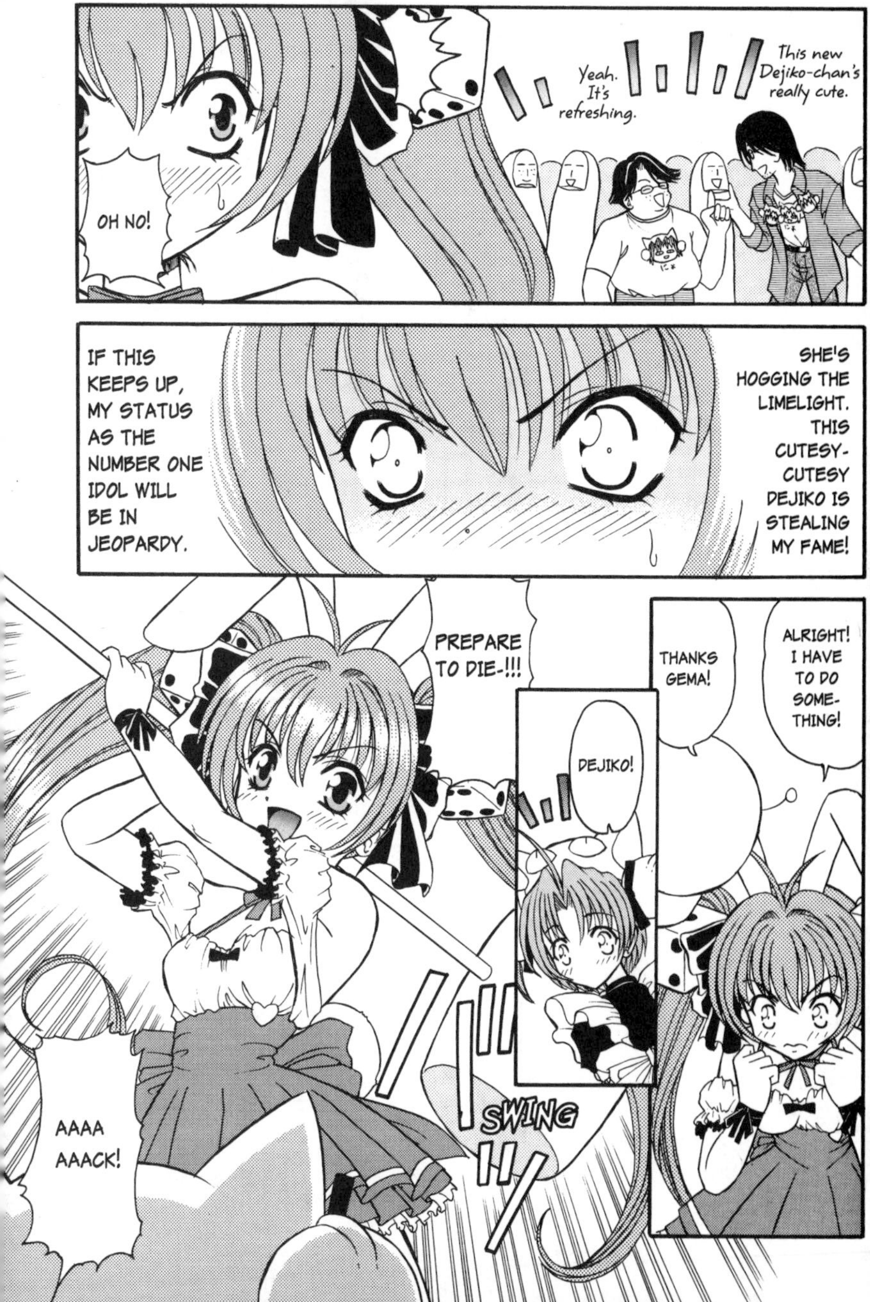
This new Dejiko-chan's really cute.
Yeah. It's refreshing.
OH NO!
SHE'S HOGGING THE LIMELIGHT. THIS CUTESY-CUTESY DEJIKO IS STEALING MY FAME!
IF THIS KEEPS UP, MY STATUS AS THE NUMBER ONE IDOL WILL BE IN JEOPARDY.
ALRIGHT! I HAVE TO DO SOME-THING!
THANKS GEMA!
DEJIKO!
PREPARE TO DIE-!!!
SWING
AAAA AAACK!

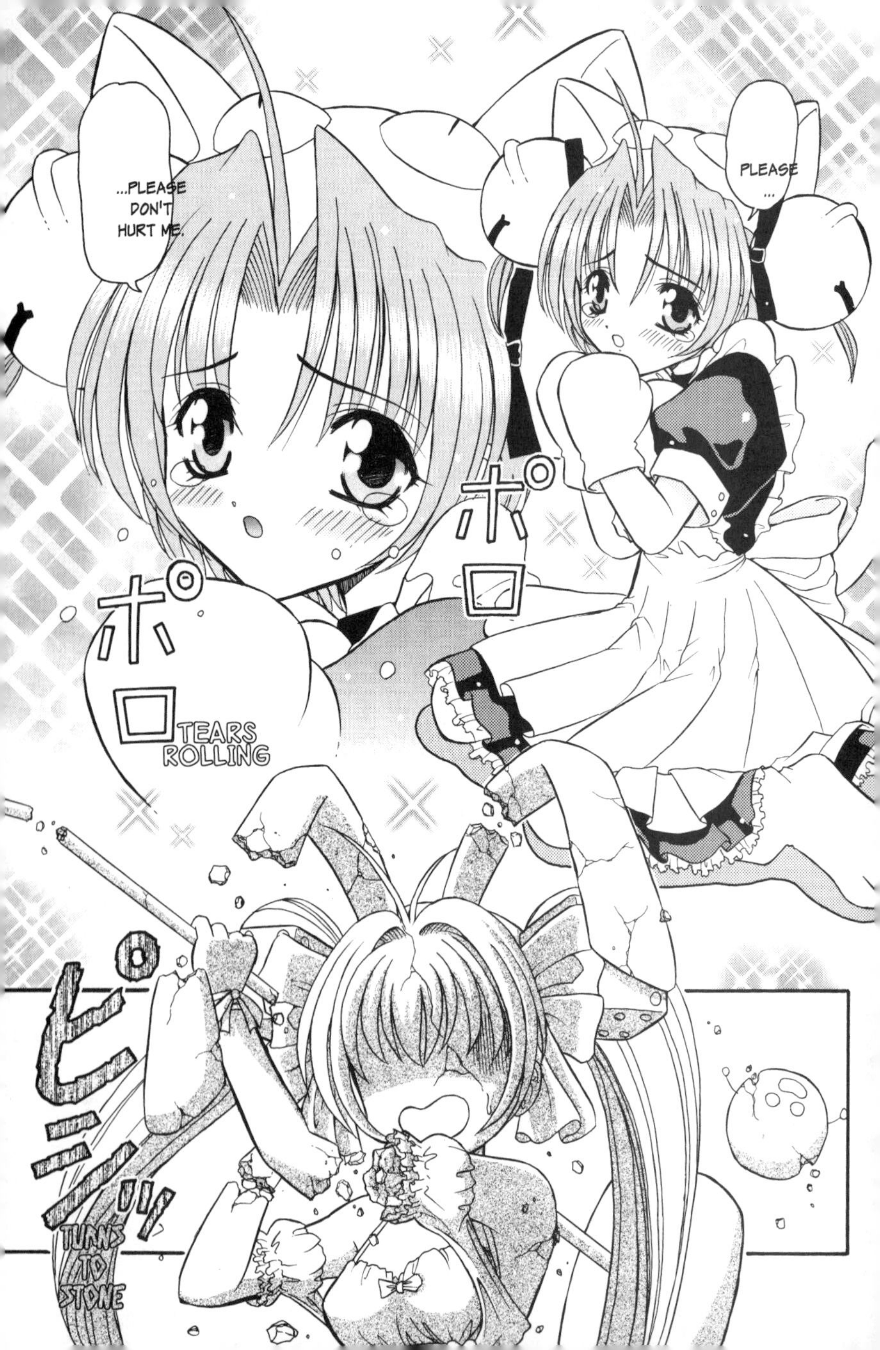
PLEASE ...
...PLEASE DON'T HURT ME.
ポロ
ポロ
TEARS ROLLING
TURNS TO STONE

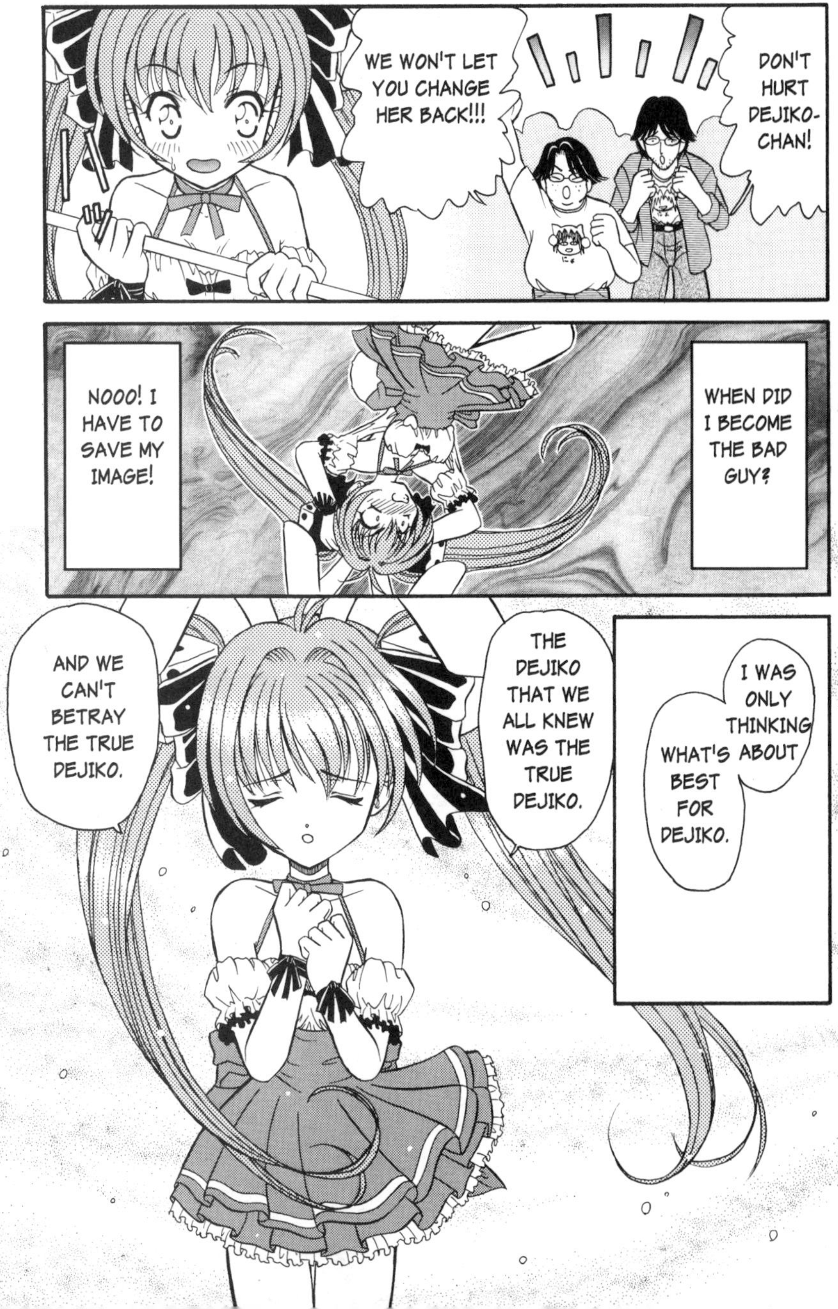
DON'T HURT DEJIKO-CHAN!
WE WON'T LET YOU CHANGE HER BACK!!!
WHEN DID I BECOME THE BAD GUY?
NOOO! I HAVE TO SAVE MY IMAGE!
I WAS ONLY THINKING ABOUT WHAT'S BEST FOR DEJIKO.
THE DEJIKO THAT WE ALL KNEW WAS THE TRUE DEJIKO.
AND WE CAN'T BETRAY THE TRUE DEJIKO.

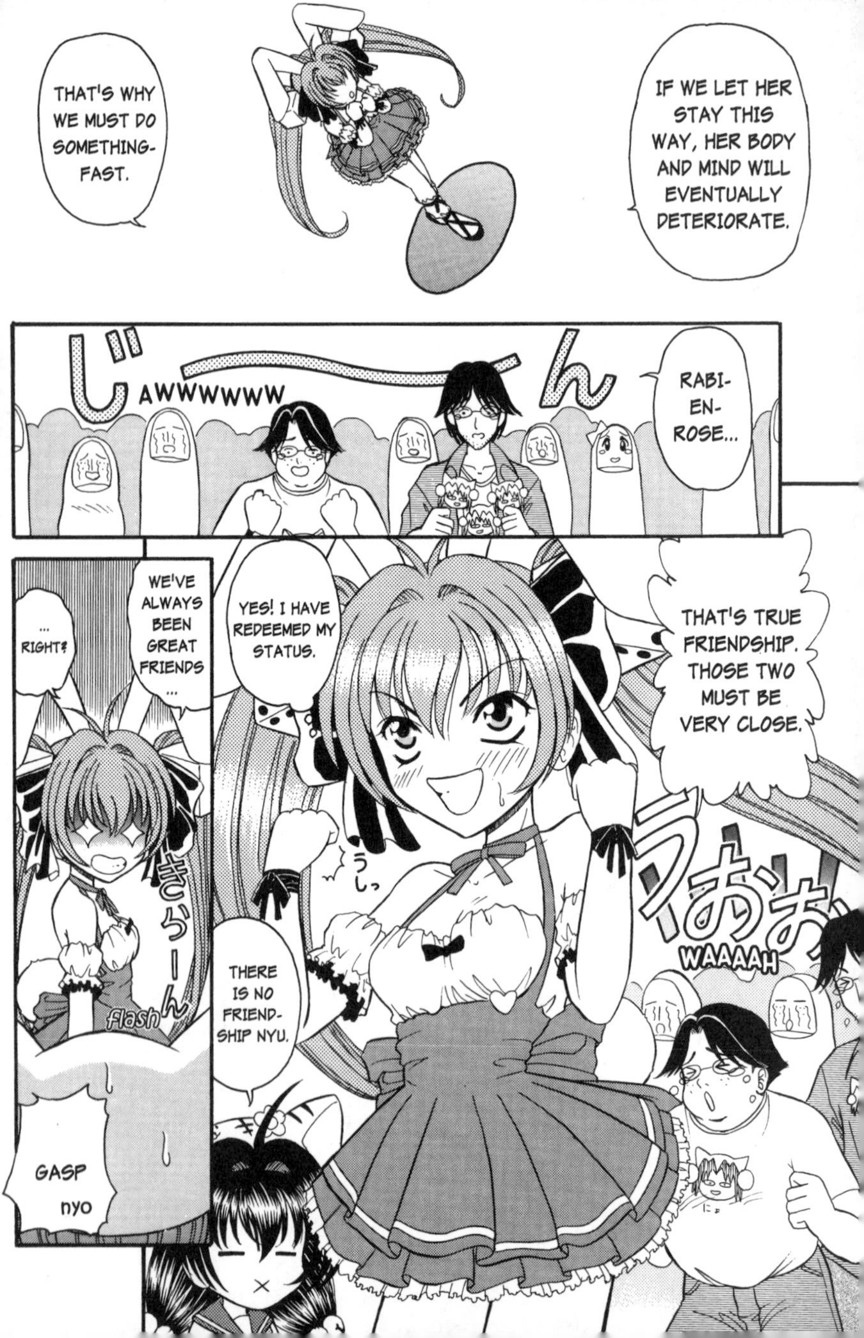
IF WE LET HER STAY THIS WAY, HER BODY AND MIND WILL EVENTUALLY DETERIORATE.
THAT'S WHY WE MUST DO SOMETHING-FAST.
RABI-EN-ROSE...
じーーん
AWWWWWWW
THAT'S TRUE FRIENDSHIP. THOSE TWO MUST BE VERY CLOSE.
YES! I HAVE REDEEMED MY STATUS.
うしっ
うおお
WAAAAH
THERE IS NO FRIEND-SHIP NYU.
WE'VE ALWAYS BEEN GREAT FRIENDS ...
... RIGHT?
きらーん
flash
GASP
nyo

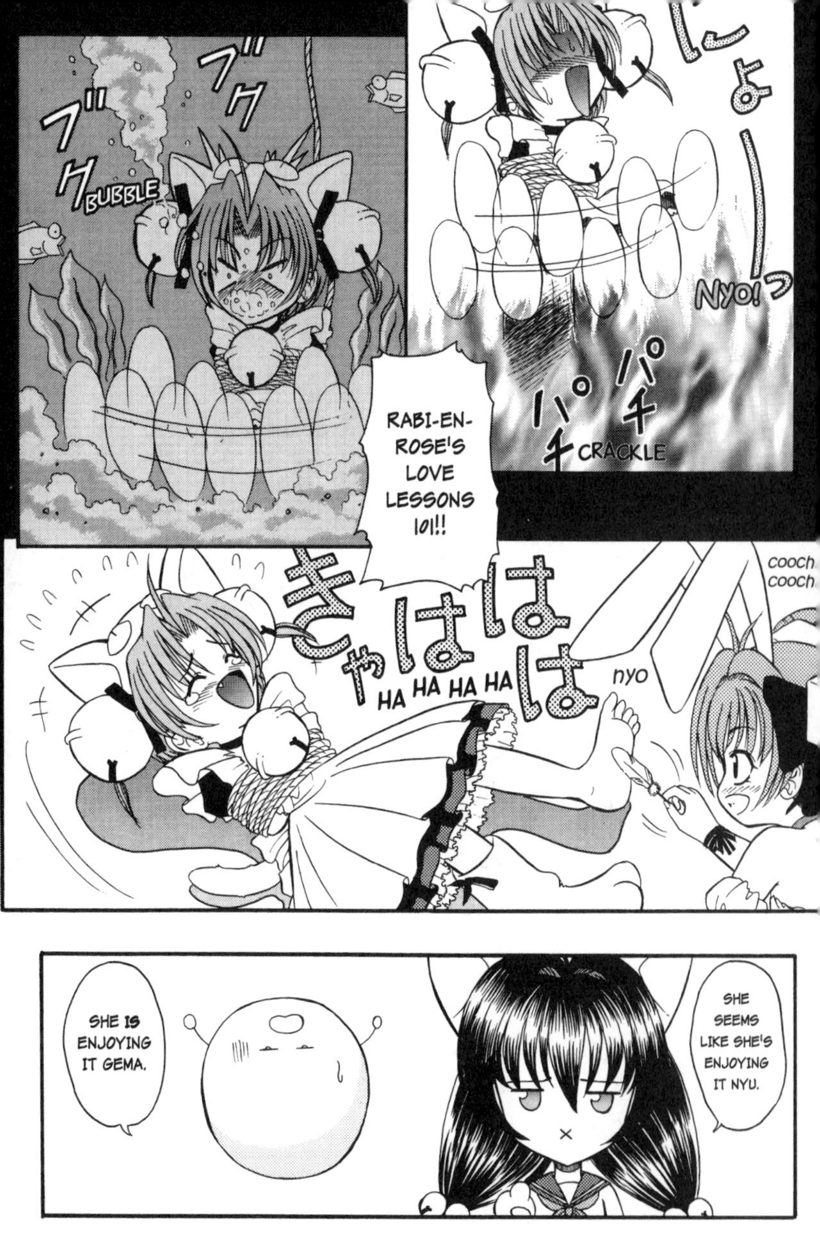
にょーっ
NYO!っ
パチパチ
CRACKLE
ブグブグ
BUBBLE
RABI-EN-ROSE'S LOVE LESSONS 101!!
cooch cooch
nyo
きゃはははは
HA HA HA HA
SHE SEEMS LIKE SHE'S ENJOYING IT NYU.
SHE IS ENJOYING IT GEMA.

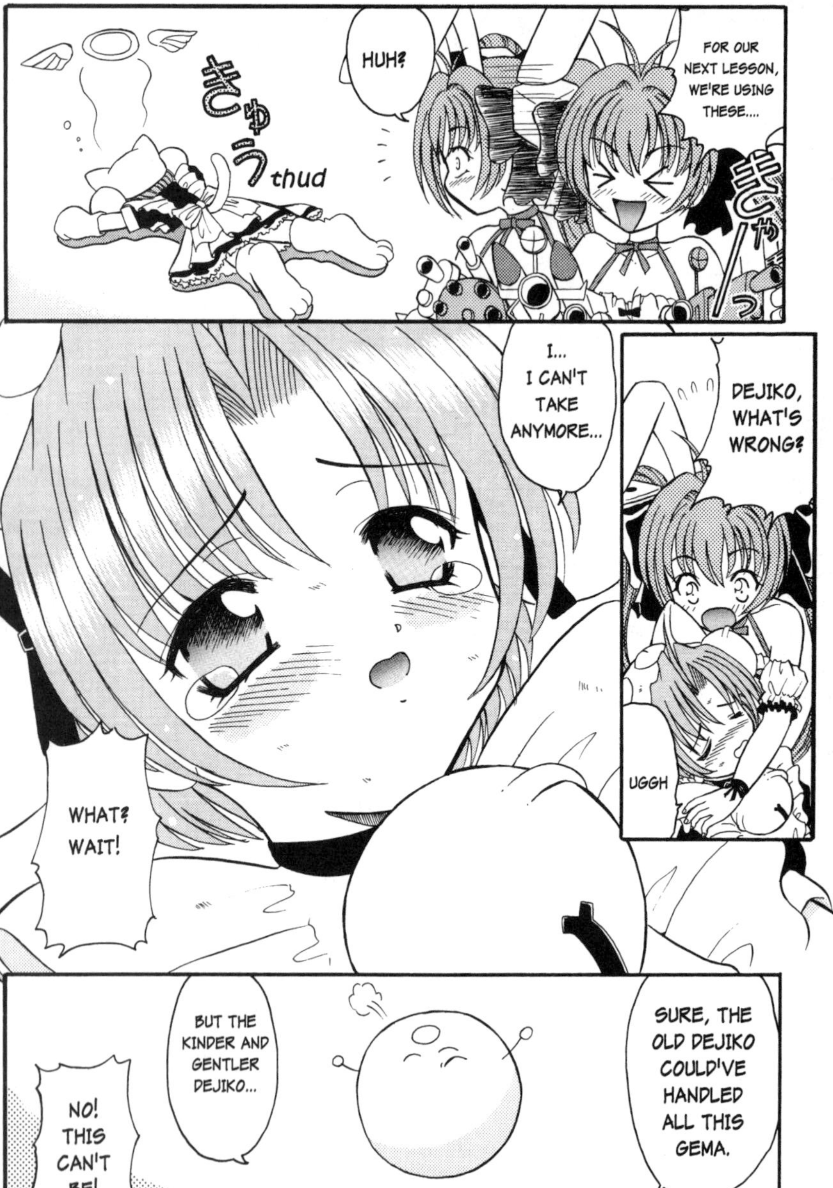

FOR OUR NEXT LESSON, WE'RE USING THESE....
きゅっ
HUH?
きゅう thud
DEJIKO, WHAT'S WRONG?
UGGH
I... I CAN'T TAKE ANYMORE...
WHAT? WAIT!
SURE, THE OLD DEJIKO COULD'VE HANDLED ALL THIS GEMA.
BUT THE KINDER AND GENTLER DEJIKO...
NO! THIS CAN'T BE!

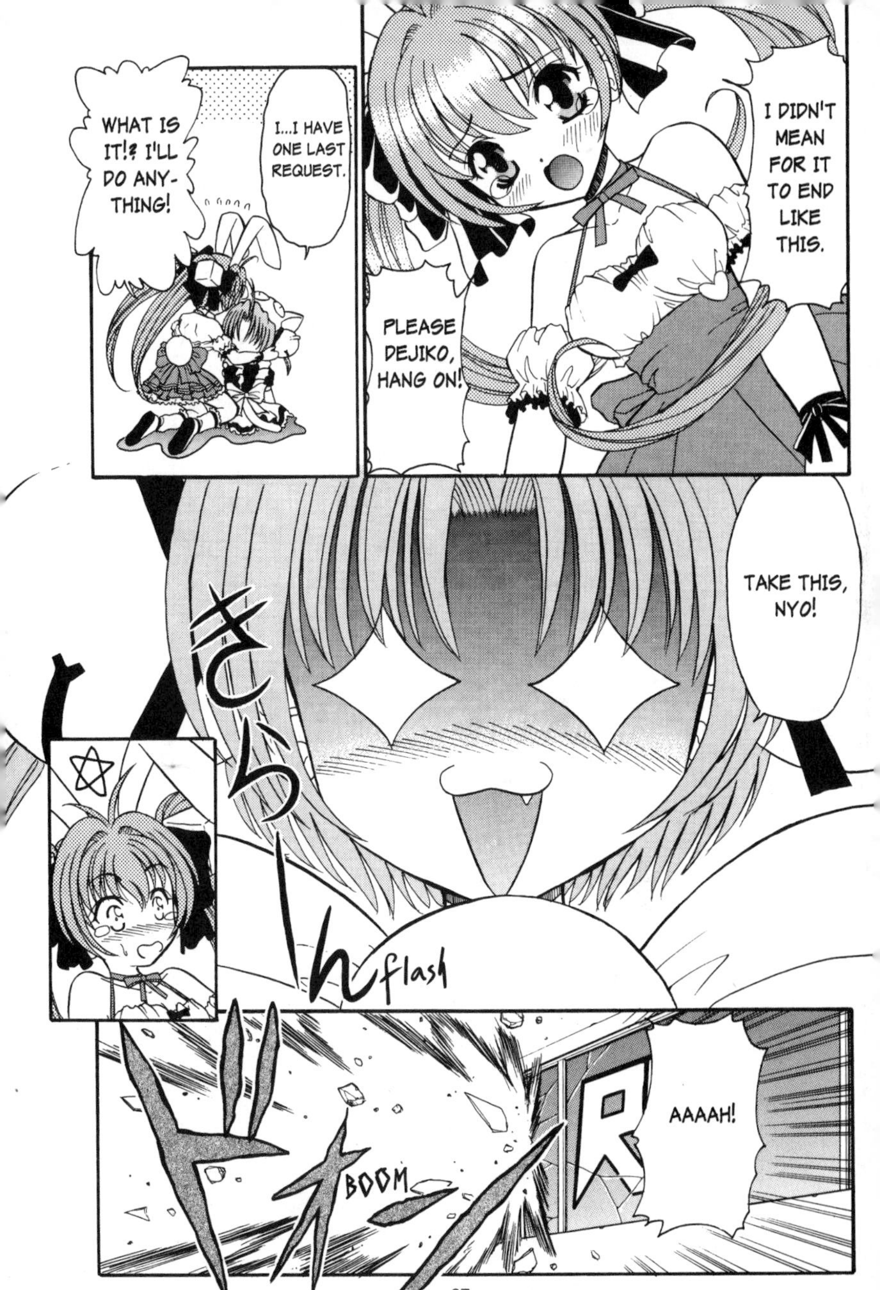
I DIDN'T MEAN FOR IT TO END LIKE THIS.
PLEASE DEJIKO, HANG ON!
I...I HAVE ONE LAST REQUEST.
WHAT IS IT!? I'LL DO ANYTHING!
TAKE THIS, NYO!
flash
AAAAH!
BOOM

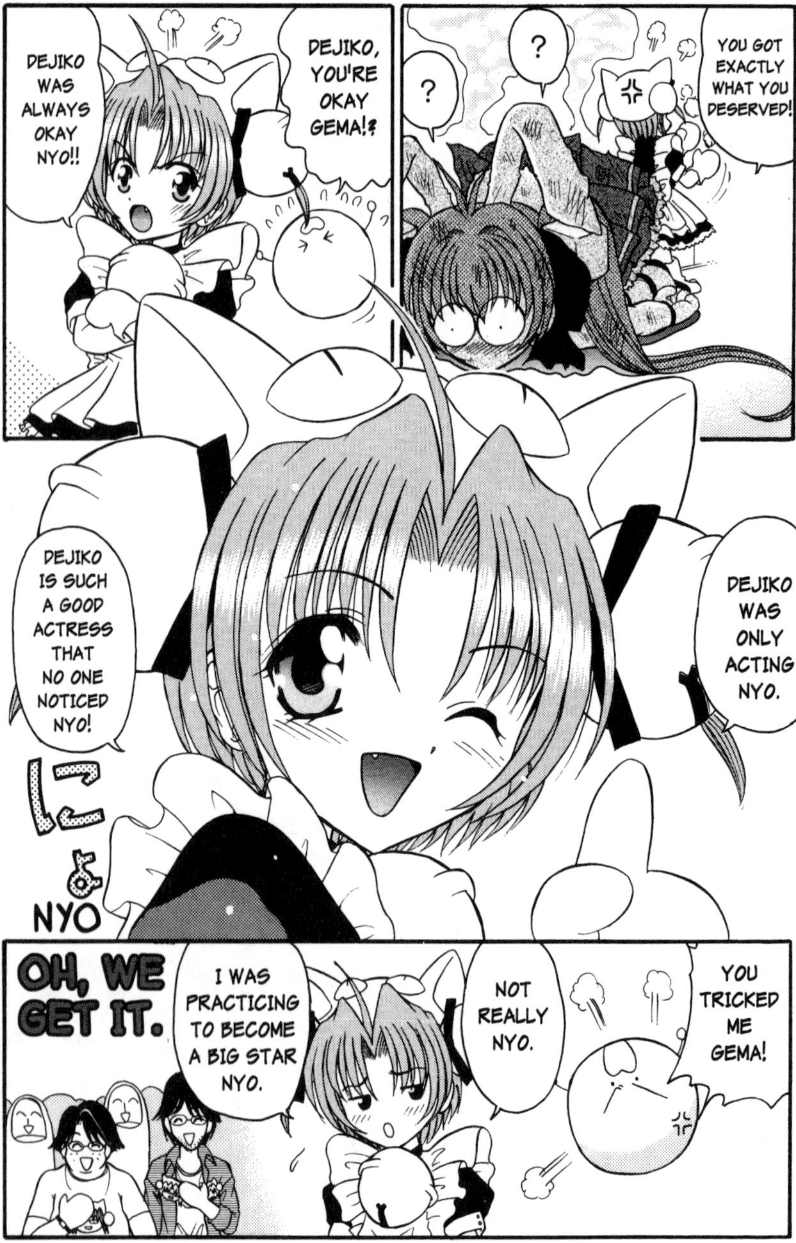
YOU GOT EXACTLY WHAT YOU DESERVED!
?
?
DEJIKO, YOU'RE OKAY GEMA!?
DEJIKO WAS ALWAYS OKAY NYO!!
DEJIKO WAS ONLY ACTING NYO.
DEJIKO IS SUCH A GOOD ACTRESS THAT NO ONE NOTICED NYO!
NYO
YOU TRICKED ME GEMA!
NOT REALLY NYO.
I WAS PRACTICING TO BECOME A BIG STAR NYO.
OH, WE GET IT.

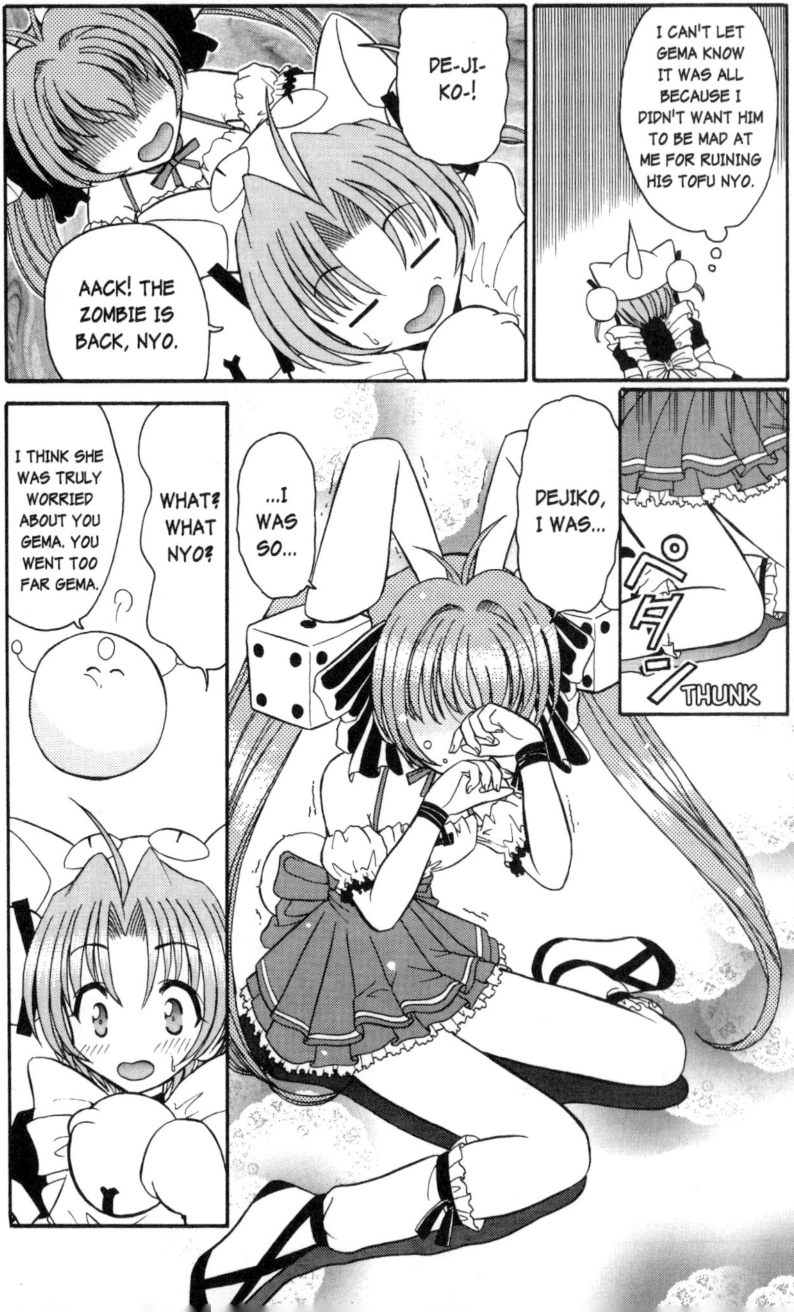
I CAN'T LET GEMA KNOW IT WAS ALL BECAUSE I DIDN'T WANT HIM TO BE MAD AT ME FOR RUINING HIS TOFU NYO.
DE-JI-KO-!
AACK! THE ZOMBIE IS BACK, NYO.
THUNK
DEJIKO, I WAS...
...I WAS SO...
WHAT? WHAT NYO?
I THINK SHE WAS TRULY WORRIED ABOUT YOU GEMA. YOU WENT TOO FAR GEMA.

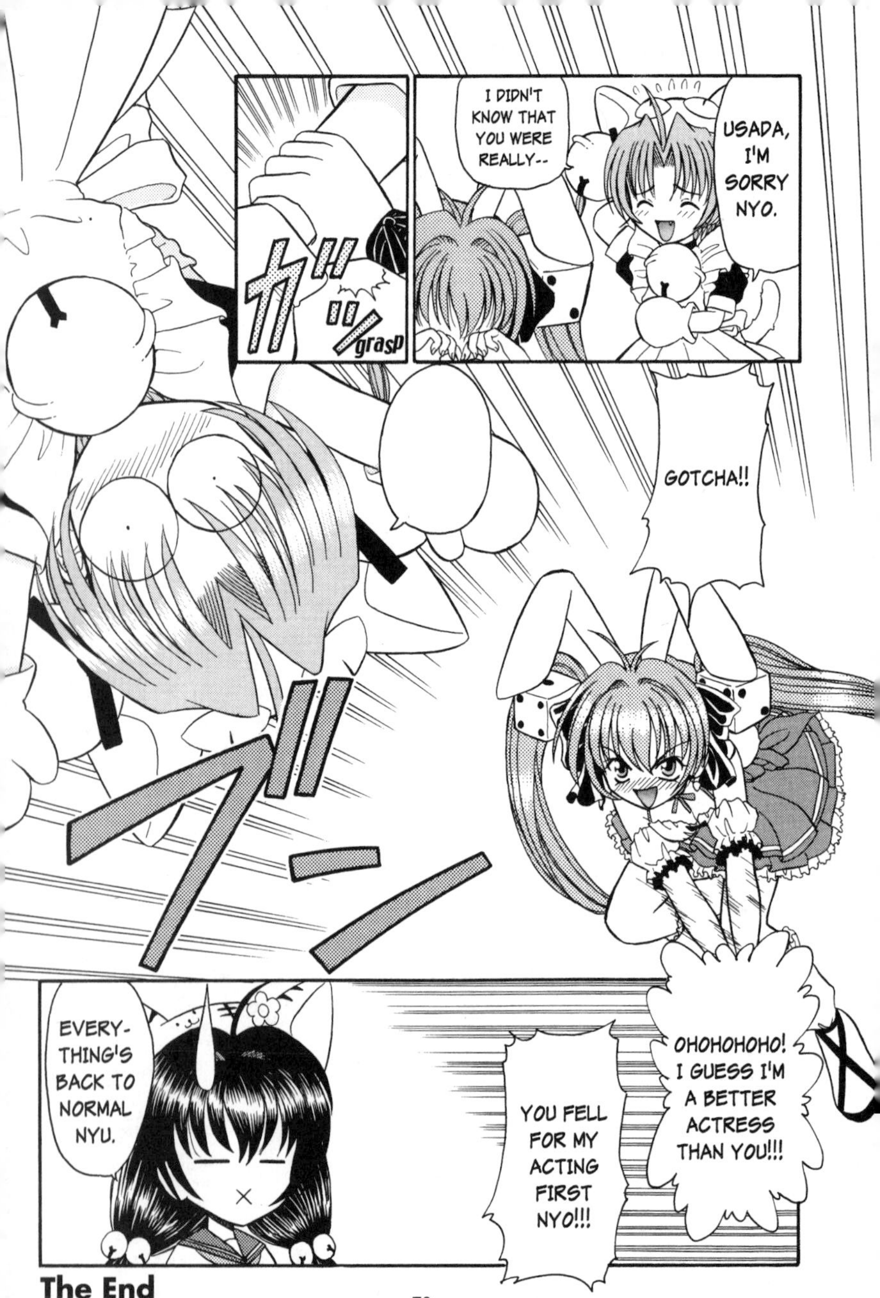
USADA, I'M SORRY NYO.
I DIDN'T KNOW THAT YOU WERE REALLY--
grasp
GOTCHA!!
OHOHOHOHO! I GUESS I'M A BETTER ACTRESS THAN YOU!!!
YOU FELL FOR MY ACTING FIRST NYO!!!
EVERY-THING'S BACK TO NORMAL NYU.

The End

Who's your favorite character in Di Gi Charat?

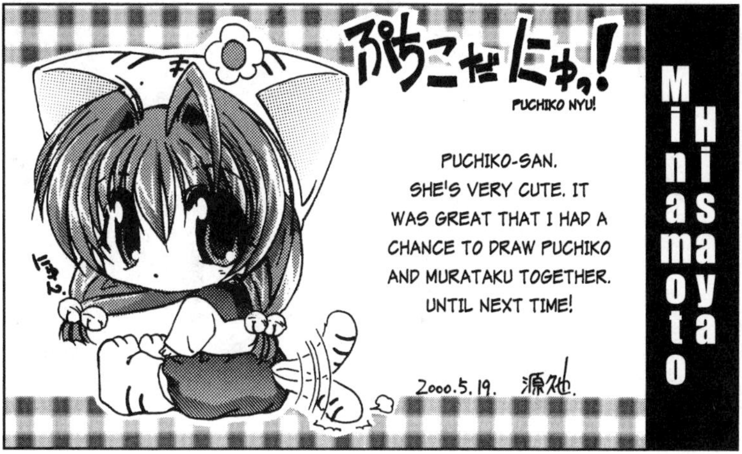
ぷちこだにゅっ!
PUCHIKO NYU!
PUCHIKO-SAN. SHE'S VERY CUTE. IT WAS GREAT THAT I HAD A CHANCE TO DRAW PUCHIKO AND MURATAKU TOGETHER. UNTIL NEXT TIME!
2000.5.19. 源久也.
Minamoto Hisaya

Who's your favorite character in Di Gi Charat?

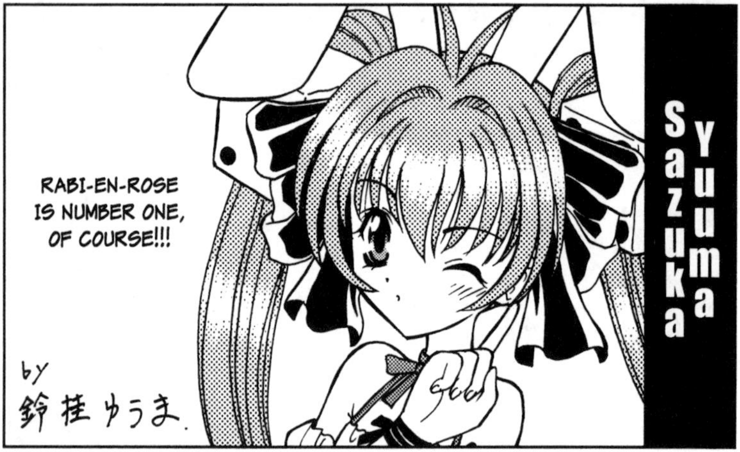
Syuuma Sazuka
RABI-EN-ROSE IS NUMBER ONE, OF COURSE!!!
by
鈴桂ゆうま.

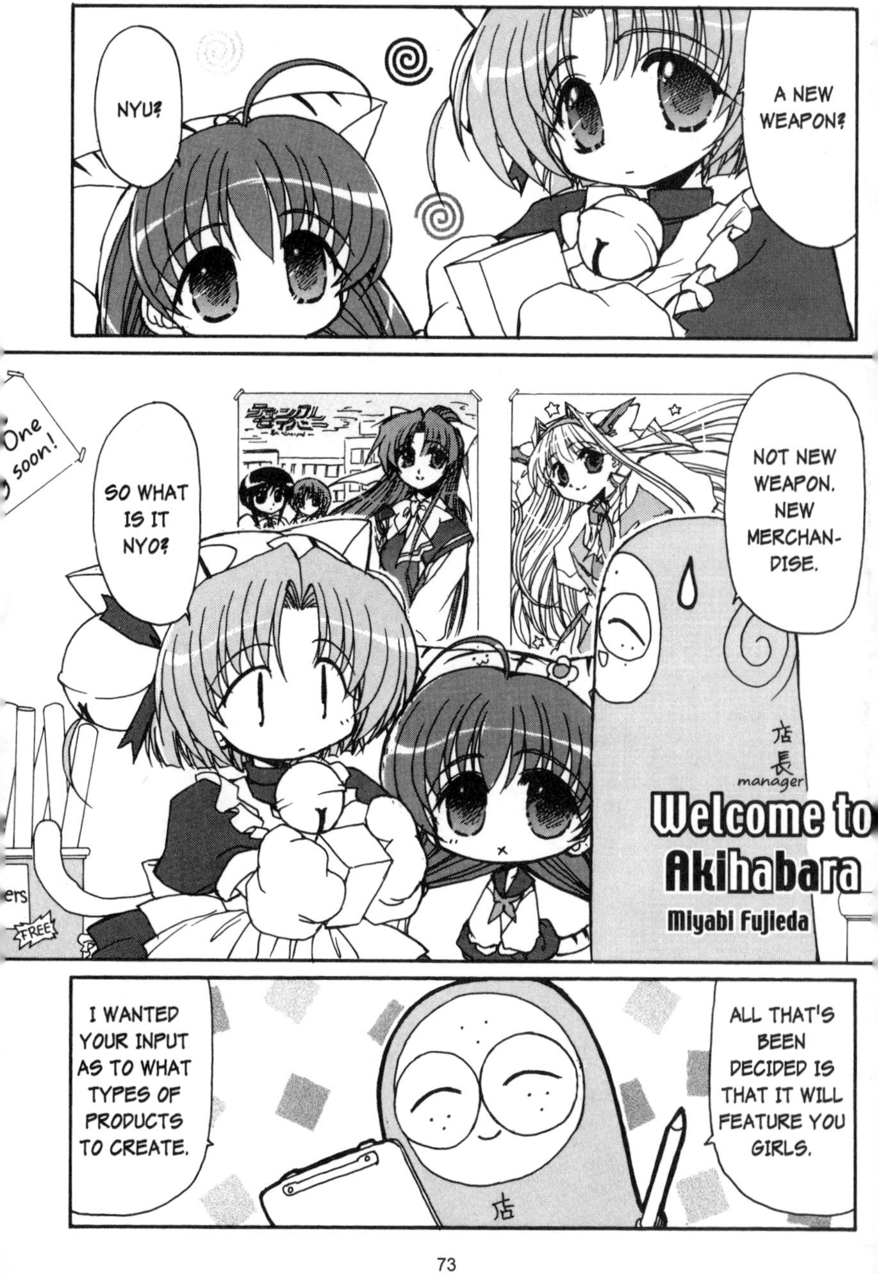
A NEW WEAPON?
NYU?
NOT NEW WEAPON. NEW MERCHANDISE.
SO WHAT IS IT NYO?
店長
manager
Welcome to Akihabara
Miyabi Fujieda
FREE
ALL THAT'S BEEN DECIDED IS THAT IT WILL FEATURE YOU GIRLS.
I WANTED YOUR INPUT AS TO WHAT TYPES OF PRODUCTS TO CREATE.
店

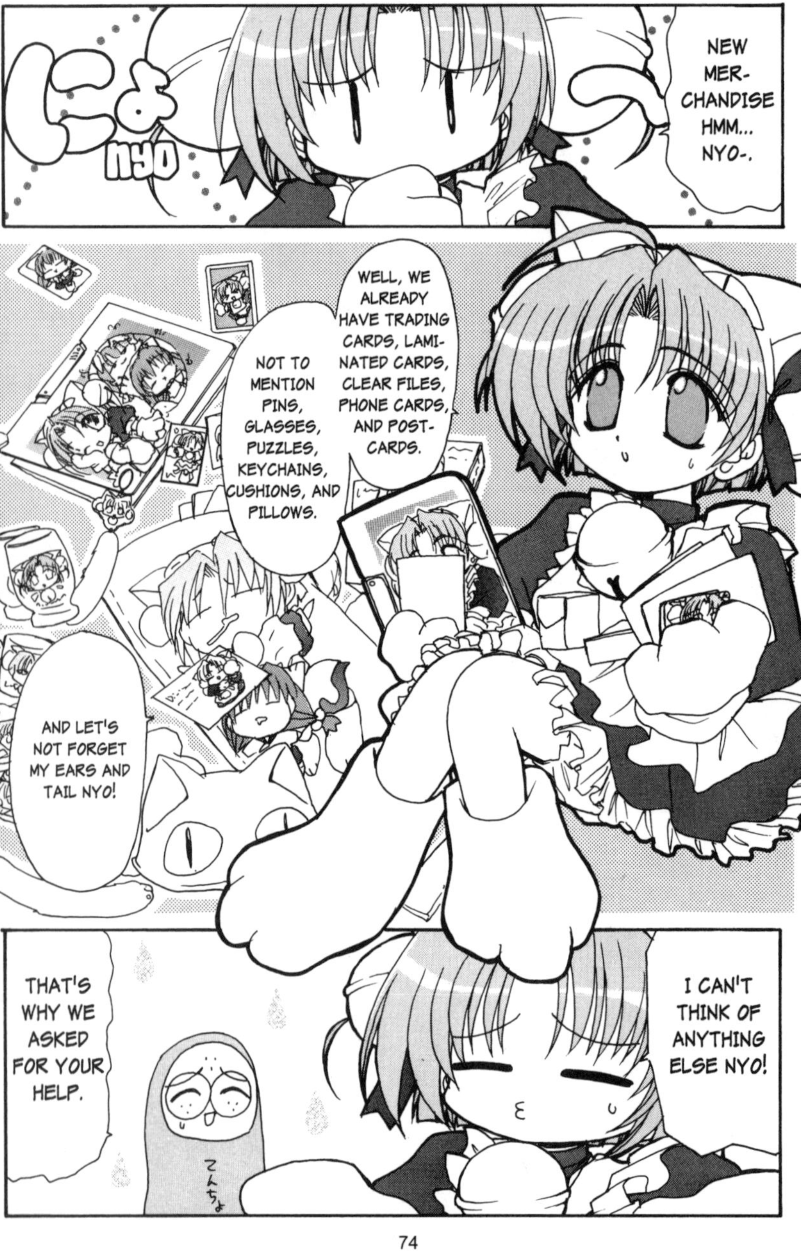
NEW MER- CHANDISE HMM... NYO-.
にょ nyo
WELL, WE ALREADY HAVE TRADING CARDS, LAMI- NATED CARDS, CLEAR FILES, PHONE CARDS, AND POST- CARDS.
NOT TO MENTION PINS, GLASSES, PUZZLES, KEYCHAINS, CUSHIONS, AND PILLOWS.
AND LET'S NOT FORGET MY EARS AND TAIL NYO!
I CAN'T THINK OF ANYTHING ELSE NYO!
THAT'S WHY WE ASKED FOR YOUR HELP.

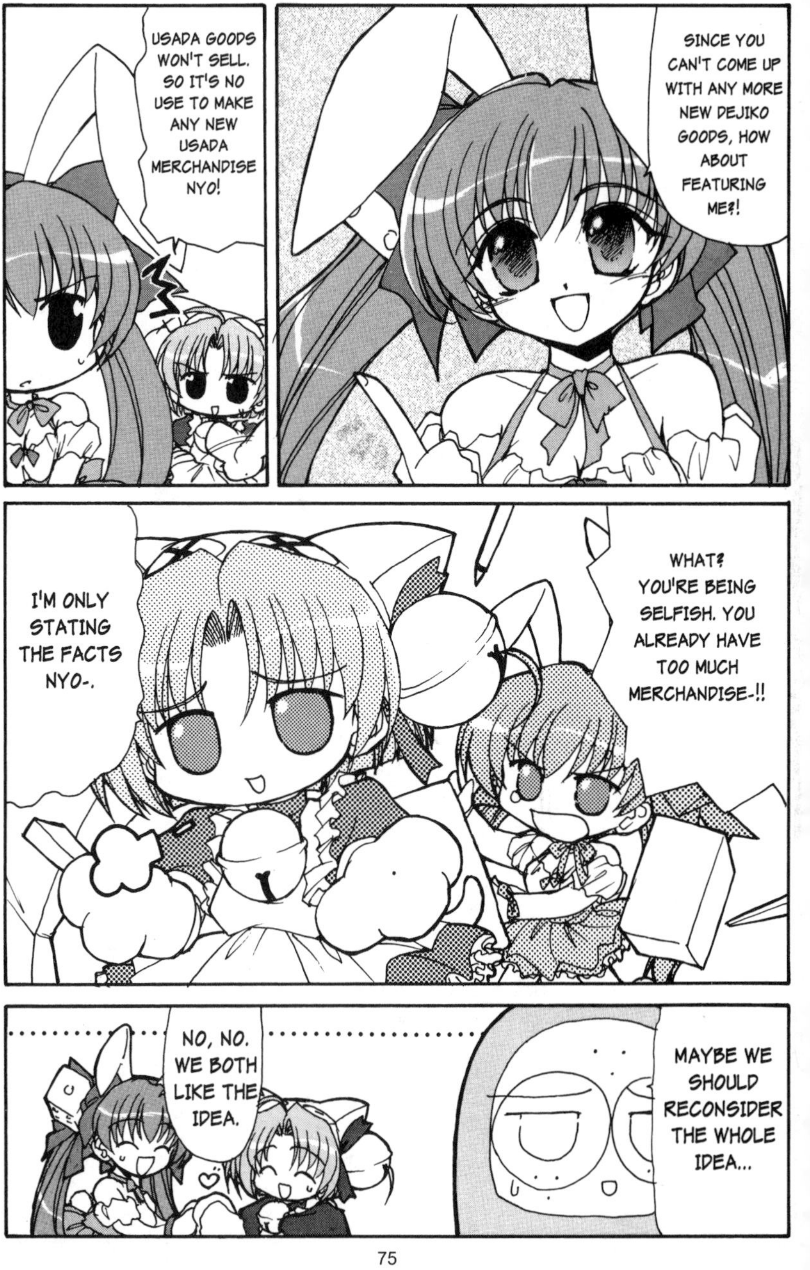
SINCE YOU CAN'T COME UP WITH ANY MORE NEW DEJIKO GOODS, HOW ABOUT FEATURING ME?!
USADA GOODS WON'T SELL. SO IT'S NO USE TO MAKE ANY NEW USADA MERCHANDISE NYO!
WHAT? YOU'RE BEING SELFISH. YOU ALREADY HAVE TOO MUCH MERCHANDISE-!!
I'M ONLY STATING THE FACTS NYO-.
MAYBE WE SHOULD RECONSIDER THE WHOLE IDEA...
NO, NO. WE BOTH LIKE THE IDEA.

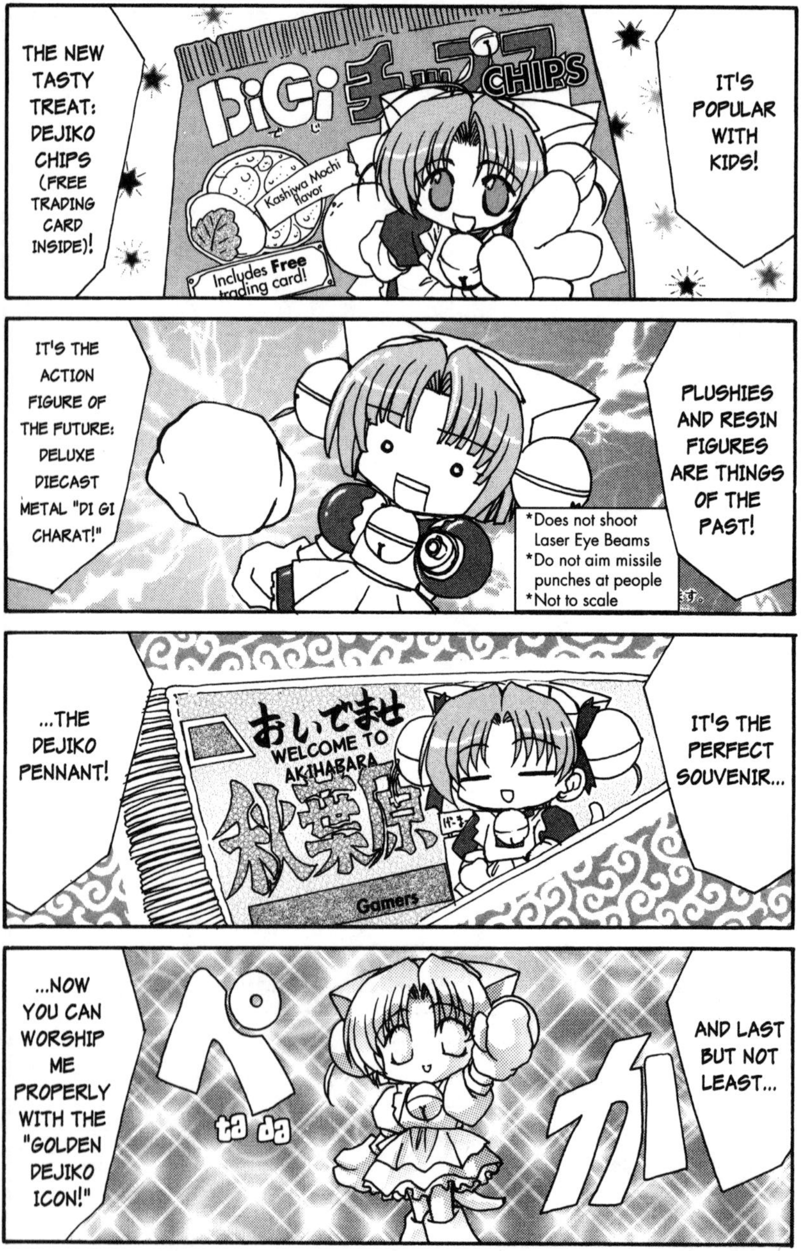
IT'S POPULAR WITH KIDS!
THE NEW TASTY TREAT: DEJIKO CHIPS (FREE TRADING CARD INSIDE)!
DiGi CHIPS
Kashiwa Mochi flavor
Includes Free trading card!
PLUSHIES AND RESIN FIGURES ARE THINGS OF THE PAST!
IT'S THE ACTION FIGURE OF THE FUTURE: DELUXE DIECAST METAL "DI GI CHARAT!"
*Does not shoot Laser Eye Beams
*Do not aim missile punches at people
*Not to scale
IT'S THE PERFECT SOUVENIR...
...THE DEJIKO PENNANT!
おいでませ
WELCOME TO AKIHABARA
秋葉原
Gamers
AND LAST BUT NOT LEAST...
ペカ
ta da
...NOW YOU CAN WORSHIP ME PROPERLY WITH THE "GOLDEN DEJIKO ICON!"

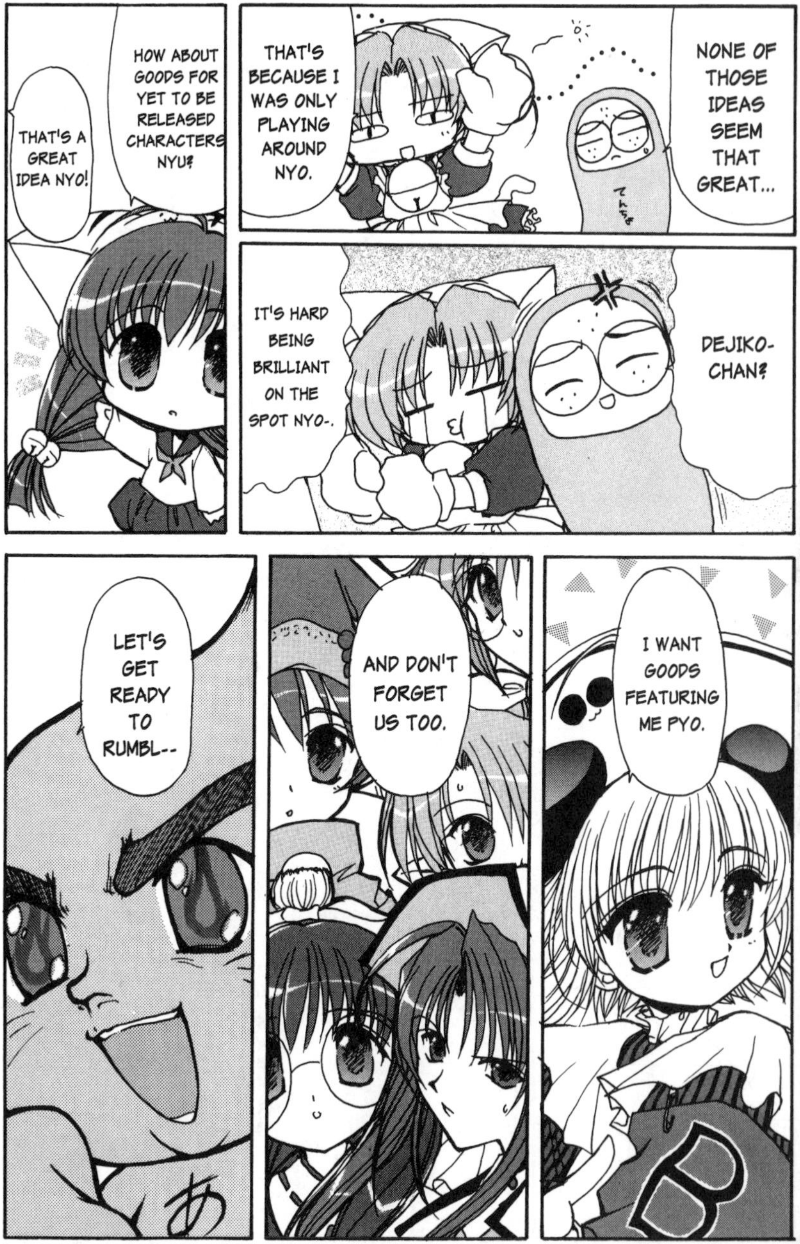
NONE OF THOSE IDEAS SEEM THAT GREAT...
THAT'S BECAUSE I WAS ONLY PLAYING AROUND NYO.
DEJIKO-CHAN?
IT'S HARD BEING BRILLIANT ON THE SPOT NYO-.
HOW ABOUT GOODS FOR YET TO BE RELEASED CHARACTERS NYU?
THAT'S A GREAT IDEA NYO!
I WANT GOODS FEATURING ME PYO.
AND DON'T FORGET US TOO.
LET'S GET READY TO RUMBL--
あ

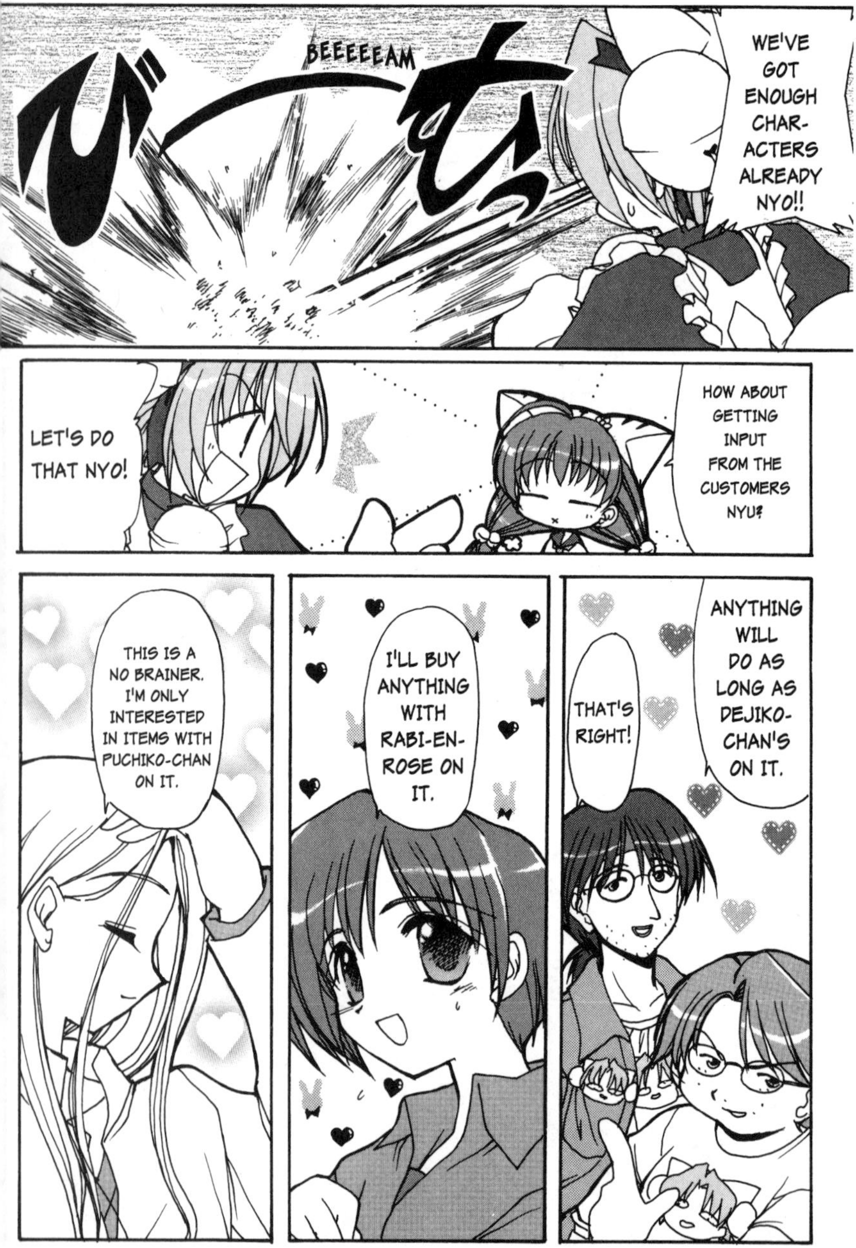
WE'VE GOT ENOUGH CHAR-ACTERS ALREADY NYO!!
BEEEEEEAM
HOW ABOUT GETTING INPUT FROM THE CUSTOMERS NYU?
LET'S DO THAT NYO!
ANYTHING WILL DO AS LONG AS DEJIKO-CHAN'S ON IT.
THAT'S RIGHT!
I'LL BUY ANYTHING WITH RABI-EN-ROSE ON IT.
THIS IS A NO BRAINER. I'M ONLY INTERESTED IN ITEMS WITH PUCHIKO-CHAN ON IT.

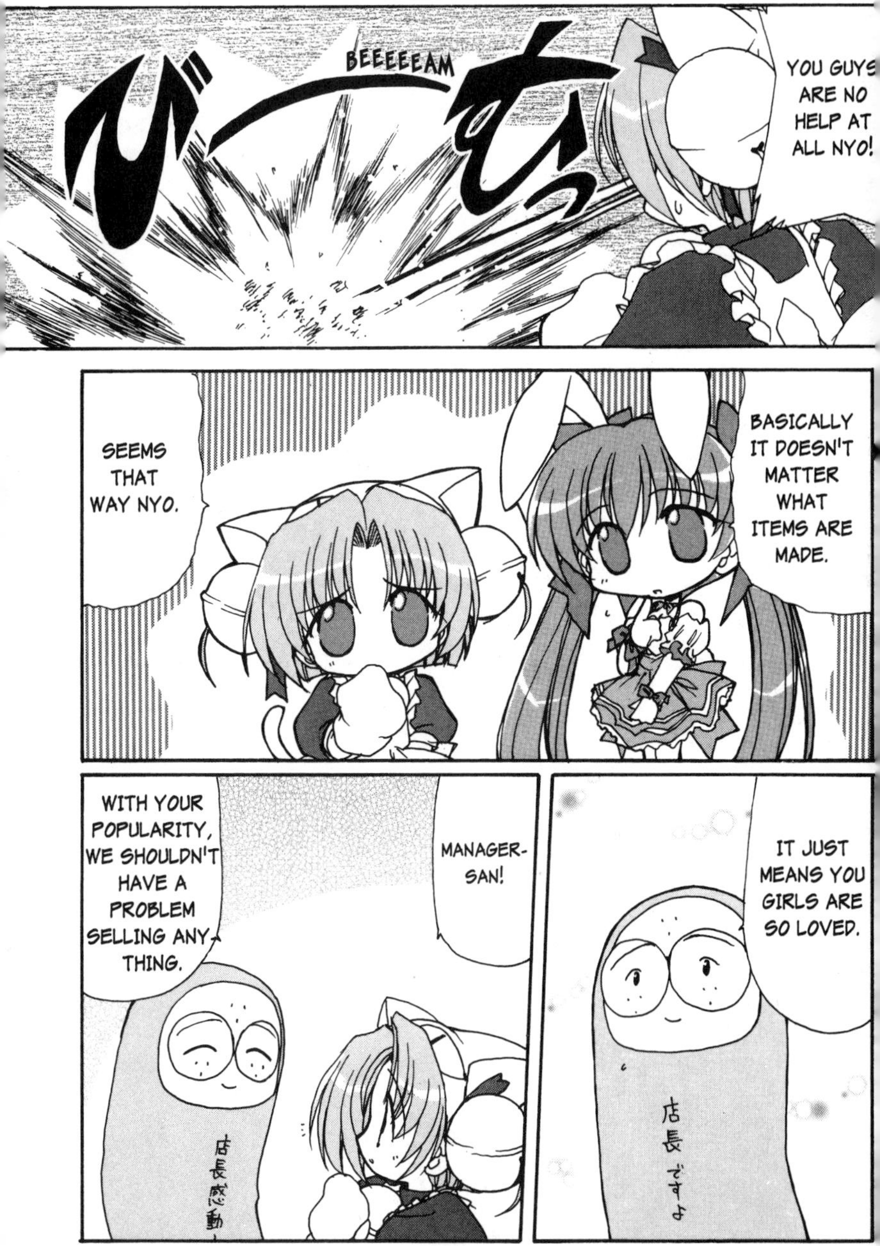
びーむっ
BEEEEEAM
YOU GUYS ARE NO HELP AT ALL NYO!
BASICALLY IT DOESN'T MATTER WHAT ITEMS ARE MADE.
SEEMS THAT WAY NYO.
IT JUST MEANS YOU GIRLS ARE SO LOVED.
店長ですよ
MANAGER-SAN!
WITH YOUR POPULARITY, WE SHOULDN'T HAVE A PROBLEM SELLING ANY-THING.
店長感動ー

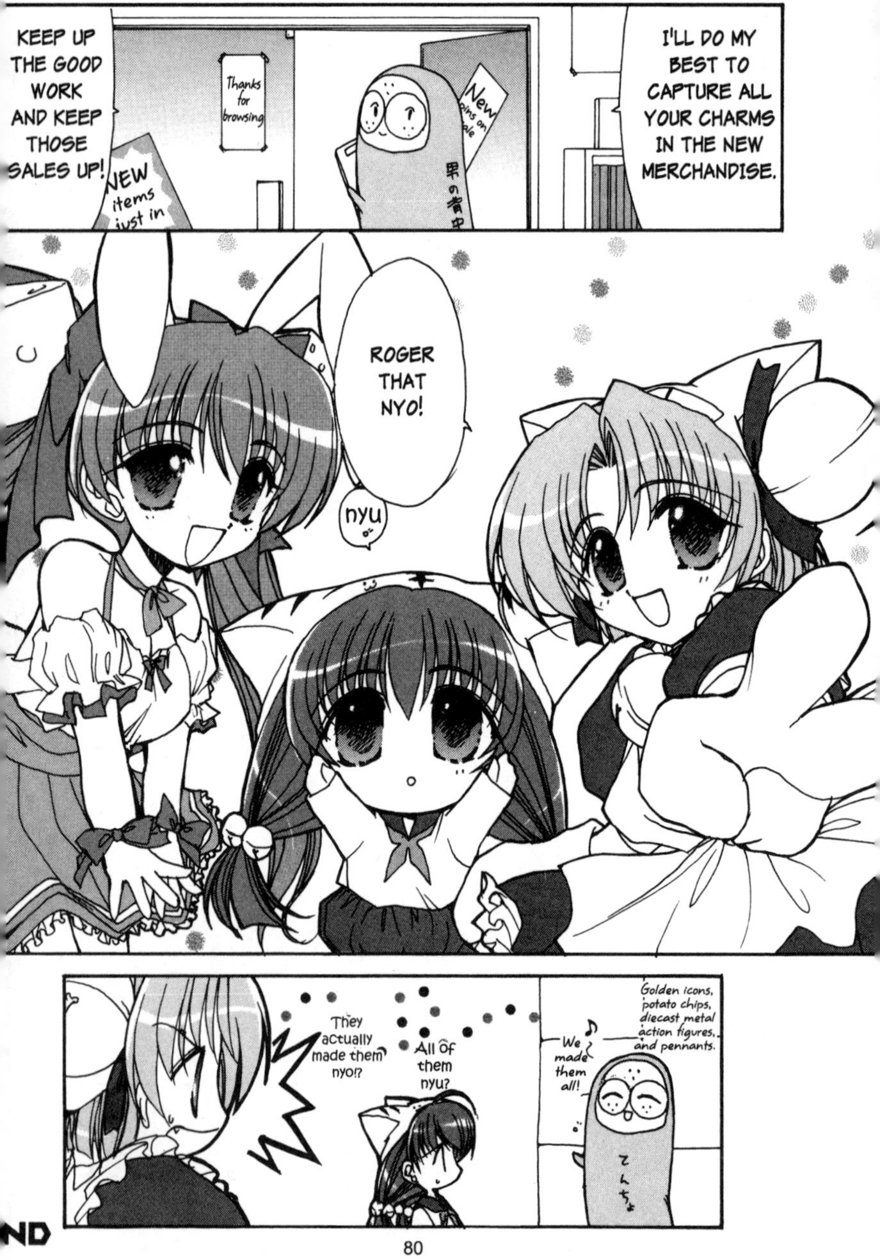

I'LL DO MY BEST TO CAPTURE ALL YOUR CHARMS IN THE NEW MERCHANDISE.
KEEP UP THE GOOD WORK AND KEEP THOSE SALES UP!
Thanks for browsing
NEW items just in
ROGER THAT NYO!
nyu
Golden icons, potato chips, diecast metal action figures, and pennants.
We made them all!
All of them nyu?
They actually made them nyo!?
ND

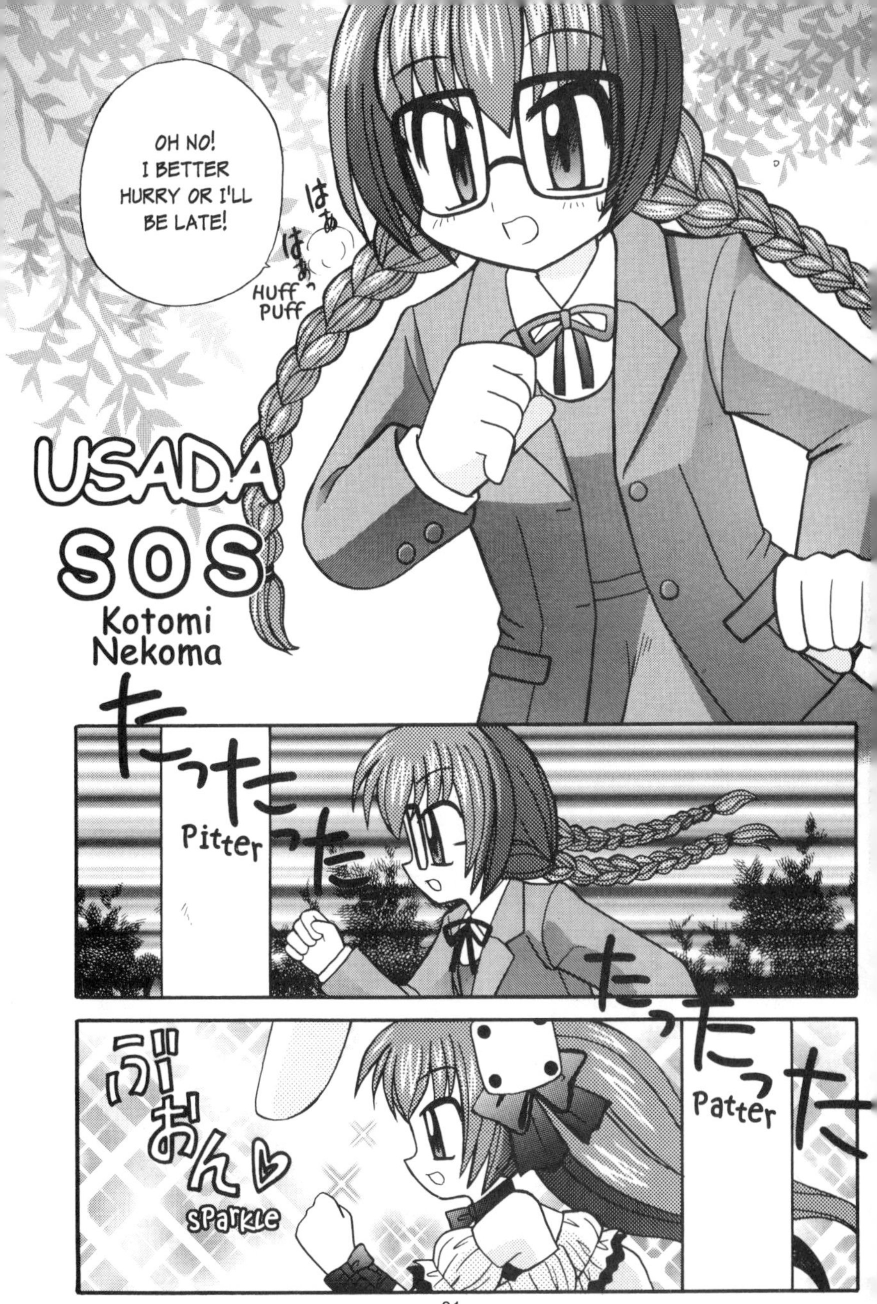
OH NO! I BETTER HURRY OR I'LL BE LATE!
はぁ はぁっ
HUFF PUFF
USADA SOS
Kotomi Nekoma
たったった
Pitter
たったった
Patter
ぶぉん♥
sparkle

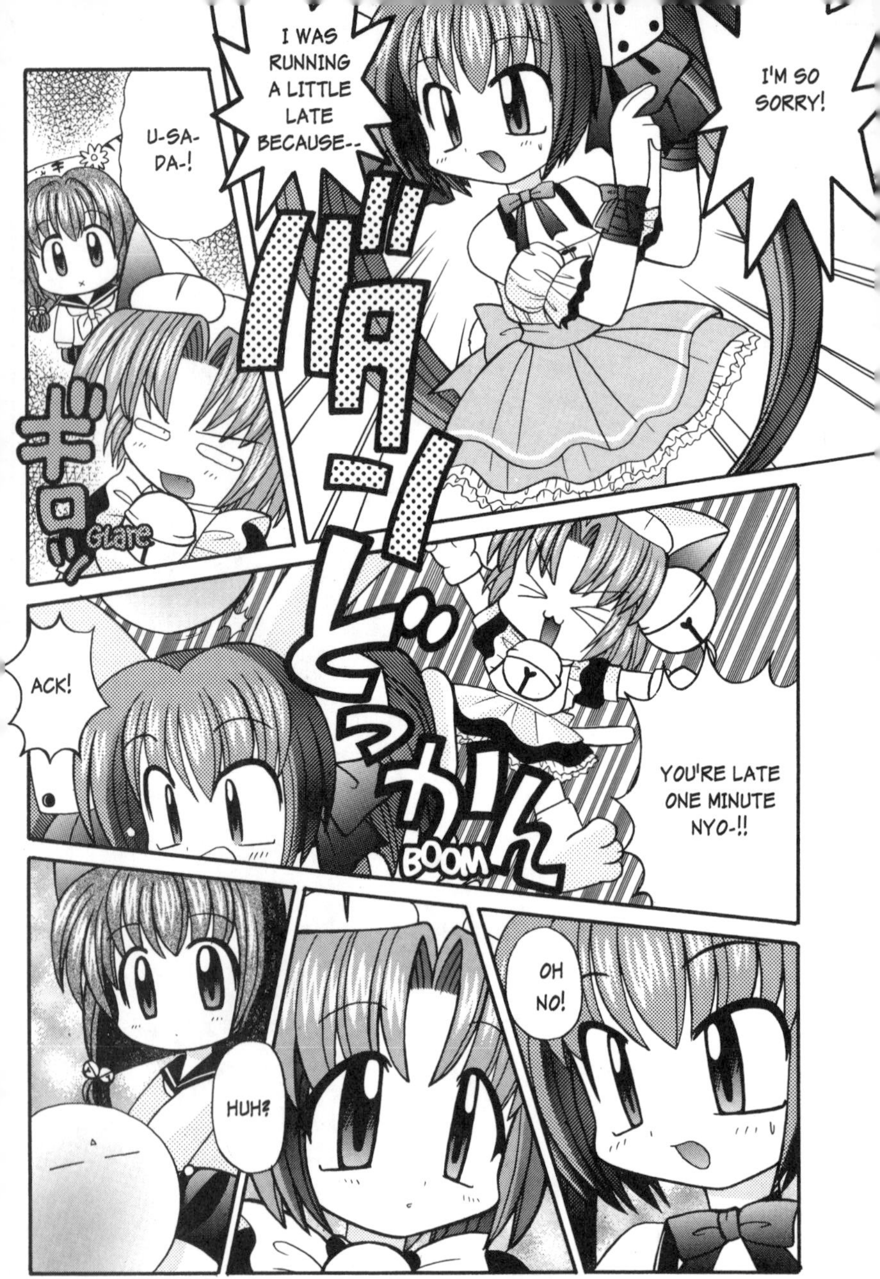
I'M SO SORRY!
I WAS RUNNING A LITTLE LATE BECAUSE--
U-SA-DA-!
GLARE
YOU'RE LATE ONE MINUTE NYO-!!
BOOM
ACK!
OH NO!
HUH?

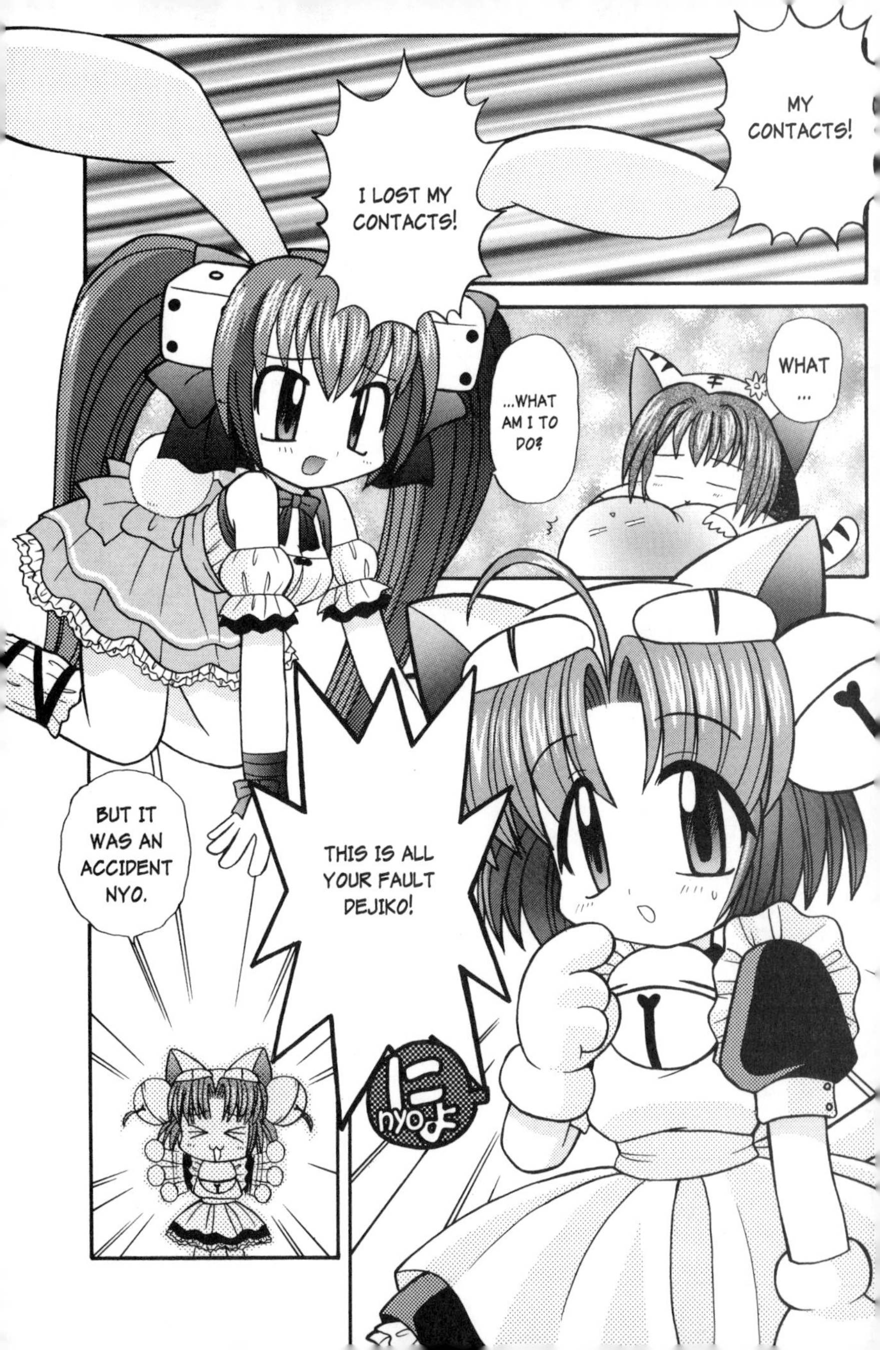
MY CONTACTS!
I LOST MY CONTACTS!
WHAT ...
...WHAT AM I TO DO?
THIS IS ALL YOUR FAULT DEJIKO!
にnyoよ
BUT IT WAS AN ACCIDENT NYO.

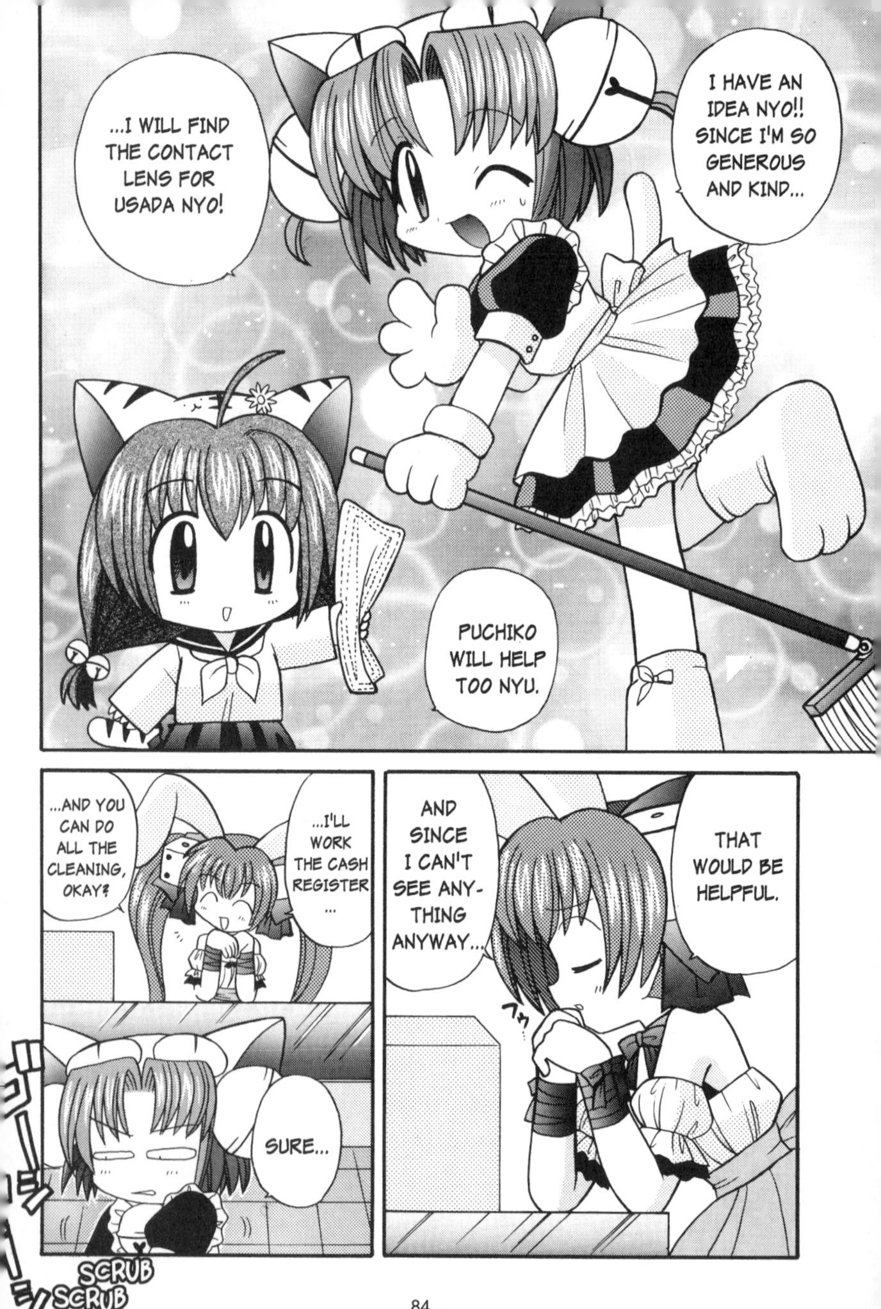
I HAVE AN IDEA NYO!! SINCE I'M SO GENEROUS AND KIND...
...I WILL FIND THE CONTACT LENS FOR USADA NYO!
PUCHIKO WILL HELP TOO NYU.
THAT WOULD BE HELPFUL.
AND SINCE I CAN'T SEE ANY-THING ANYWAY...
...I'LL WORK THE CASH REGISTER ...
...AND YOU CAN DO ALL THE CLEANING, OKAY?
SURE...
SCRUB SCRUB

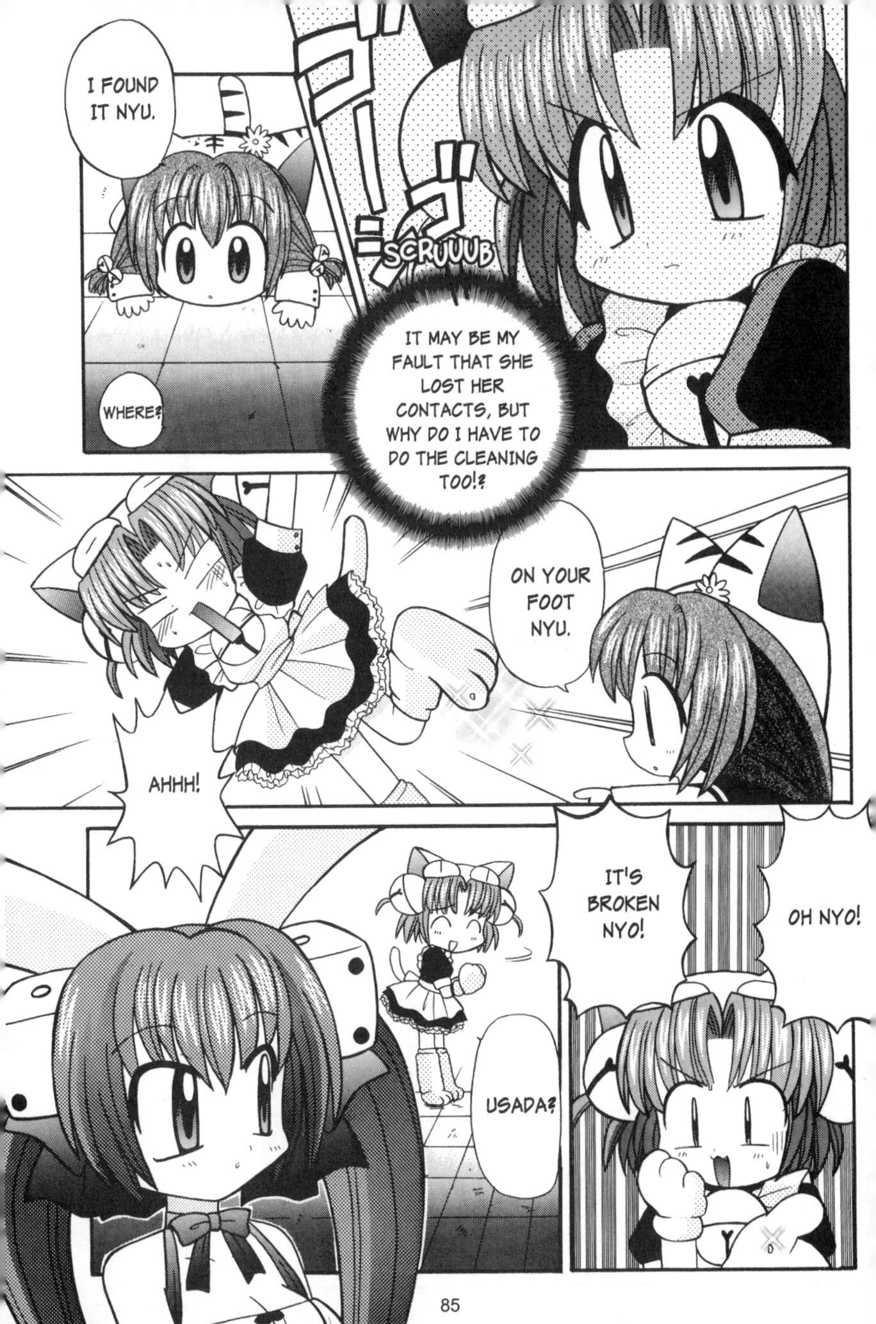
SCRUUUB
IT MAY BE MY FAULT THAT SHE LOST HER CONTACTS, BUT WHY DO I HAVE TO DO THE CLEANING TOO!?
I FOUND IT NYU.
WHERE?!
ON YOUR FOOT NYU.
AHHH!
OH NYO!
IT'S BROKEN NYO!
USADA?!

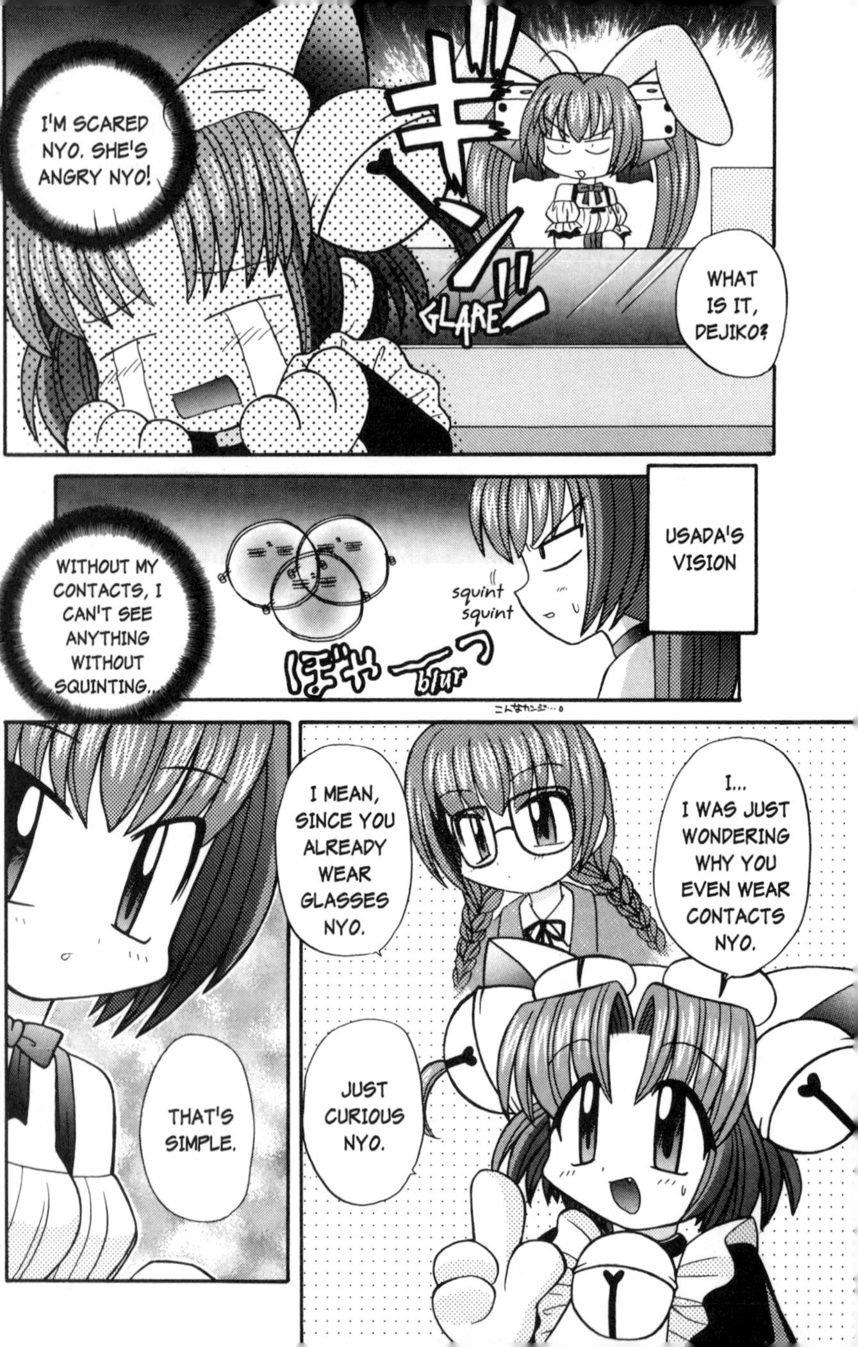
WHAT IS IT, DEJIKO?
GLARE
I'M SCARED NYO. SHE'S ANGRY NYO!
USADA'S VISION
squint squint
blur
WITHOUT MY CONTACTS, I CAN'T SEE ANYTHING WITHOUT SQUINTING...
こんなカンジ…。
I... I WAS JUST WONDERING WHY YOU EVEN WEAR CONTACTS NYO.
I MEAN, SINCE YOU ALREADY WEAR GLASSES NYO.
JUST CURIOUS NYO.
THAT'S SIMPLE.

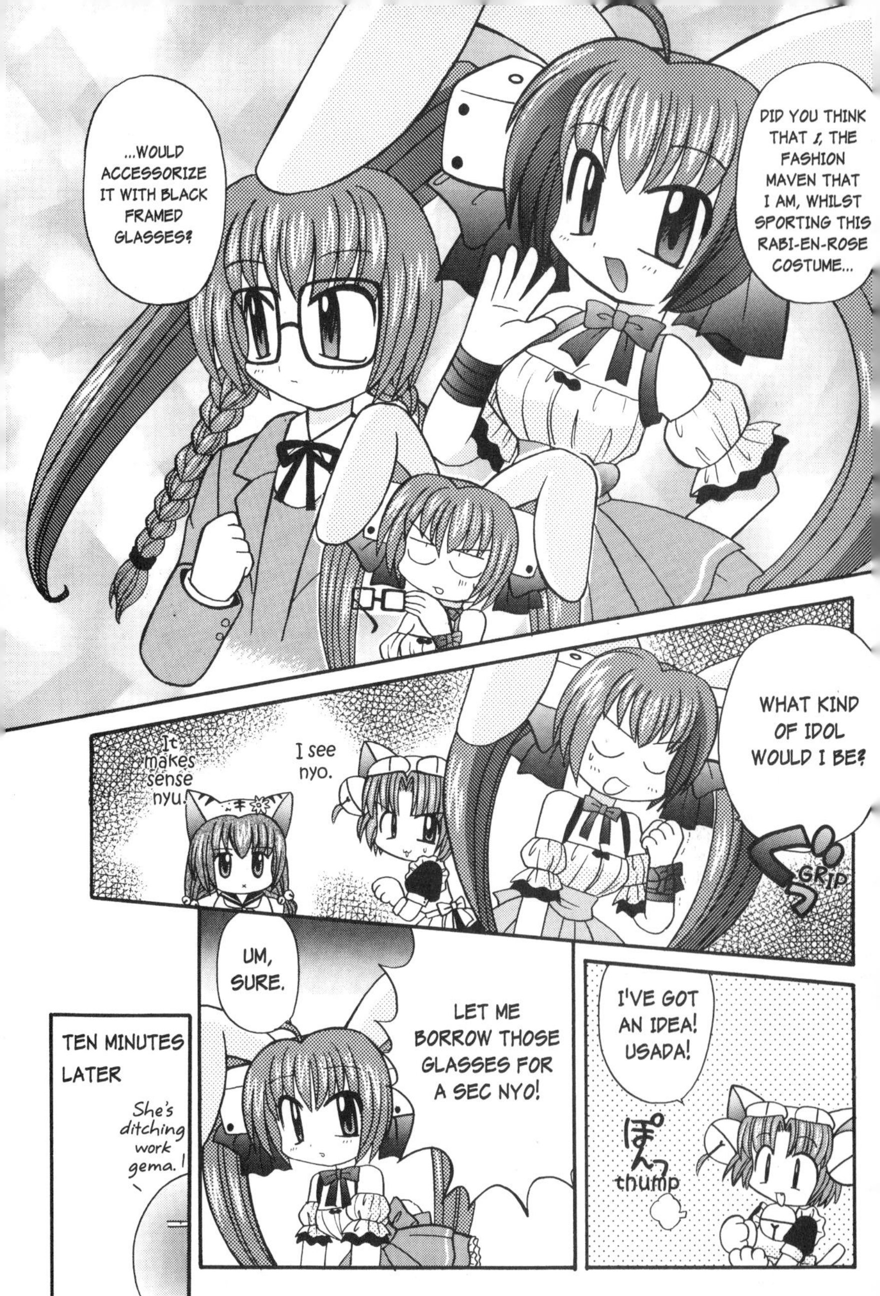
DID YOU THINK THAT I, THE FASHION MAVEN THAT I AM, WHILST SPORTING THIS RABI-EN-ROSE COSTUME...
...WOULD ACCESSORIZE IT WITH BLACK FRAMED GLASSES?
WHAT KIND OF IDOL WOULD I BE?
GRIP
I see nyo.
It makes sense nyu.
I'VE GOT AN IDEA! USADA!
ぽんっ
thump
LET ME BORROW THOSE GLASSES FOR A SEC NYO!
UM, SURE.
TEN MINUTES LATER
She's ditching work gema.!

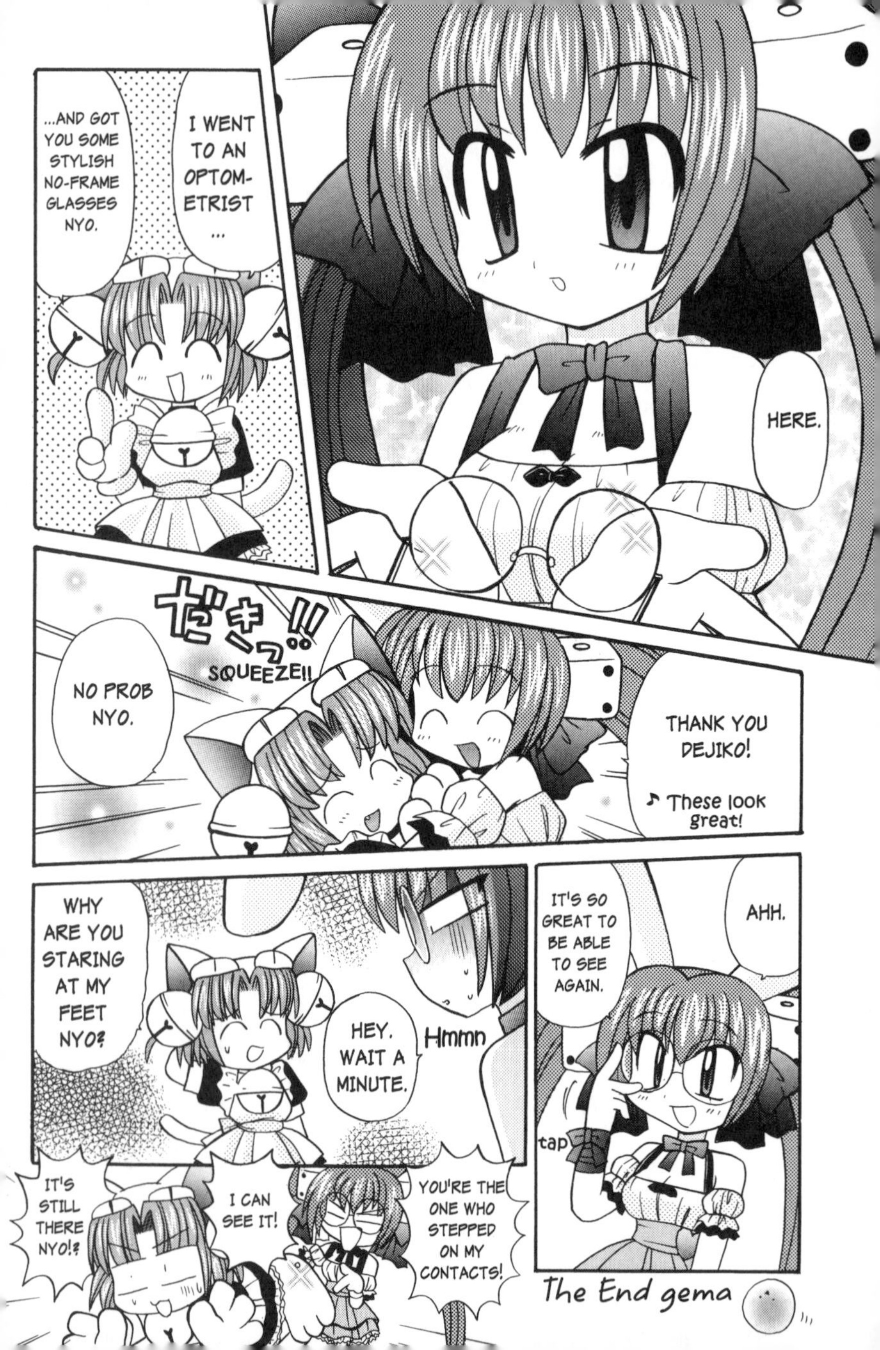
HERE.
I WENT TO AN OPTOMETRIST ...
...AND GOT YOU SOME STYLISH NO-FRAME GLASSES NYO.
THANK YOU DEJIKO! ♪ These look great!
だきっ!!
SQUEEZE!!
NO PROB NYO.
AHH.
IT'S SO GREAT TO BE ABLE TO SEE AGAIN.
tap
Hmmn
HEY. WAIT A MINUTE.
WHY ARE YOU STARING AT MY FEET NYO?
YOU'RE THE ONE WHO STEPPED ON MY CONTACTS!
I CAN SEE IT!
IT'S STILL THERE NYO!?
The End gema

Who's your favorite character in Di Gi Charat?

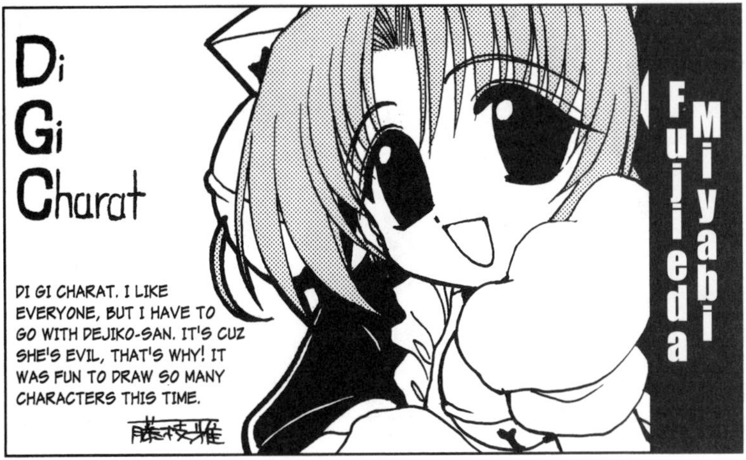
Di Gi Charat
DI GI CHARAT. I LIKE EVERYONE, BUT I HAVE TO GO WITH DEJIKO-SAN. IT'S CUZ SHE'S EVIL, THAT'S WHY! IT WAS FUN TO DRAW SO MANY CHARACTERS THIS TIME.
藤枝雅
Fujieda Miyabi

Who's your favorite character in Di Gi Charat?

DEJIKO-SAMA IS NUMBER ONE NYO!!

でじこ様が1番にょ!!

BUT, THIS TIME I DREW ABOUT USADA. USADA, I LOVE YOU TOO!

http://www.age.ne.jp/x/kotomura/kotorun
BY 猫間ことみ.

Nekoma Kotomai

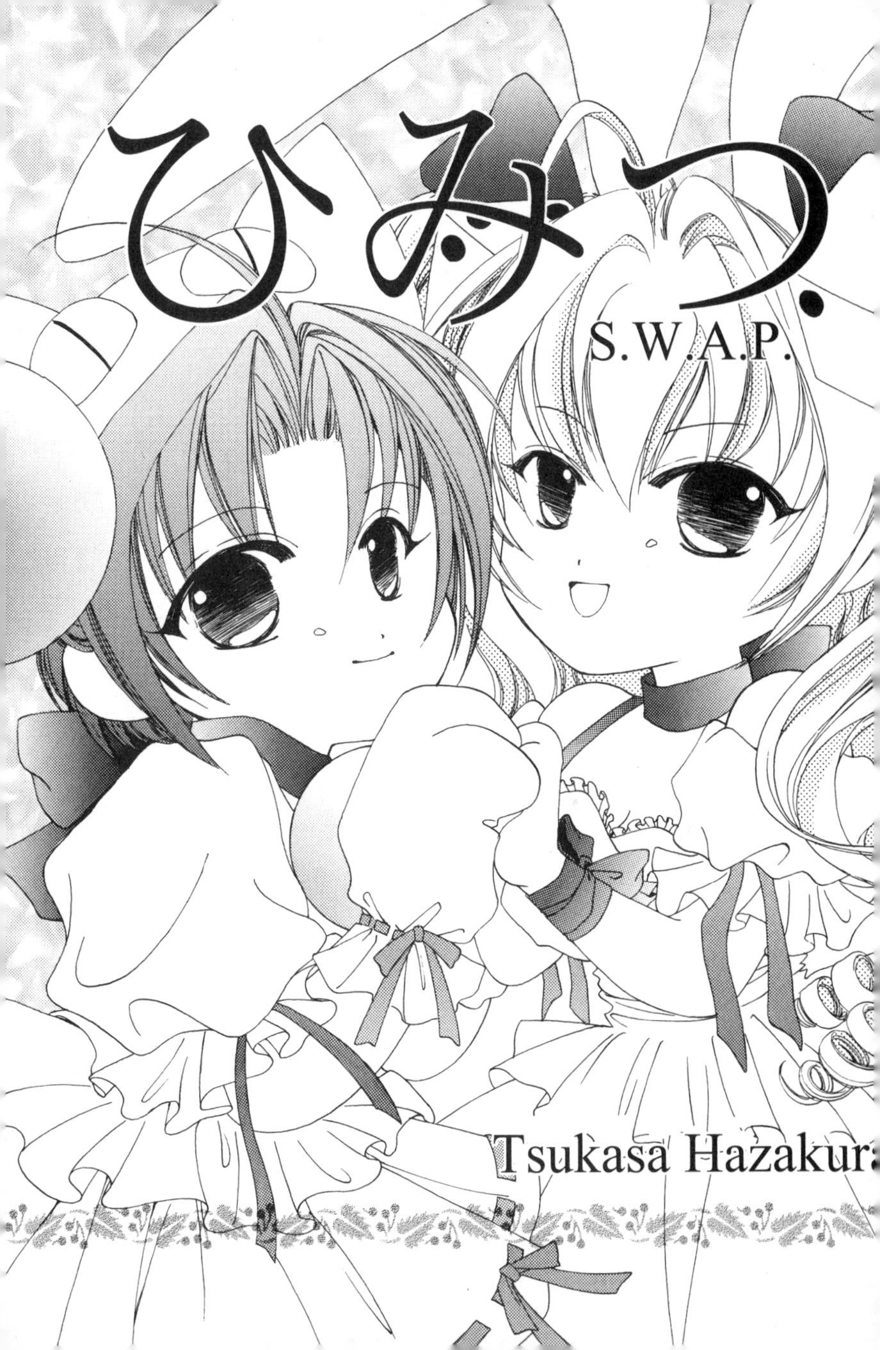
ひみつ
S.W.A.P.
Tsukasa Hazakur

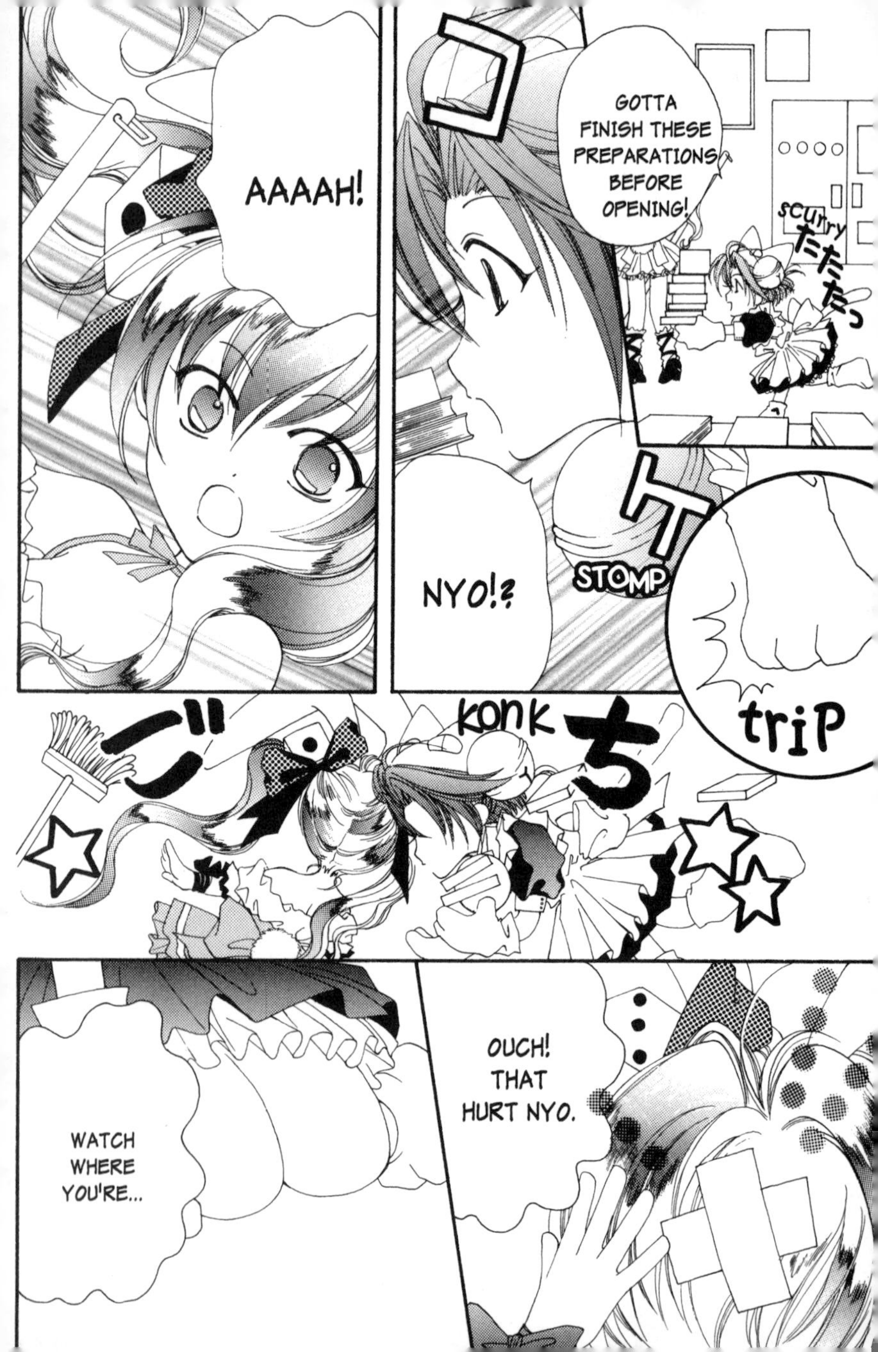
GOTTA FINISH THESE PREPARATIONS BEFORE OPENING!
scurry
たたたっ
NYO!?
ケ
STOMP
trip
AAAAH!
konk
ごち
...
OUCH! THAT HURT NYO.
WATCH WHERE YOU'RE...

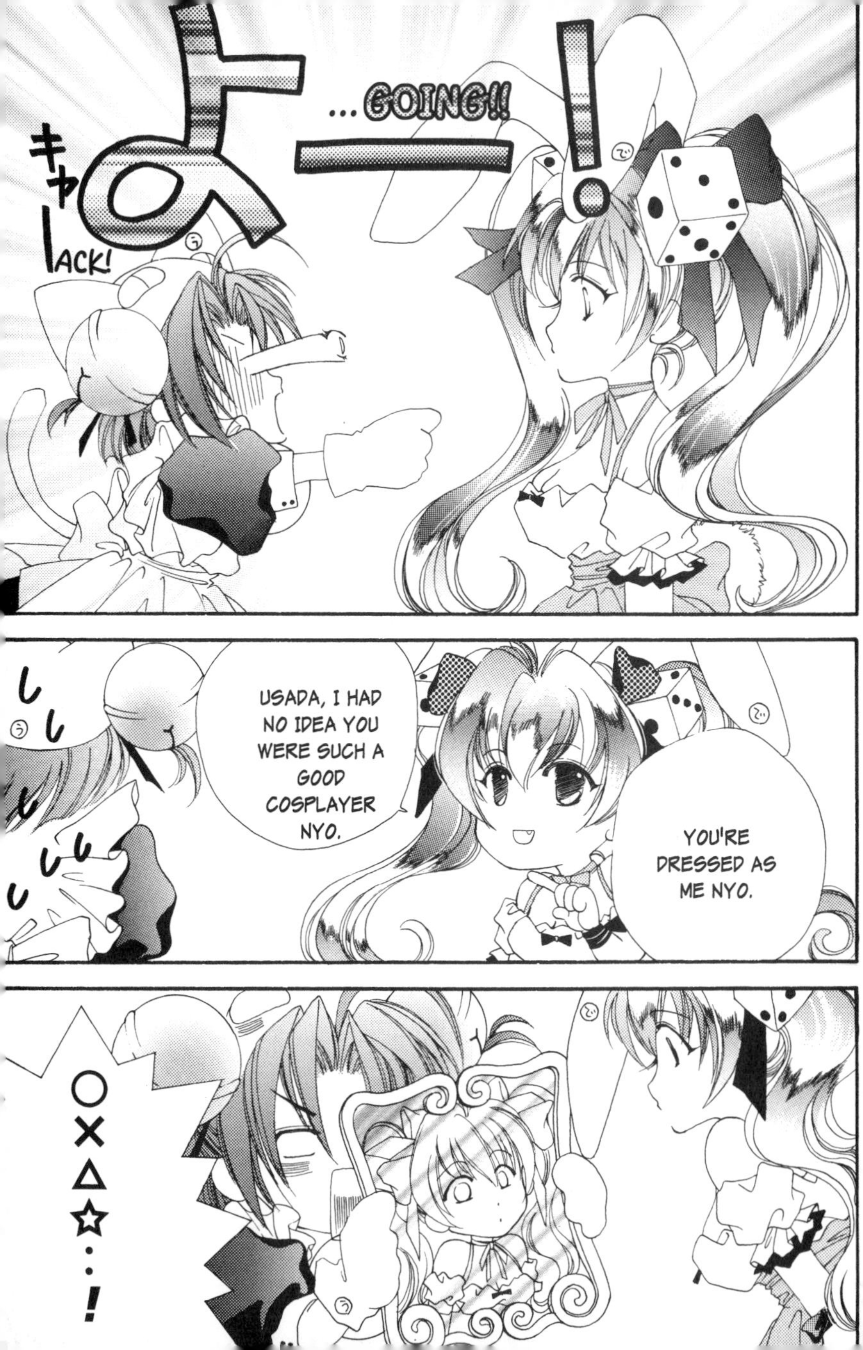
よー！
...GOING!!
キャ
ACK!
YOU'RE DRESSED AS ME NYO.
USADA, I HAD NO IDEA YOU WERE SUCH A GOOD COSPLAYER NYO.
○×△☆...!

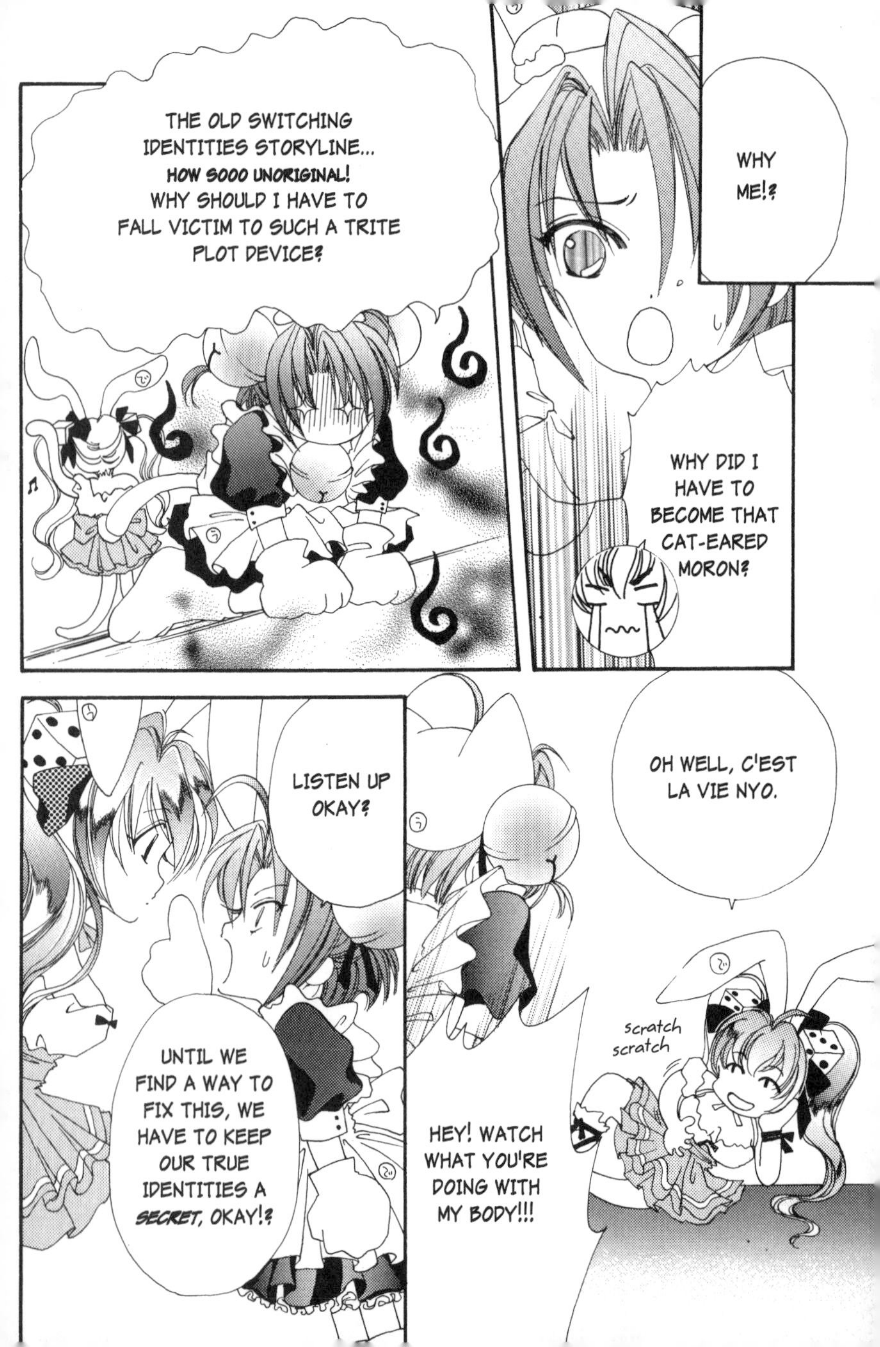
WHY ME!?
WHY DID I HAVE TO BECOME THAT CAT-EARED MORON?
THE OLD SWITCHING IDENTITIES STORYLINE... HOW SOOO UNORIGINAL! WHY SHOULD I HAVE TO FALL VICTIM TO SUCH A TRITE PLOT DEVICE?
OH WELL, C'EST LA VIE NYO.
scratch scratch
HEY! WATCH WHAT YOU'RE DOING WITH MY BODY!!!
LISTEN UP OKAY?
UNTIL WE FIND A WAY TO FIX THIS, WE HAVE TO KEEP OUR TRUE IDENTITIES A SECRET, OKAY!?

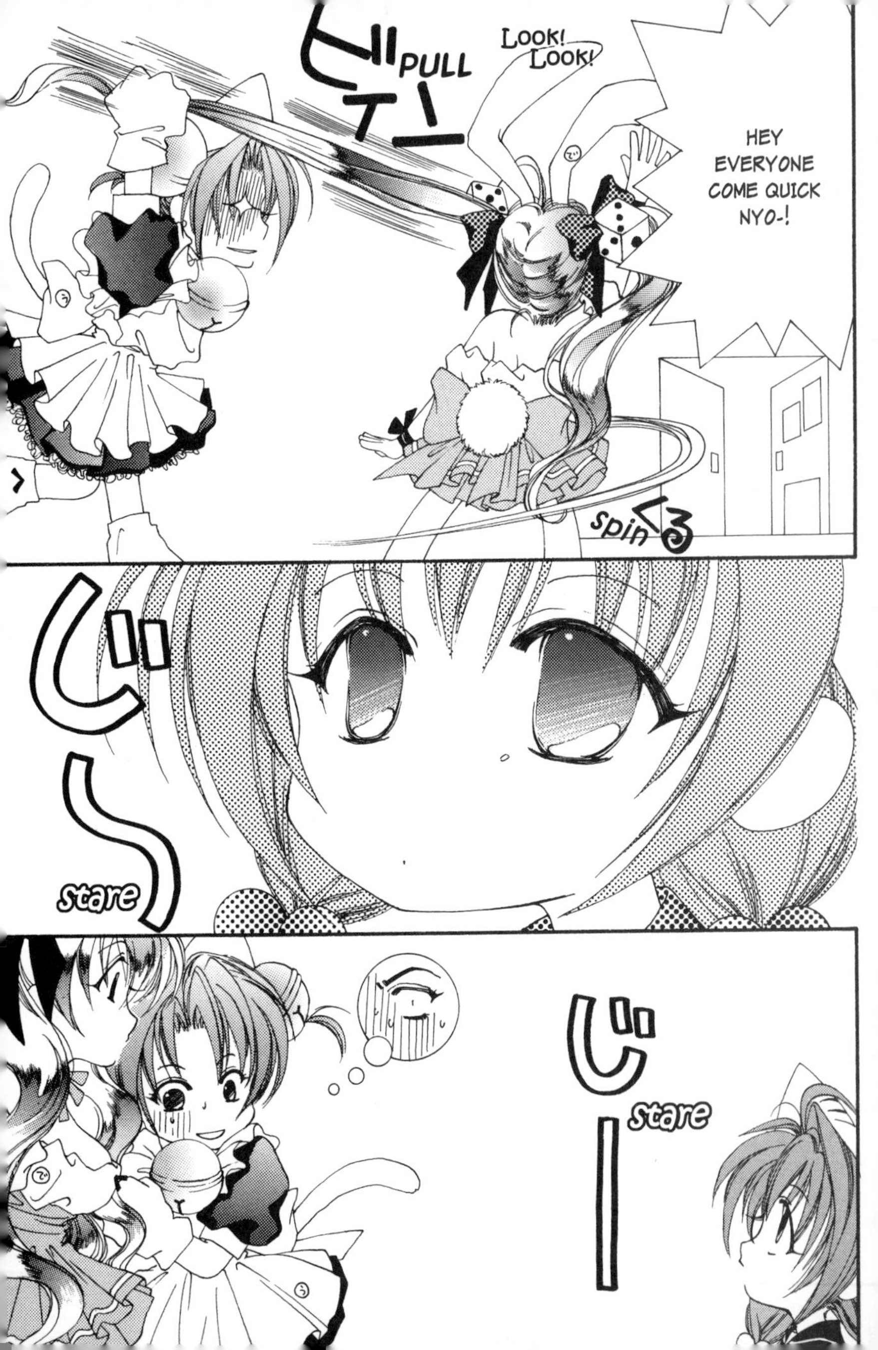
HEY EVERYONE COME QUICK NYO-!
LOOK! LOOK!
PULL
くる
spin
stare
stare

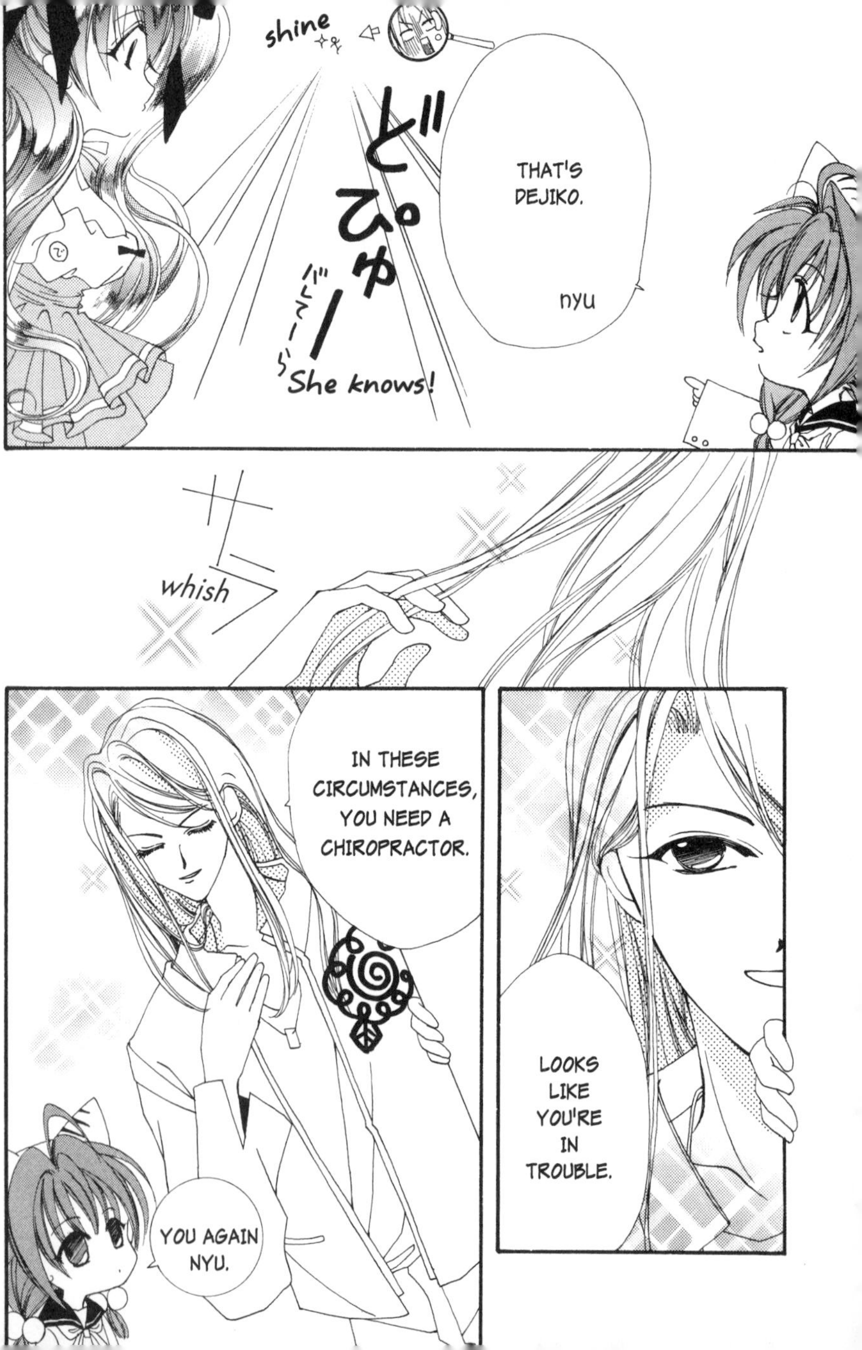
THAT'S DEJIKO.
nyu
shine
どひゅー
She knows!
whish
LOOKS LIKE YOU'RE IN TROUBLE.
IN THESE CIRCUMSTANCES, YOU NEED A CHIROPRACTOR.
YOU AGAIN NYU.

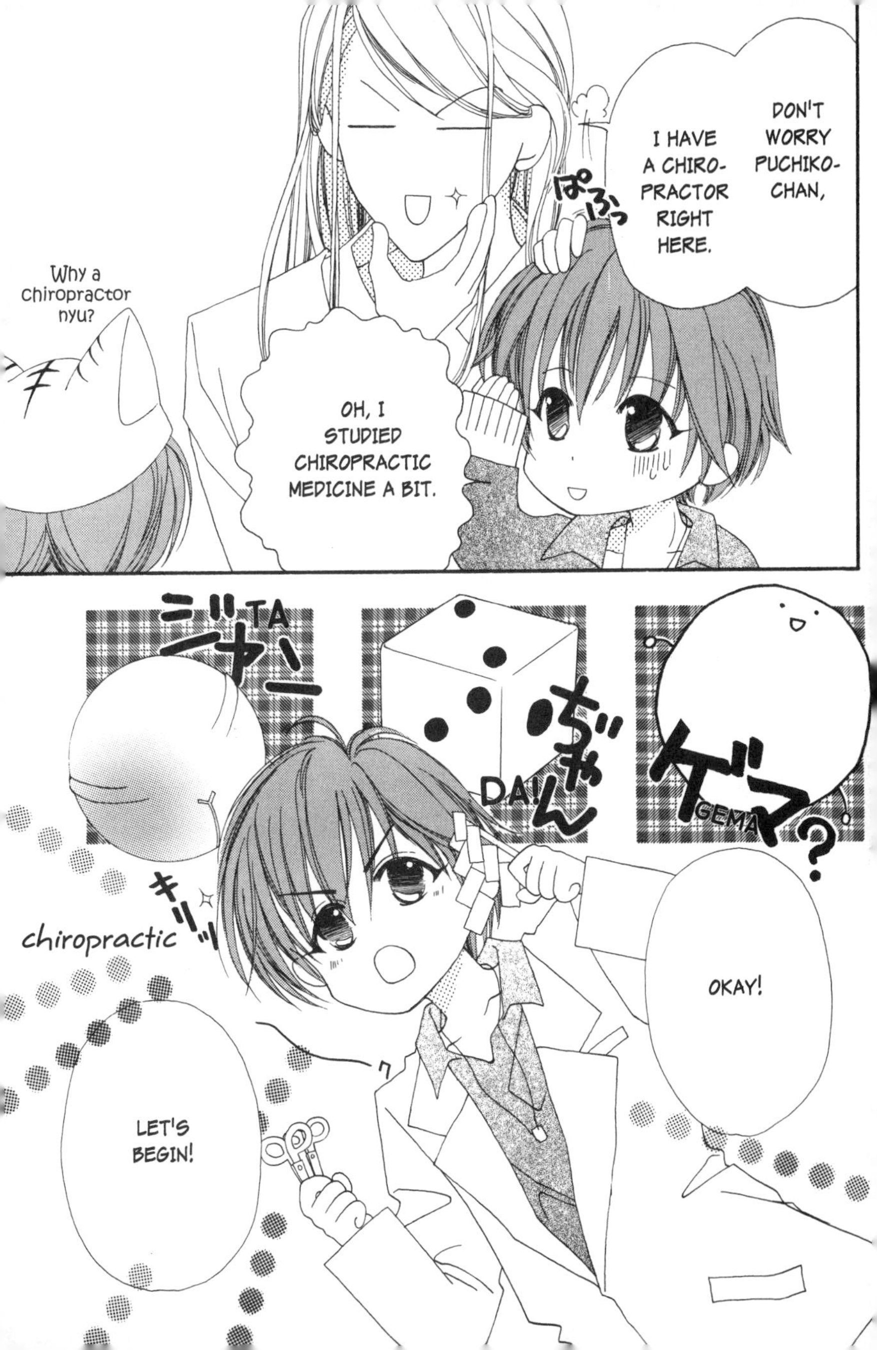
DON'T WORRY PUCHIKO-CHAN,
I HAVE A CHIRO-PRACTOR RIGHT HERE.
ぱふっ
OH, I STUDIED CHIROPRACTIC MEDICINE A BIT.
Why a chiropractor nyu?
ゲマ GEMA ?
ぢゃん DA!
ジャーン TA
OKAY!
キリッ chiropractic
LET'S BEGIN!

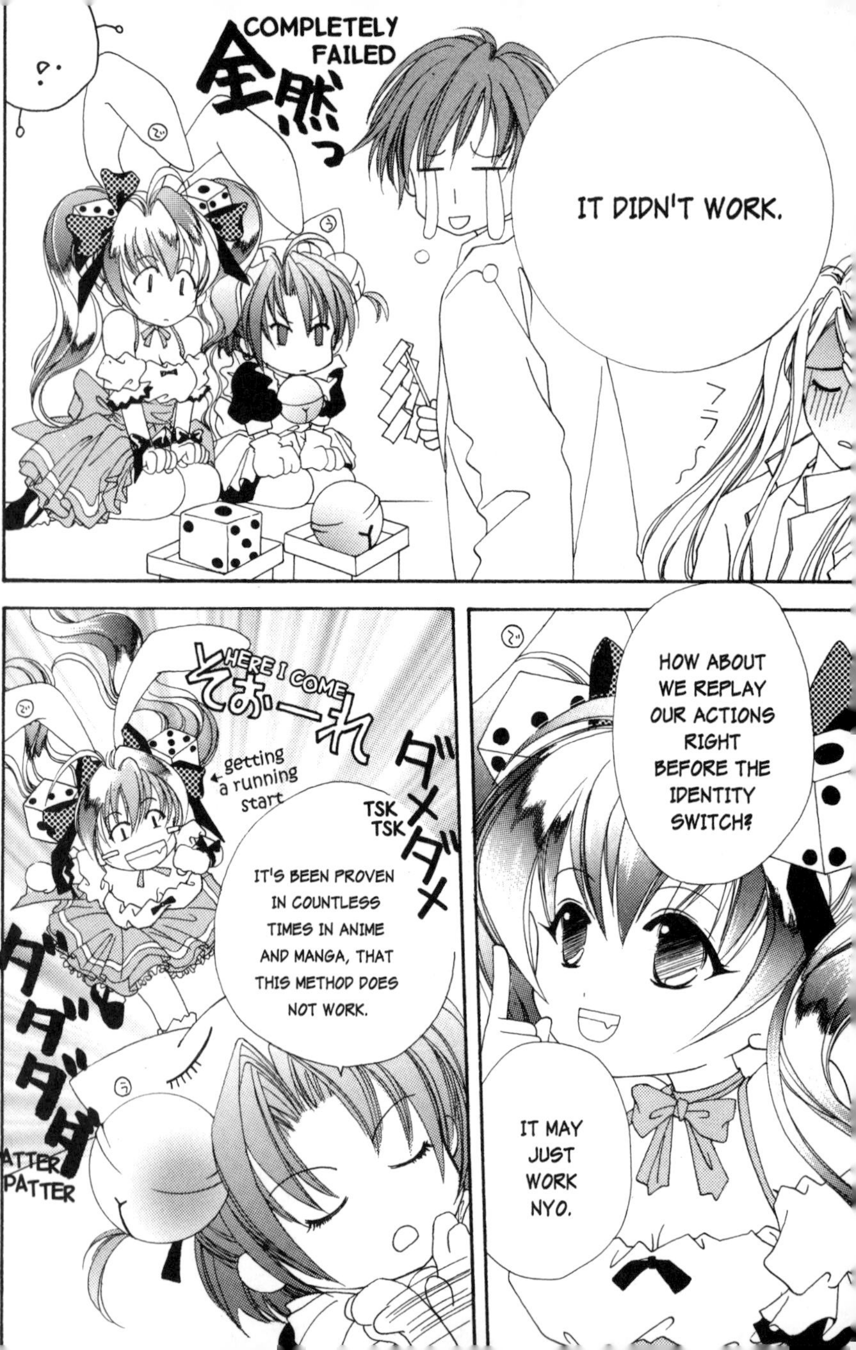
IT DIDN'T WORK.
COMPLETELY FAILED
全然っ
フラ～
HOW ABOUT WE REPLAY OUR ACTIONS RIGHT BEFORE THE IDENTITY SWITCH?
IT MAY JUST WORK NYO.
TSK TSK
ダメダメ
HERE I COME
そぉーれ
getting a running start
IT'S BEEN PROVEN IN COUNTLESS TIMES IN ANIME AND MANGA, THAT THIS METHOD DOES NOT WORK.
PATTER PATTER
ダダダダ

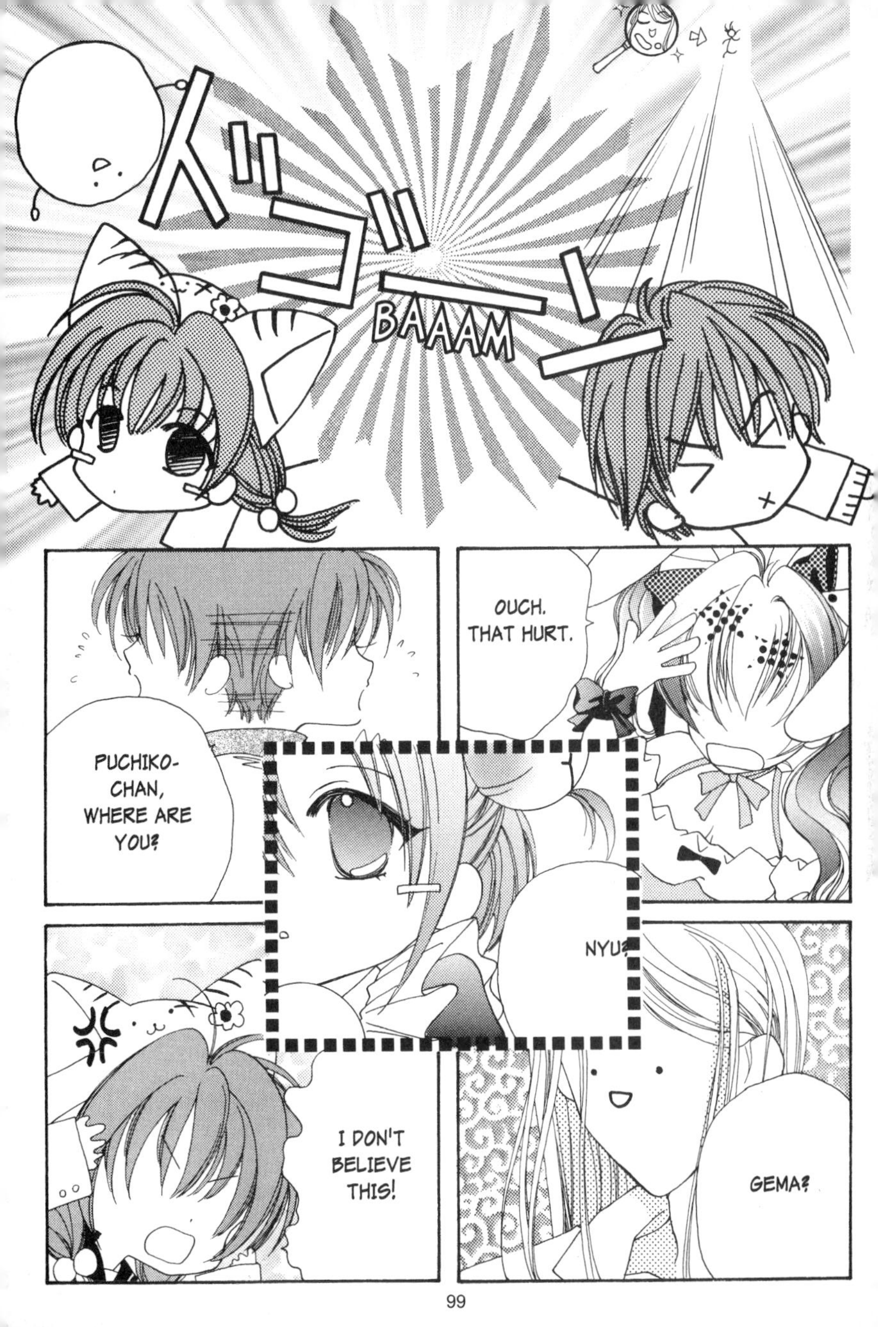
BAAAM
OUCH. THAT HURT.
PUCHIKO-CHAN, WHERE ARE YOU?
NYU?
GEMA?
I DON'T BELIEVE THIS!

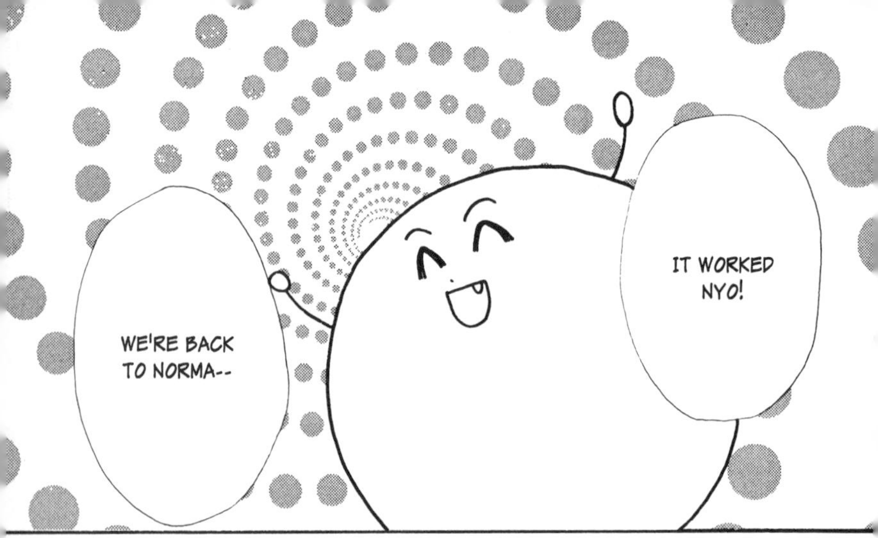
IT WORKED NYO!
WE'RE BACK TO NORMA--

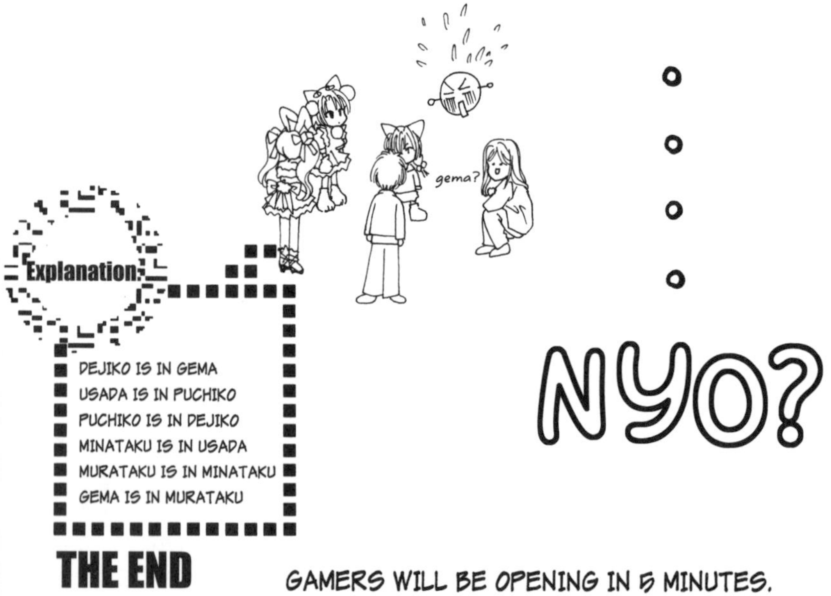
. . . . NYO?
gema?
Explanation
DEJIKO IS IN GEMA
USADA IS IN PUCHIKO
PUCHIKO IS IN DEJIKO
MINATAKU IS IN USADA
MURATAKU IS IN MINATAKU
GEMA IS IN MURATAKU
THE END
GAMERS WILL BE OPENING IN 5 MINUTES.

Hokke Mirin's Secret

Hina.

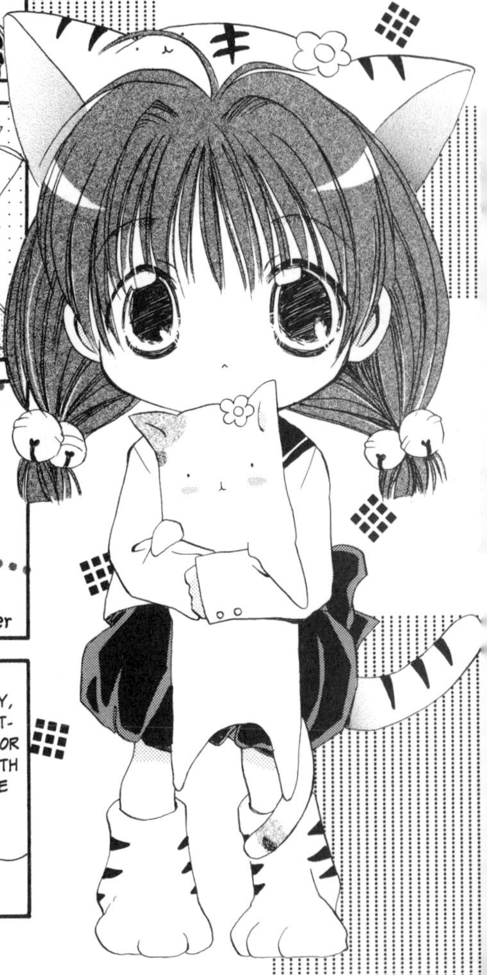

BEWARE!

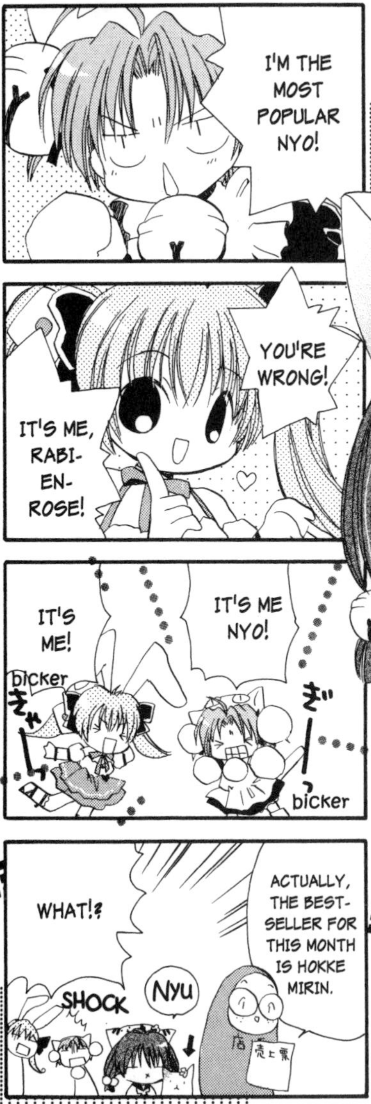
I'M THE MOST POPULAR NYO!
YOU'RE WRONG!
IT'S ME, RABI-EN-ROSE!
IT'S ME NYO!
IT'S ME!
bicker
bicker
ACTUALLY, THE BEST-SELLER FOR THIS MONTH IS HOKKE MIRIN.
WHAT!?
NYU
SHOCK

Hokke Mirin Goods

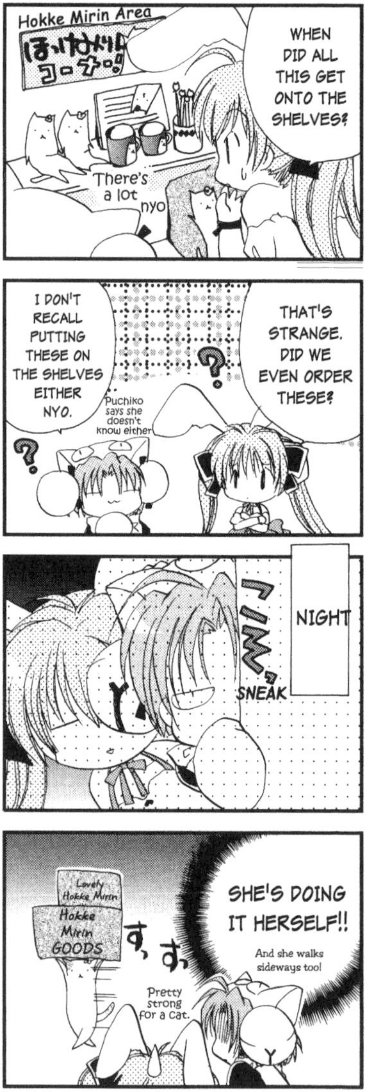
WHEN DID ALL THIS GET ONTO THE SHELVES?
Hokke Mirin Area
There's a lot nyo
THAT'S STRANGE. DID WE EVEN ORDER THESE?
I DON'T RECALL PUTTING THESE ON THE SHELVES EITHER NYO.
Puchiko says she doesn't know either
NIGHT
SNEAK
SHE'S DOING IT HERSELF!!
And she walks sideways too!
Lovely Hokke Mirin
Hokke Mirin GOODS
す、す、
Pretty strong for a cat.

Meanwhile Puchiko...

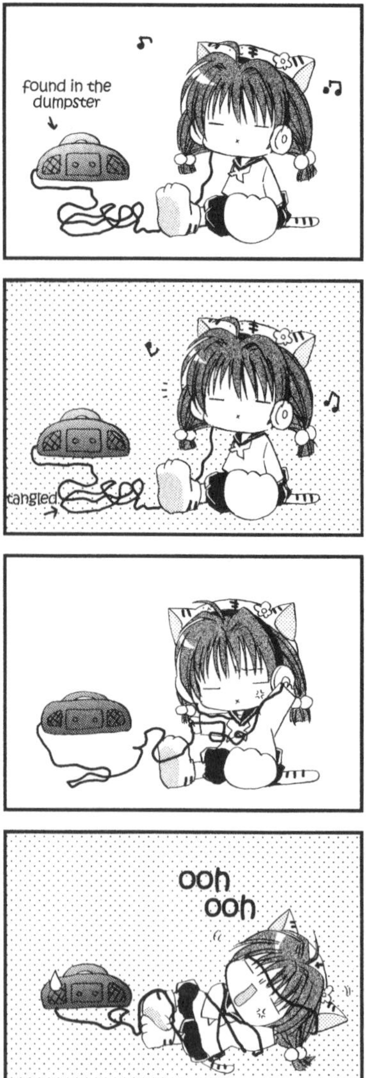
found in the dumpster
tangled
ooh ooh

The Pursuit

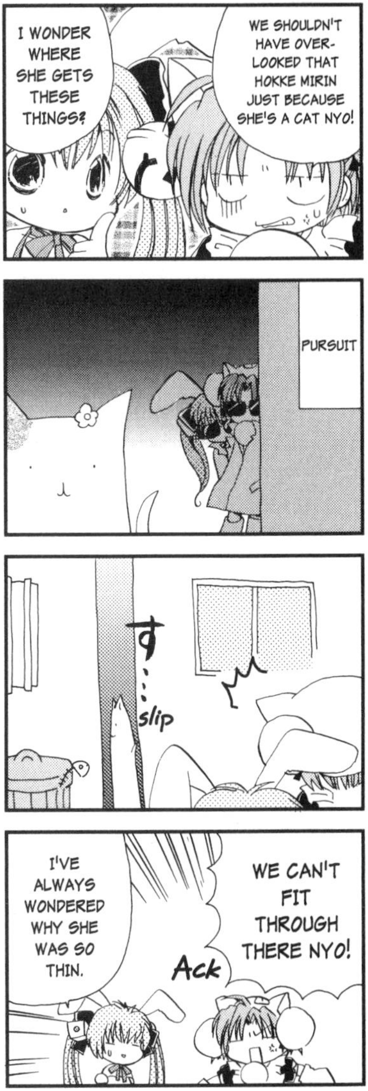
WE SHOULDN'T HAVE OVER-LOOKED THAT HOKKE MIRIN JUST BECAUSE SHE'S A CAT NYO!
I WONDER WHERE SHE GETS THESE THINGS?
PURSUIT
す
slip
WE CAN'T FIT THROUGH THERE NYO!
Ack
I'VE ALWAYS WONDERED WHY SHE WAS SO THIN.

The Secret Hideout

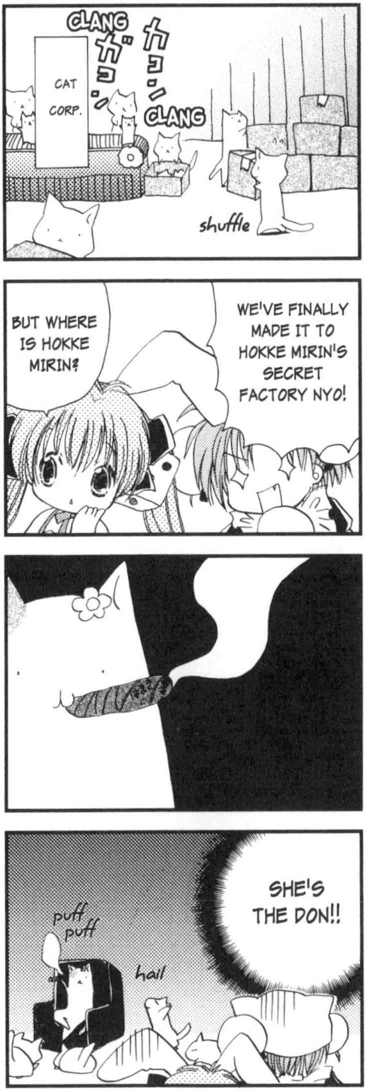
CLANG
CLANG
CAT CORP.
shuffle
WE'VE FINALLY MADE IT TO HOKKE MIRIN'S SECRET FACTORY NYO!
BUT WHERE IS HOKKE MIRIN?
SHE'S THE DON!!
hail
puff puff

The Lovely Hokke Mirin

Didn't want to see that nyo.

THE END

Who's your favorite character in Di Gi Charat?

Hazakura Tsukasa
I AM REALLY INTERESTED IN THIS GIRL. I DON'T KNOW HER NAME YET, BUT SHE SEEMS TO BE THE HEAD OF THE BLACK GEMA GEMA GANG, SO I NICKNAMED HER "DON-CHAN." (ERR... SO LAME.) I WANT TO KNOW HER IDENTITY! SHE'S A PANDA, RIGHT?
はざくら つかさ.

Who's your favorite character in Di Gi Charat?

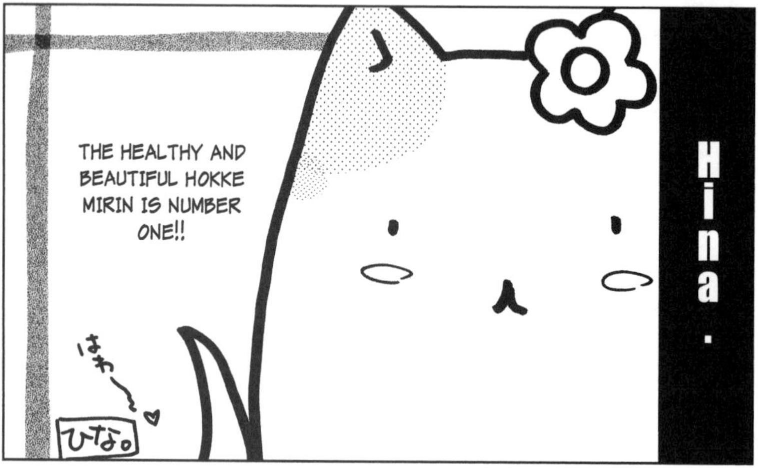
THE HEALTHY AND BEAUTIFUL HOKKE MIRIN IS NUMBER ONE!!
はわ〜〜♡
ひな。
Hina.

A Message from Clim

By pure luck, Majin Gappa was able to join the Di Gi Charat family. And wow, he's going to join in on Dejiko's US debut too!

He's awfully quiet, and he doesn't appear much, but I hope you enjoy his company.

- Clim

木谷高明

代表取締役社長

A Message from the CEO

In 2003, Di Gi Charat celebrates her 5th anniversary. But I must confess that we at Broccoli have more than one thing to celebrate. Di Gi Charat has finally made her way to the U.S., and it is indeed the perfect timing for Dejiko to make her American debut.

I hope that you enjoy *Di Gi Charat Theater - Dejiko's Summer Vacation.* It is only the beginning of what's in store.

Thank you to all the fans who have supported Dejiko in the U.S. and around the world. We would not be here without you. I would also like to take the time to welcome new fans. I hope you come to love Dejiko and the rest of the *Di Gi Charat* world as much as we do.

Sincerely,
Takaaki Kidani
CEO, Broccoli Co, Ltd.

Profile
Takaaki Kidani founded Broccoli Co., Ltd in 1994. Since then, he has been one of the major players responsible for creating media such as *Di Gi Charat*, *Galaxy Angel*, *Aquarian Age*, and *Neppu Kairiku Bushi Lord*.

What is Gema Gema?

Gema Gema is the title of a 4-panel comic series featured in the monthly informational magazine *From Gamers.* While only Dejiko and Gema appeared at first, Gema Gema was eventually the springboard for other *Di Gi Charat* characters like Rabi~en~Rose and Piyoko.

Gema Gema is still currently featured in *From Gamers*, and Koge-Donbo hand draws and colors them each month. The hardcore industry jokes and random announcements make Gema Gema a very popular section of the magazine.

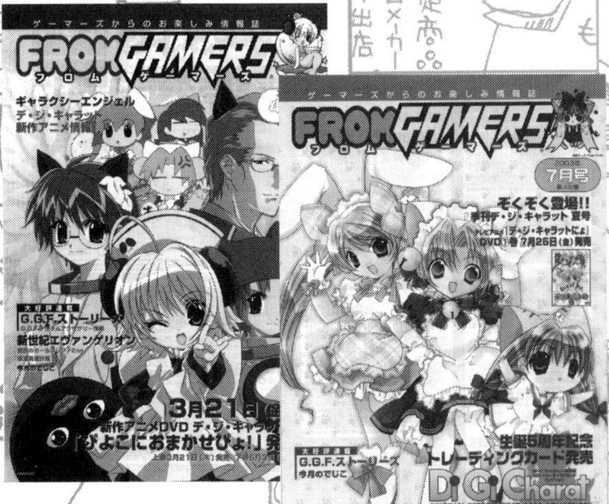
ゲーマーズからのお楽しみ情報誌
FROMGAMERS
フロムゲーマーズ
ギャラクシーエンジェル
デ・ジ・キャラット
新作アニメ情報
G.G.F.ストーリーズ
新世紀エヴァンゲリオン
3月21日
ゲーマーズからのお楽しみ情報誌
FROMGAMERS
フロムゲーマーズ
7月号
ぞくぞく登場!!
季刊デ・ジ・キャラット 夏号
DVD1巻 7月25日(金)発売
G.G.F.ストーリーズ
今月のでじこ
生誕5周年記念
トレーディングカード発売
Di Gi Charat
Di Gi Charat 5th Aniversary

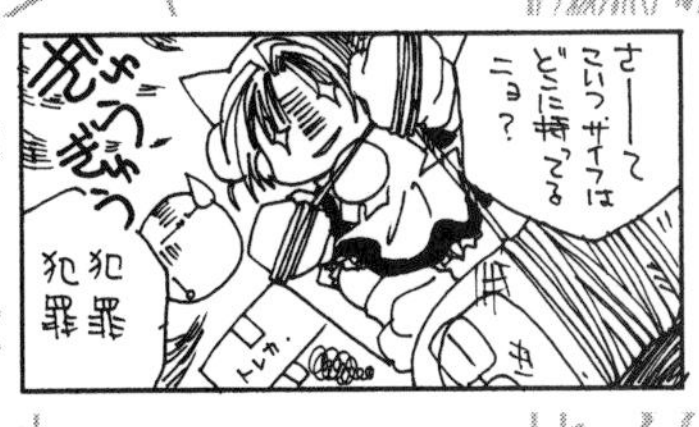
さーーって こいつサイフは どこに持ってるニョ?
犯罪 犯罪
トレカ

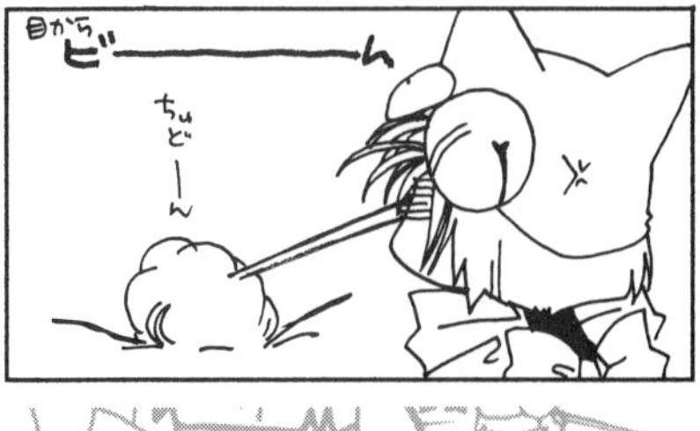
目から ビーーーーム
ちゅどーーん

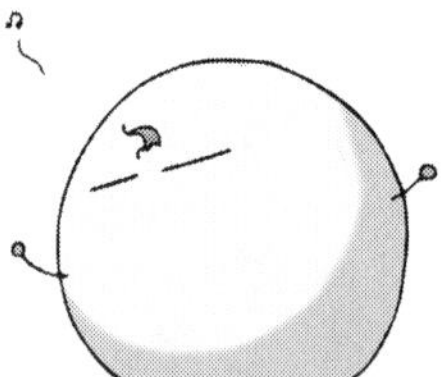

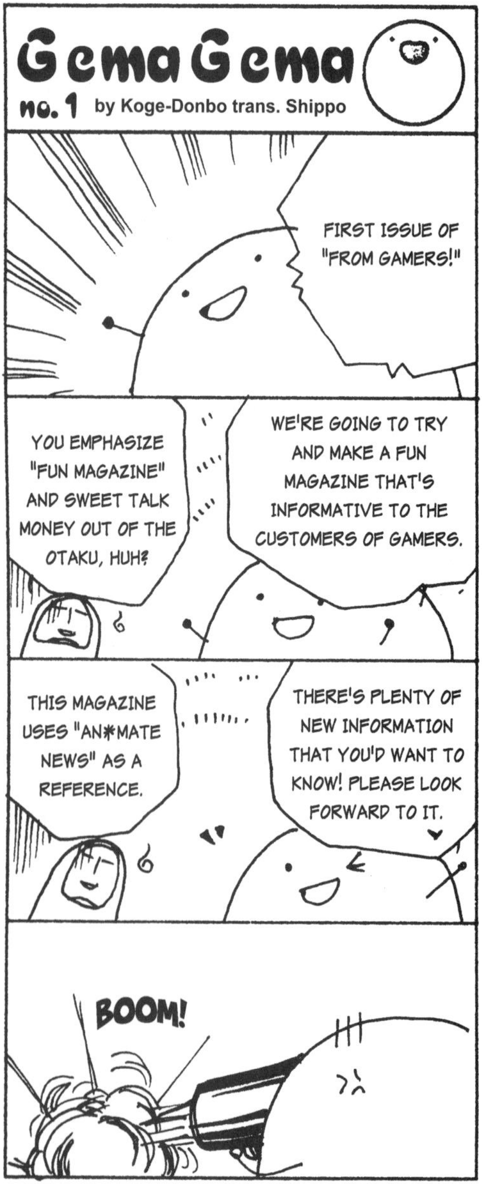
Gema Gema
no. 1 by Koge-Donbo trans. Shippo
FIRST ISSUE OF "FROM GAMERS!"
WE'RE GOING TO TRY AND MAKE A FUN MAGAZINE THAT'S INFORMATIVE TO THE CUSTOMERS OF GAMERS.
YOU EMPHASIZE "FUN MAGAZINE" AND SWEET TALK MONEY OUT OF THE OTAKU, HUH?
THERE'S PLENTY OF NEW INFORMATION THAT YOU'D WANT TO KNOW! PLEASE LOOK FORWARD TO IT.
THIS MAGAZINE USES "AN*MATE NEWS" AS A REFERENCE.
BOOM!

Gema Gema

no. 2 by Koge-Donbo trans. Shippo

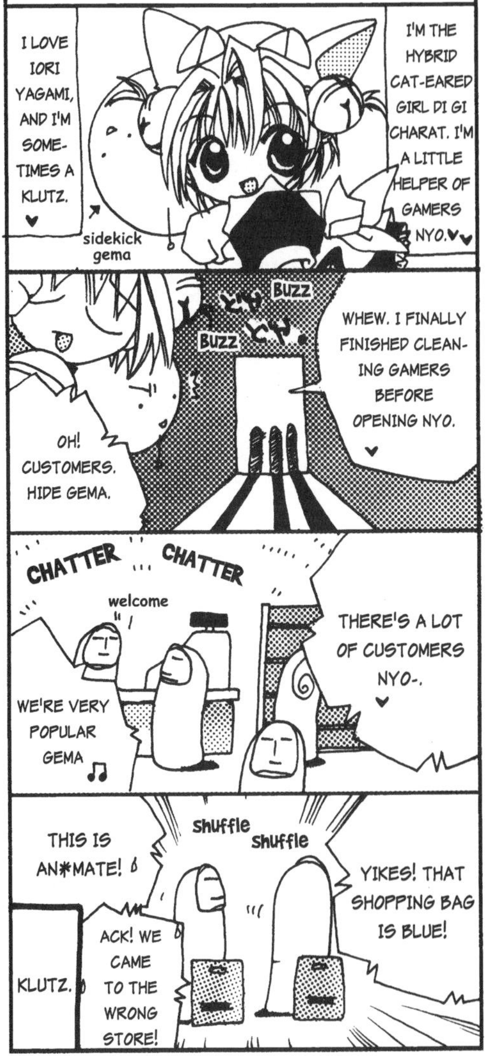
I'M THE HYBRID CAT-EARED GIRL DI GI CHARAT. I'M A LITTLE HELPER OF GAMERS NYO.♥♥
I LOVE IORI YAGAMI, AND I'M SOME-TIMES A KLUTZ. ♥
sidekick gema
Buzz
Buzz
WHEW. I FINALLY FINISHED CLEAN-ING GAMERS BEFORE OPENING NYO. ♥
OH! CUSTOMERS. HIDE GEMA.
CHATTER
CHATTER
THERE'S A LOT OF CUSTOMERS NYO-. ♥
welcome
WE'RE VERY POPULAR GEMA ♫
YIKES! THAT SHOPPING BAG IS BLUE!
shuffle
shuffle
THIS IS AN*MATE!
ACK! WE CAME TO THE WRONG STORE!
KLUTZ.

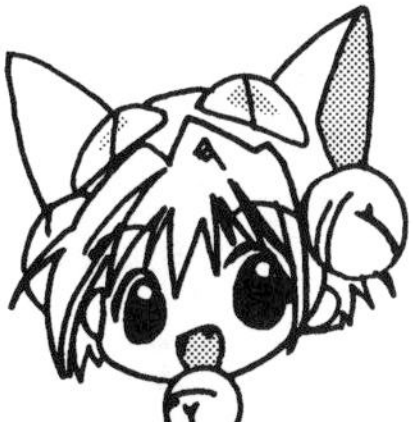

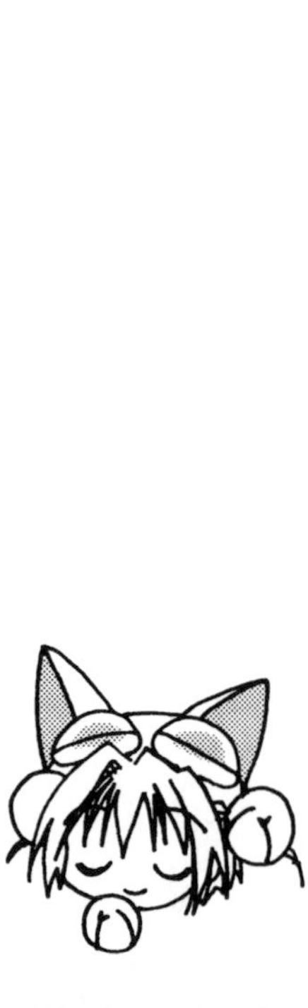

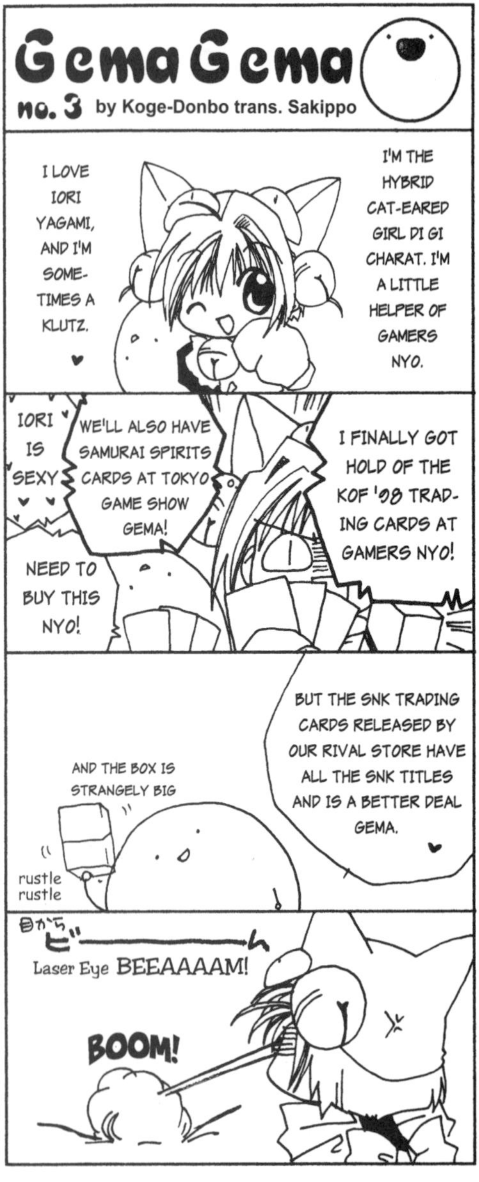
Gema Gema
no. 3 by Koge-Donbo trans. Sakippo
I'M THE HYBRID CAT-EARED GIRL DI GI CHARAT. I'M A LITTLE HELPER OF GAMERS NYO.
I LOVE IORI YAGAMI, AND I'M SOME-TIMES A KLUTZ.
I FINALLY GOT HOLD OF THE KOF '98 TRAD-ING CARDS AT GAMERS NYO!
WE'LL ALSO HAVE SAMURAI SPIRITS CARDS AT TOKYO GAME SHOW GEMA!
IORI IS SEXY
NEED TO BUY THIS NYO!
BUT THE SNK TRADING CARDS RELEASED BY OUR RIVAL STORE HAVE ALL THE SNK TITLES AND IS A BETTER DEAL GEMA.
AND THE BOX IS STRANGELY BIG
rustle rustle
目から
ビ————ム
Laser Eye BEEAAAAM!
BOOM!

Gema Gema

no. 4 by Koge-Donbo trans. Sakippo

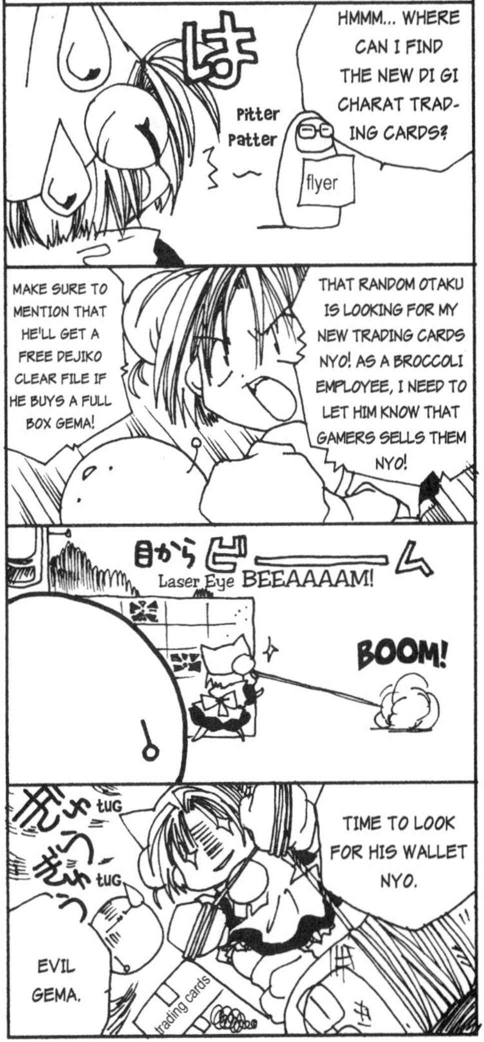
HMMM... WHERE CAN I FIND THE NEW DI GI CHARAT TRAD-ING CARDS?
は
Pitter Patter
flyer
THAT RANDOM OTAKU IS LOOKING FOR MY NEW TRADING CARDS NYO! AS A BROCCOLI EMPLOYEE, I NEED TO LET HIM KNOW THAT GAMERS SELLS THEM NYO!
MAKE SURE TO MENTION THAT HE'LL GET A FREE DEJIKO CLEAR FILE IF HE BUYS A FULL BOX GEMA!
目からビーーーム
Laser Eye BEEAAAAM!
BOOM!
TIME TO LOOK FOR HIS WALLET NYO.
tug
tug
EVIL GEMA.
trading cards

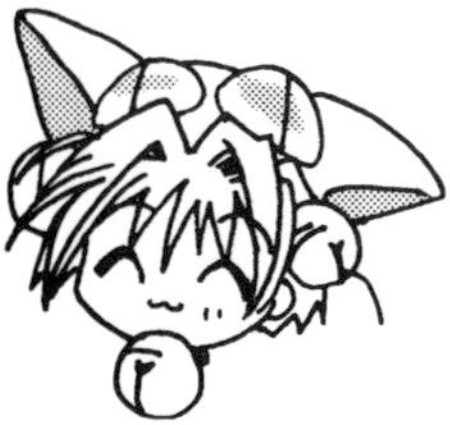

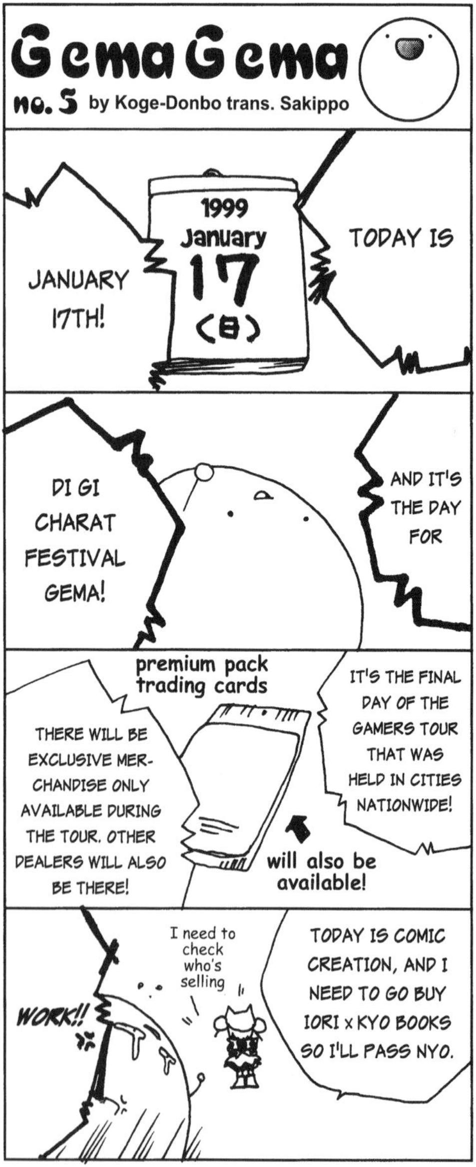
Gema Gema
no. 5 by Koge-Donbo trans. Sakippo
TODAY IS
1999 January 17 (日)
JANUARY 17TH!
AND IT'S THE DAY FOR
DI GI CHARAT FESTIVAL GEMA!
IT'S THE FINAL DAY OF THE GAMERS TOUR THAT WAS HELD IN CITIES NATIONWIDE!
premium pack trading cards
will also be available!
THERE WILL BE EXCLUSIVE MER-CHANDISE ONLY AVAILABLE DURING THE TOUR. OTHER DEALERS WILL ALSO BE THERE!
TODAY IS COMIC CREATION, AND I NEED TO GO BUY IORI x KYO BOOKS SO I'LL PASS NYO.
I need to check who's selling
WORK!!

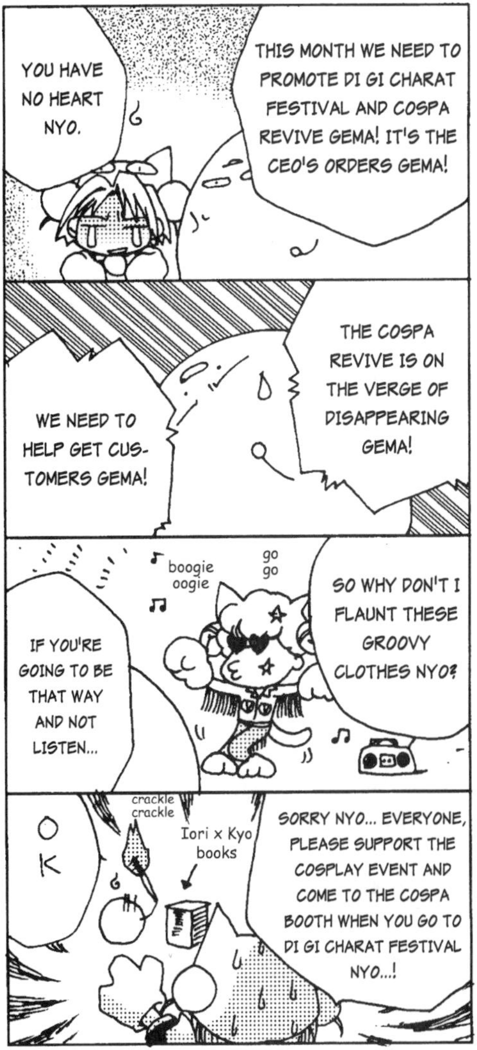
THIS MONTH WE NEED TO PROMOTE DI GI CHARAT FESTIVAL AND COSPA REVIVE GEMA! IT'S THE CEO'S ORDERS GEMA!
YOU HAVE NO HEART NYO.
THE COSPA REVIVE IS ON THE VERGE OF DISAPPEARING GEMA!
WE NEED TO HELP GET CUSTOMERS GEMA!
go go
boogie oogie
SO WHY DON'T I FLAUNT THESE GROOVY CLOTHES NYO?
IF YOU'RE GOING TO BE THAT WAY AND NOT LISTEN...
SORRY NYO... EVERYONE, PLEASE SUPPORT THE COSPLAY EVENT AND COME TO THE COSPA BOOTH WHEN YOU GO TO DI GI CHARAT FESTIVAL NYO...!
Iori x Kyo books
crackle crackle
OK

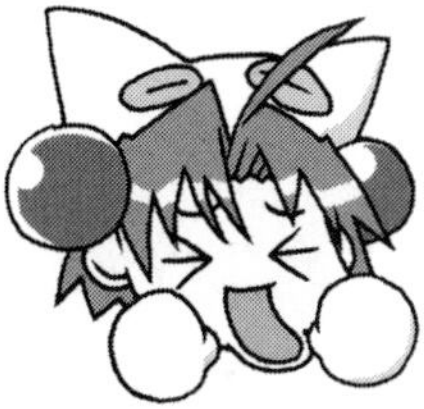

Gema Gema

no. 6 by Koge-Donbo trans. Shippo

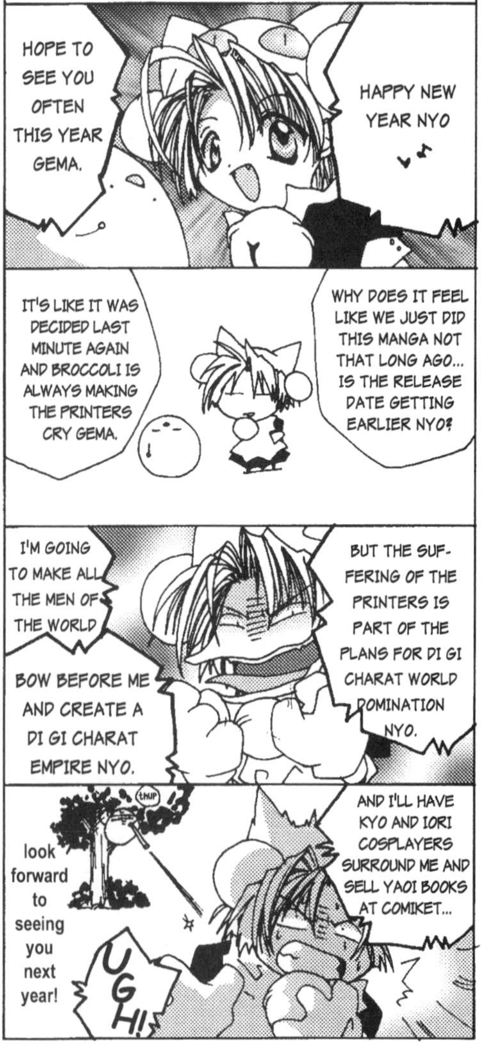
HAPPY NEW YEAR NYO
HOPE TO SEE YOU OFTEN THIS YEAR GEMA.
WHY DOES IT FEEL LIKE WE JUST DID THIS MANGA NOT THAT LONG AGO... IS THE RELEASE DATE GETTING EARLIER NYO?
IT'S LIKE IT WAS DECIDED LAST MINUTE AGAIN AND BROCCOLI IS ALWAYS MAKING THE PRINTERS CRY GEMA.
BUT THE SUF-FERING OF THE PRINTERS IS PART OF THE PLANS FOR DI GI CHARAT WORLD DOMINATION NYO.
I'M GOING TO MAKE ALL THE MEN OF THE WORLD
BOW BEFORE ME AND CREATE A DI GI CHARAT EMPIRE NYO.
AND I'LL HAVE KYO AND IORI COSPLAYERS SURROUND ME AND SELL YAOI BOOKS AT COMIKET...
thup
look forward to seeing you next year!
UGH!

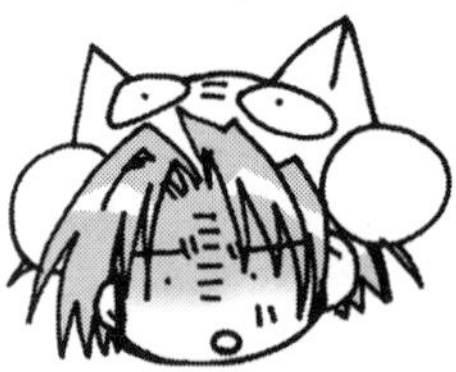

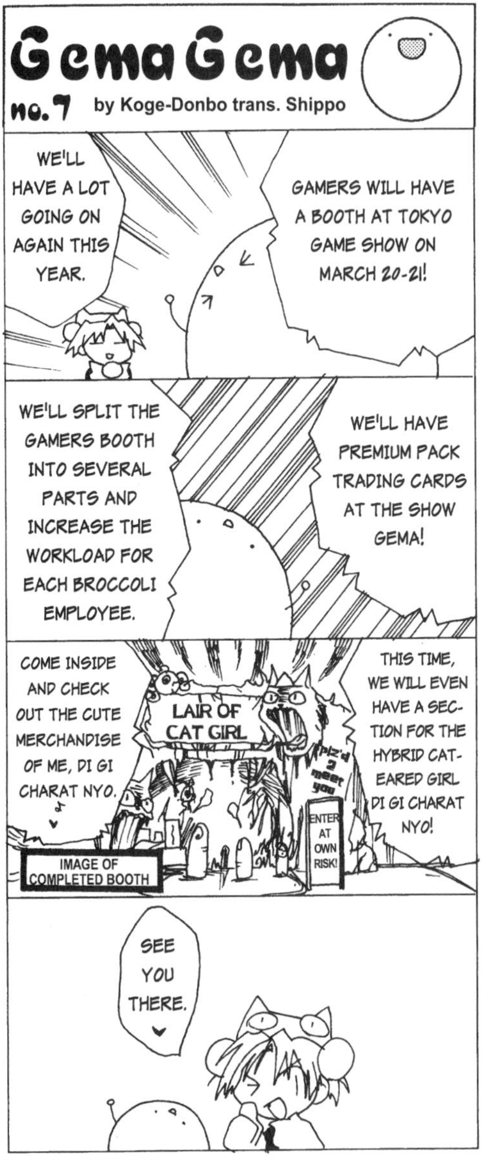
Gema Gema
no. 7 by Koge-Donbo trans. Shippo
GAMERS WILL HAVE A BOOTH AT TOKYO GAME SHOW ON MARCH 20-21!
WE'LL HAVE A LOT GOING ON AGAIN THIS YEAR.
WE'LL HAVE PREMIUM PACK TRADING CARDS AT THE SHOW GEMA!
WE'LL SPLIT THE GAMERS BOOTH INTO SEVERAL PARTS AND INCREASE THE WORKLOAD FOR EACH BROCCOLI EMPLOYEE.
THIS TIME, WE WILL EVEN HAVE A SEC-TION FOR THE HYBRID CAT-EARED GIRL DI GI CHARAT NYO!
LAIR OF CAT GIRL
plz'd 2 meet you
ENTER AT OWN RISK!
COME INSIDE AND CHECK OUT THE CUTE MERCHANDISE OF ME, DI GI CHARAT NYO.
IMAGE OF COMPLETED BOOTH
SEE YOU THERE.

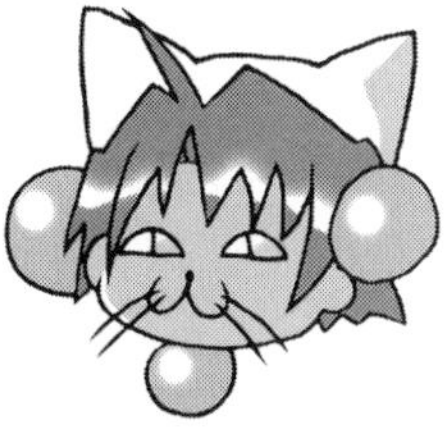

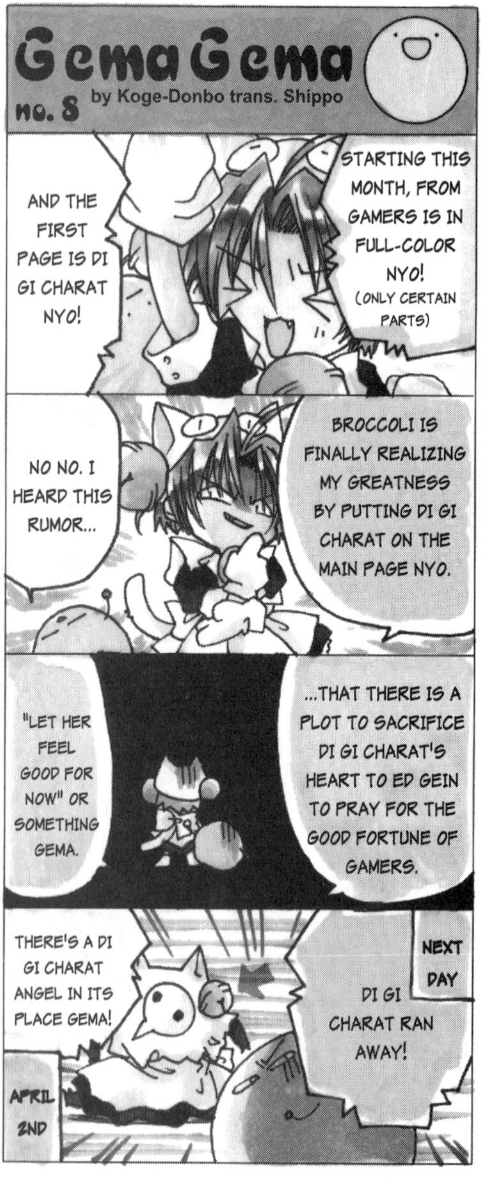
Gema Gema
no. 8
by Koge-Donbo trans. Shippo
STARTING THIS MONTH, FROM GAMERS IS IN FULL-COLOR NYO!
(ONLY CERTAIN PARTS)
AND THE FIRST PAGE IS DI GI CHARAT NYO!
BROCCOLI IS FINALLY REALIZING MY GREATNESS BY PUTTING DI GI CHARAT ON THE MAIN PAGE NYO.
NO NO. I HEARD THIS RUMOR...
...THAT THERE IS A PLOT TO SACRIFICE DI GI CHARAT'S HEART TO ED GEIN TO PRAY FOR THE GOOD FORTUNE OF GAMERS.
"LET HER FEEL GOOD FOR NOW" OR SOMETHING GEMA.
NEXT DAY
DI GI CHARAT RAN AWAY!
THERE'S A DI GI CHARAT ANGEL IN ITS PLACE GEMA!
APRIL 2ND

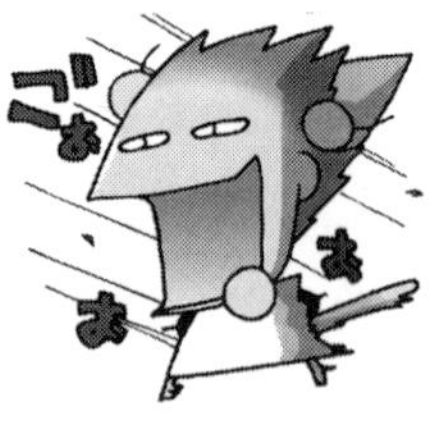

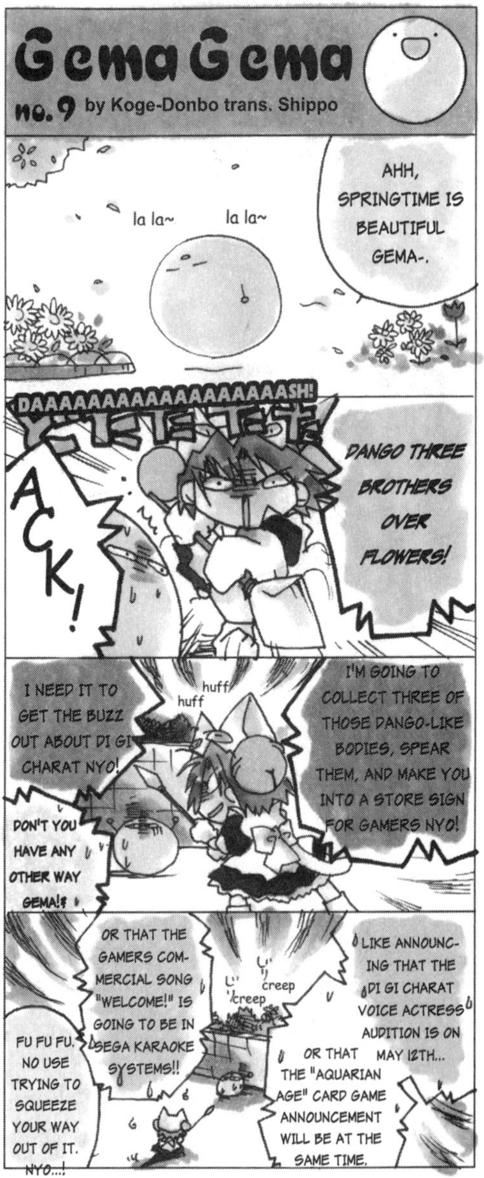
Gema Gema
no. 9 by Koge-Donbo trans. Shippo
AHH, SPRINGTIME IS BEAUTIFUL GEMA-.
la la~
la la~
DAAAAAAAAAAAAAAAAAASH!
DANGO THREE BROTHERS OVER FLOWERS!
ACK!
I'M GOING TO COLLECT THREE OF THOSE DANGO-LIKE BODIES, SPEAR THEM, AND MAKE YOU INTO A STORE SIGN FOR GAMERS NYO!
huff
huff
I NEED IT TO GET THE BUZZ OUT ABOUT DI GI CHARAT NYO!
DON'T YOU HAVE ANY OTHER WAY GEMA!?
LIKE ANNOUNCING THAT THE DI GI CHARAT VOICE ACTRESS AUDITION IS ON MAY 12TH...
OR THAT THE "AQUARIAN AGE" CARD GAME ANNOUNCEMENT WILL BE AT THE SAME TIME.
creep
creep
OR THAT THE GAMERS COMMERCIAL SONG "WELCOME!" IS GOING TO BE IN SEGA KARAOKE SYSTEMS!!
FU FU FU. NO USE TRYING TO SQUEEZE YOUR WAY OUT OF IT. NYO...!

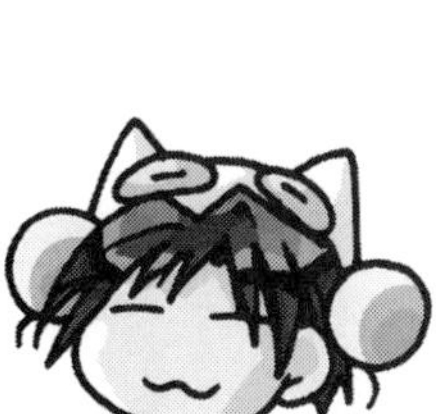

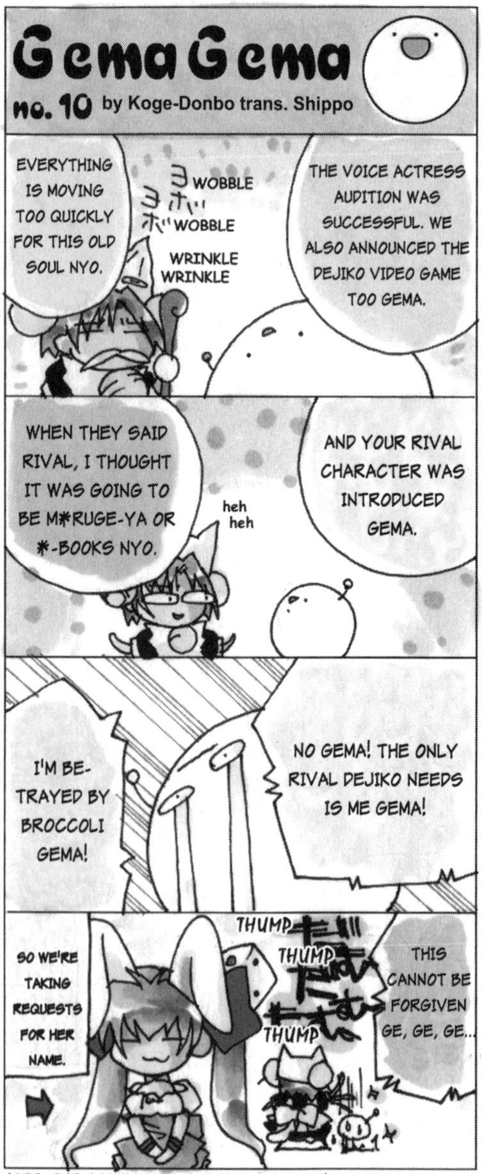
Gema Gema
no. 10 by Koge-Donbo trans. Shippo
THE VOICE ACTRESS AUDITION WAS SUCCESSFUL. WE ALSO ANNOUNCED THE DEJIKO VIDEO GAME TOO GEMA.
WOBBLE
WOBBLE
WRINKLE WRINKLE
EVERYTHING IS MOVING TOO QUICKLY FOR THIS OLD SOUL NYO.
AND YOUR RIVAL CHARACTER WAS INTRODUCED GEMA.
heh heh
WHEN THEY SAID RIVAL, I THOUGHT IT WAS GOING TO BE M*RUGE-YA OR *-BOOKS NYO.
NO GEMA! THE ONLY RIVAL DEJIKO NEEDS IS ME GEMA!
I'M BE-TRAYED BY BROCCOLI GEMA!
THIS CANNOT BE FORGIVEN GE, GE, GE...
THUMP
THUMP
THUMP
SO WE'RE TAKING REQUESTS FOR HER NAME.

NOTE: THE SUBMISSION FOR RABI-EN-ROSE'S NAME IS NOW COMPLETED.

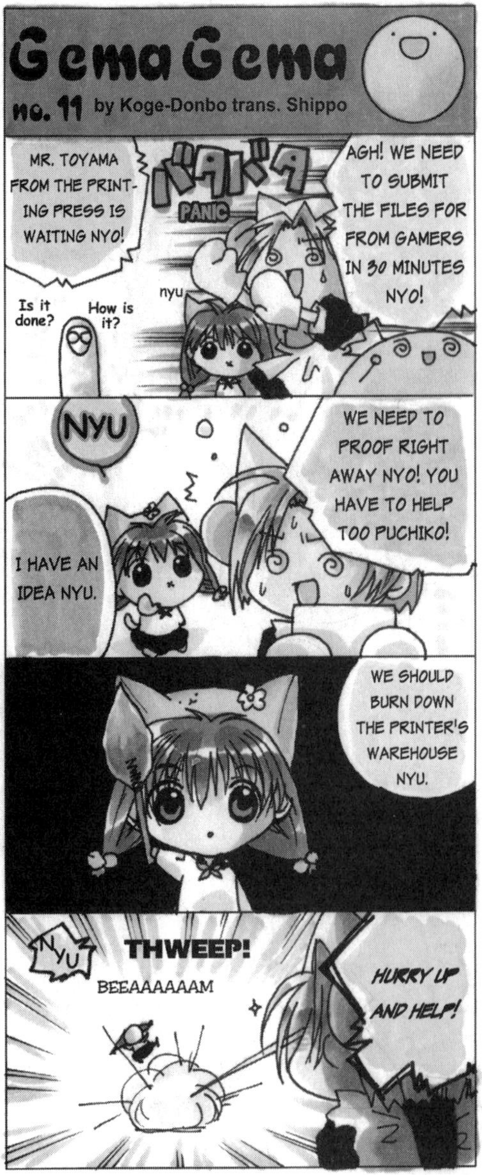
Gema Gema
no. 11 by Koge-Donbo trans. Shippo
AGH! WE NEED TO SUBMIT THE FILES FOR FROM GAMERS IN 30 MINUTES NYO!
PANIC
MR. TOYAMA FROM THE PRINT-ING PRESS IS WAITING NYO!
nyu
How is it?
Is it done?
WE NEED TO PROOF RIGHT AWAY NYO! YOU HAVE TO HELP TOO PUCHIKO!
NYU
I HAVE AN IDEA NYU.
WE SHOULD BURN DOWN THE PRINTER'S WAREHOUSE NYU.
HURRY UP AND HELP!
THWEEP!
NYU
BEEAAAAAAAM

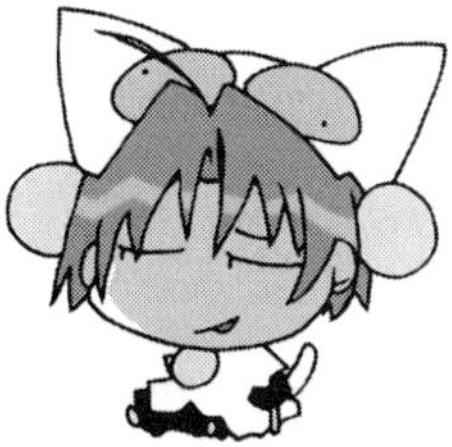

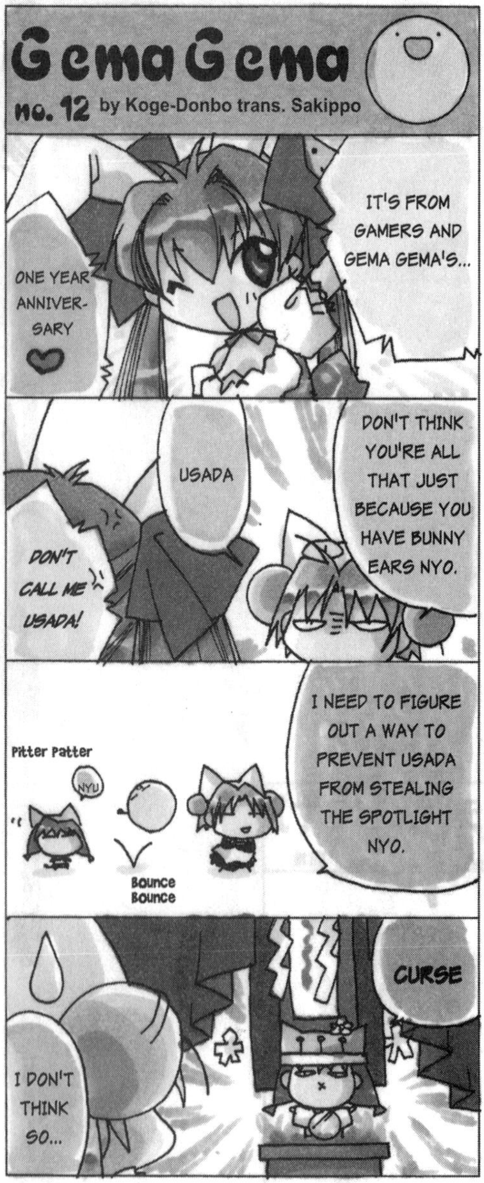
Gema Gema
no. 12 by Koge-Donbo trans. Sakippo
IT'S FROM GAMERS AND GEMA GEMA'S...
ONE YEAR ANNIVER-SARY
USADA
DON'T THINK YOU'RE ALL THAT JUST BECAUSE YOU HAVE BUNNY EARS NYO.
DON'T CALL ME USADA!
I NEED TO FIGURE OUT A WAY TO PREVENT USADA FROM STEALING THE SPOTLIGHT NYO.
Pitter Patter
NYU
Bounce Bounce
CURSE
I DON'T THINK SO...

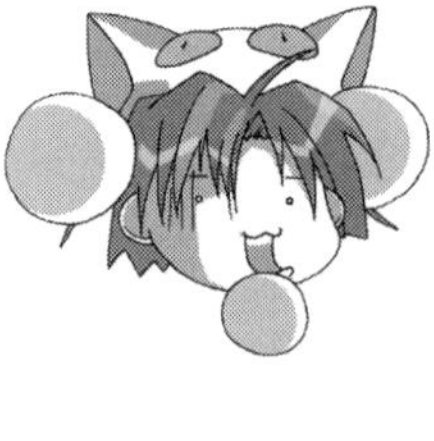

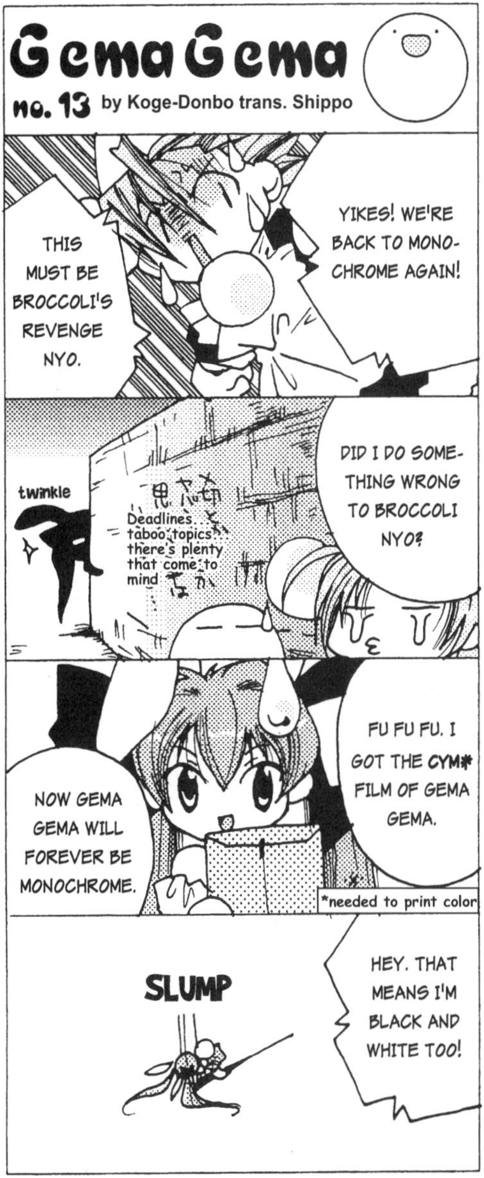
Gema Gema
no. 13 by Koge-Donbo trans. Shippo
YIKES! WE'RE BACK TO MONO-CHROME AGAIN!
THIS MUST BE BROCCOLI'S REVENGE NYO.
DID I DO SOME-THING WRONG TO BROCCOLI NYO?
Deadlines taboo topics there's plenty that come to mind
twinkle
FU FU FU. I GOT THE CYM* FILM OF GEMA GEMA.
NOW GEMA GEMA WILL FOREVER BE MONOCHROME.
*needed to print color
HEY. THAT MEANS I'M BLACK AND WHITE TOO!
SLUMP

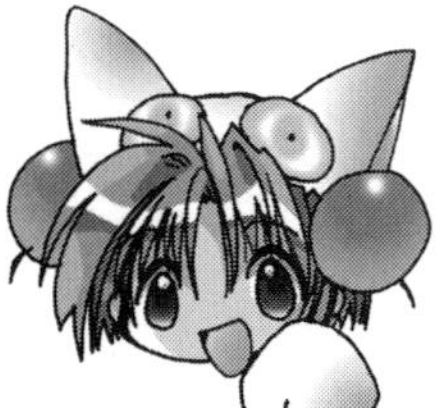

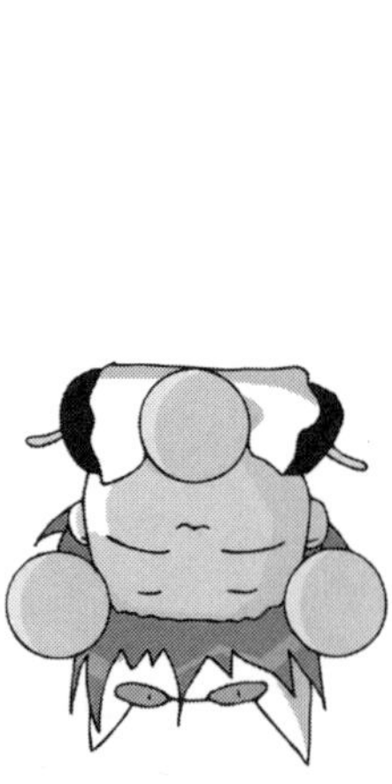

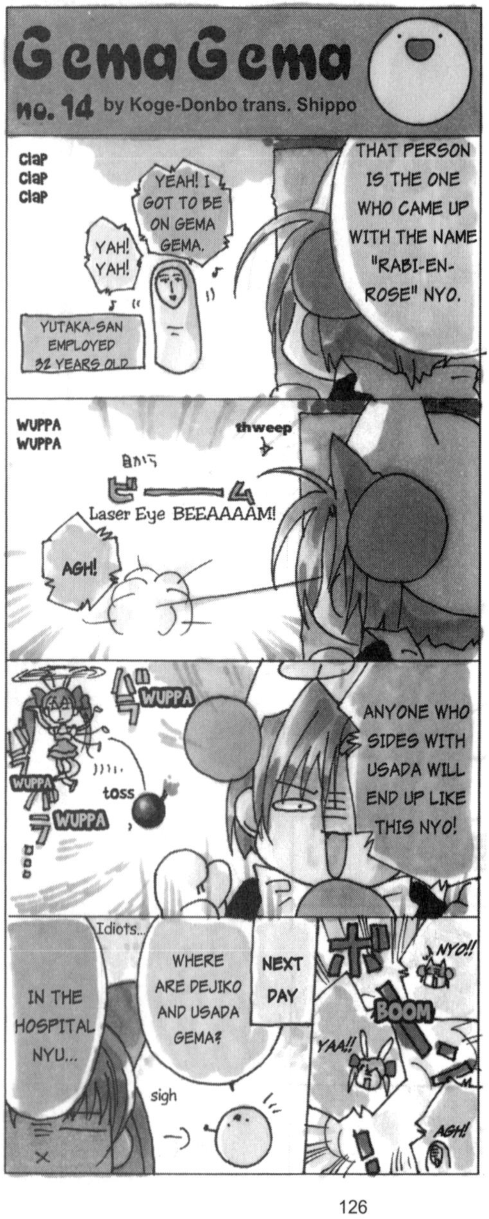
Gema Gema
no. 14 by Koge-Donbo trans. Shippo
THAT PERSON IS THE ONE WHO CAME UP WITH THE NAME "RABI-EN-ROSE" NYO.
YEAH! I GOT TO BE ON GEMA GEMA.
Clap Clap Clap
YAH! YAH!
YUTAKA-SAN EMPLOYED 32 YEARS OLD
thweep
WUPPA WUPPA
目から
ビーーーム
Laser Eye BEEAAAAM!
AGH!
ANYONE WHO SIDES WITH USADA WILL END UP LIKE THIS NYO!
WUPPA
WUPPA
toss
WUPPA
NYO!!
BOOM
YAA!!
AGH!
NEXT DAY
WHERE ARE DEJIKO AND USADA GEMA?
Idiots...
IN THE HOSPITAL NYU...
sigh

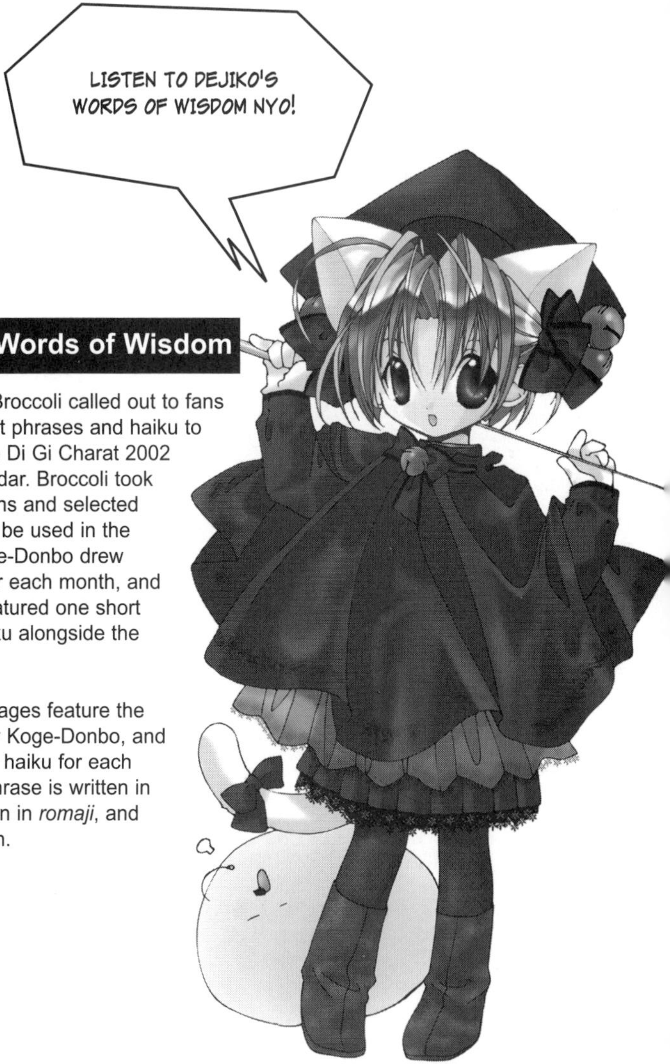
LISTEN TO DEJIKO'S WORDS OF WISDOM NYO!

Dejiko's Words of Wisdom

In Fall 2001, Broccoli called out to fans to submit short phrases and haiku to be used in the Di Gi Charat 2002 Weekly Calendar. Broccoli took the submissions and selected 52 phrases to be used in the calendar. Koge-Donbo drew illustrations for each month, and each week featured one short phrase or haiku alongside the illustration.

The next 12 pages feature the illustrations by Koge-Donbo, and one phrase or haiku for each month. The phrase is written in Japanese, then in *romaji*, and then in English.

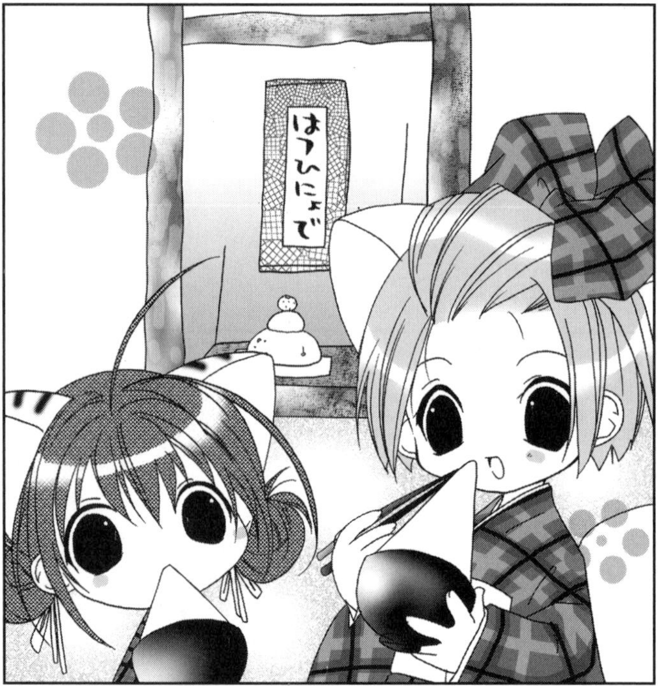
はつひにょで

January

でじこも歩けば　パンダ娘に当たる

Dejiko mo arukeba, panda musume ni ataru.

If Dejiko walks, she bumps into the Panda-girl.

By Nu-Pon

February

赤は止まれ 青は進め 黄色はゲマ

Aka wa tomare, Ao wa susume, Kiiro wa Gema.

Red is for stop. Green is for go. Yellow is for Gema.

By Usa-mimi Seibishi

March

Bゲマ団　みんな一緒に　悪の道
Black Gema Dan. Minna issho ni aku no michi.
Black Gema Gang. Together we can all follow the
path of evil.

By Kandagawa Ryuku

April

丸い生き物にも　五分の魂

Marui ikimono ni mo gobu no tamashii.

Even in round creatures, there is half a soul.

By Mr. Violence III

May

ほっけみりんは踊る　されど進まず

Hokke Mirin wa odoru, saredo susumazu.

Hokke Mirin dances, but doesn't move forward.

By Don't-Call-Me-Rabi~en~Rosebud

June

ヲの字取りが　ヲの字になる

O no Ji tori ga O no Ji ni naru.

Otaku-catcher becomes the Otaku.

By Tennai Kenko

July

ゲマはムカツクうちに打て

Gema wa mukatsuku uchi ni ute.

Hit Gema as soon as he pisses you off.

By Munek

August

ああ悲惨　目からビームが　直撃ゲマー

Aah hisan. Me kara beam ga chokugeki gema-.

Ah, the tragedy. Another Laser Eye Beam hit me gema.

By Kondo Ryuma

September

Bゲマ団　一日一悪　がんばるぴょ

Black Gema Dan. Ichi-nichi ichi-aku ganbaru pyo.

Black Gema Gang. An evil a day. I'll work hard, pyo.

By Kandagawa Ryuku

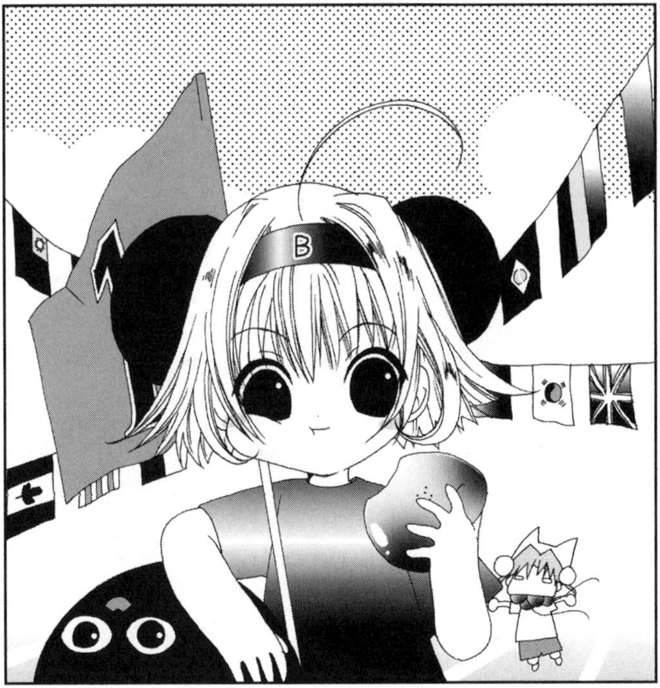
B

October

余り物はクウに食わすな

Amari-mono wa Coo ni kuwasuna.

Don't let Coo eat leftovers.

By Umiga

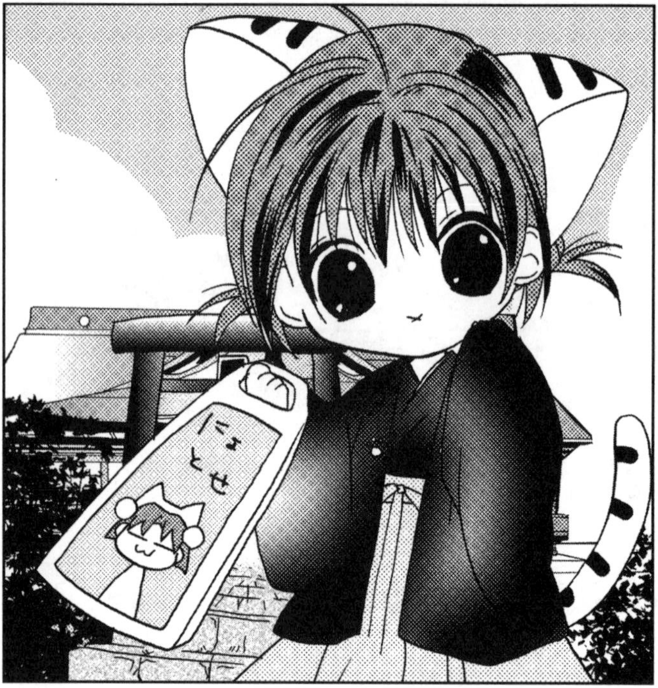
にょとせ

November

ぴょに交われば　黒くなる

Pyo ni majiwareba kuroku naru.

When you encounter the pyo, you become black.

By Narecchi Man'ei

December

急いてはグッズを買いそこねる

Seite wa goods wo kaisokoneru.

If you rush, you will miss buying some products.

By Yumesano☆Pa~shia

Interview with Koge-Donbo

This interview took place when Koge-Donbo visited the Los Angeles Anime Gamers store for an autograph session in July of 2002. Anime Gamers accepted submissions from Koge-Donbo fans worldwide, and randomly chose questions for Koge-Donbo to answer.

Please note that the information here is based on the time of the interview back in 2002.

From: Highlander
Age: 14
Cleveland, OH
Where did Hokke Mirin's name come from?
Hokke Mirin is a dish in Japan, and the cat I drew for the series looks like it, so that's where I got her name.

From: Deji Devil
Age: 17
Yokohama, Japan
If you were to compare yourself to an animal, what would you be?
Um, I don't know... Hamster? Some people say that I am like a hamster.

From: Mi-ke Neko Girl
Age: 24
Lancaster, CA
I heard that you started learning English, is this true?
Uh...No. I wish I can get better...

From: Hideki
Age: 31
Chicago, IL
Do you have any pets?
No, I don't. If I could have one, I would want a cat or a dog.

From: Sara Paulina Aramburo Vasquez
Age: 15
Guadalajara, Jalisco, Mexico
Who is your favorite character from Pita-Ten?
Hmm... I can't choose just one character; I like all of them. I have a bit of my personality and characteristic in each one.

From: kj1980
Age: 21
Los Angeles, CA
I heard that Saga (A Little Snow Fairy Sugar) was designed based on your childhood, but is this true?
Huh!? (Laughs). Um, I don't know where that came from, but no. I designed the characters by just imagining them up when I heard the character settings.

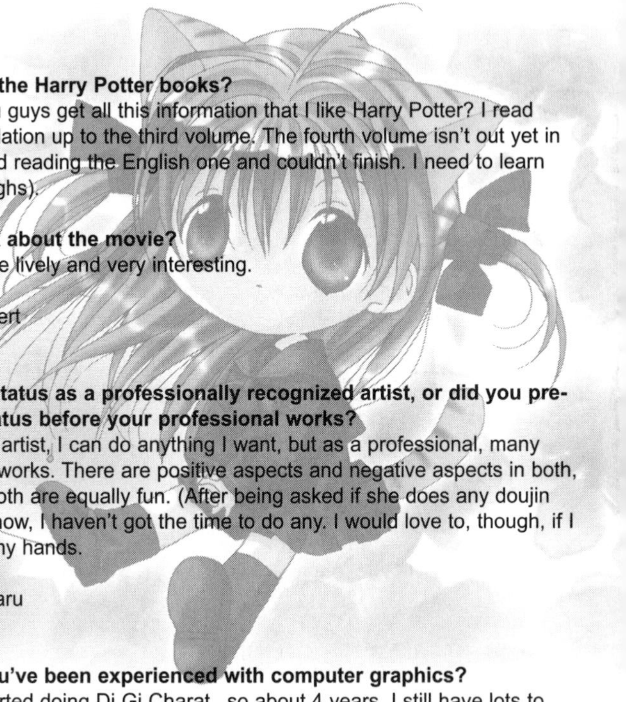

From: Polly
Age: 13
Seattle, WA
Have you read all the Harry Potter books?
Wow, where do you guys get all this information that I like Harry Potter? I read the Japanese translation up to the third volume. The fourth volume isn't out yet in translation, so I tried reading the English one and couldn't finish. I need to learn more English. (Laughs).

What do you think about the movie?
The characters were lively and very interesting.

From: Jesse Lampert
Age: 18
Richmond, VA
Do you like your status as a professionally recognized artist, or did you prefer your career status before your professional works?
Umm... As a doujin artist, I can do anything I want, but as a professional, many people will see my works. There are positive aspects and negative aspects in both, so I don't know... Both are equally fun. (After being asked if she does any doujin work lately). Right now, I haven't got the time to do any. I would love to, though, if I had more time on my hands.

From: Rinde Tsumaru
Age: 13
Sunnyvale, CA
How long have you've been experienced with computer graphics?
It's been since I started doing Di Gi Charat...so about 4 years. I still have lots to learn, though.

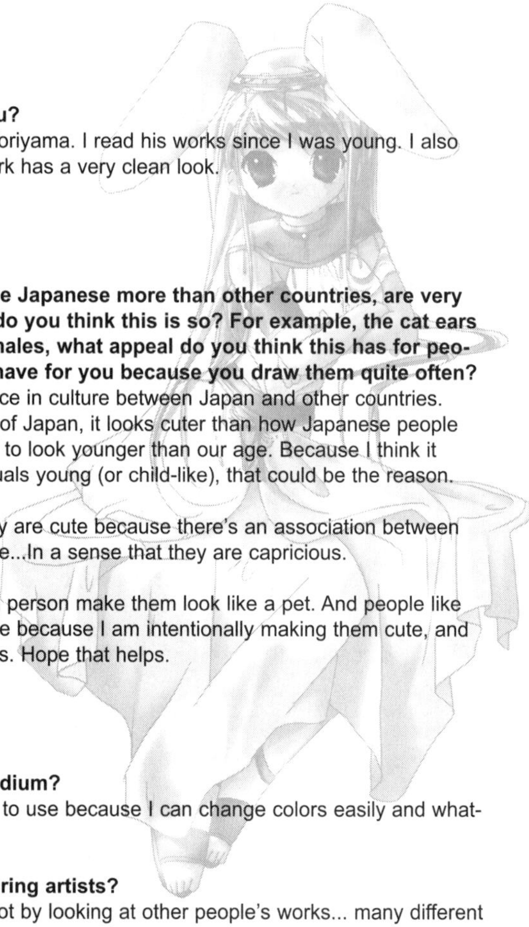

From: Neko Mimi Musume
Age: 20
Escondido, CA
Which artists influenced you?
I am a great big fan of Akira Toriyama. I read his works since I was young. I also like Fumiko Tanigawa; her work has a very clean look.

From: Shirong
Age: 19
Los Angeles, CA
Sometimes, it seems that the Japanese more than other countries, are very attached to cuteness. Why do you think this is so? For example, the cat ears drawn on females or even males, what appeal do you think this has for people, or what appeal does it have for you because you draw them quite often?
First of all, there's the difference in culture between Japan and other countries. Maybe for the people outside of Japan, it looks cuter than how Japanese people would see it because we tend to look younger than our age. Because I think it looks normal to us. If cute equals young (or child-like), that could be the reason.

As for the cat ears, I think they are cute because there's an association between cats and girls. Girls are cat-like...In a sense that they are capricious.

Also, I think that cat ears on a person make them look like a pet. And people like pets. I draw cat ears on people because I am intentionally making them cute, and Japanese people like cuteness. Hope that helps.

From: Chibi
Age: 18
Traverse City, MI
What is your favorite art medium?
The computer. It's the easiest to use because I can change colors easily and what-not.

Do you have advice for aspiring artists?
I think that you could learn a lot by looking at other people's works... many different kinds of work. Also, looking at other people's work can stimulate you, and I think that's important in improving your own art.

From: Eric
Age: 27
Davis, CA
What do you eat for breakfast?
Uh...I know it's bad for me, but I don't eat breakfast.

From: Chris
Age: 23
Los Angeles, CA
Have you ever based your designs on actual people?
Um... No. I usually get the basic concept in designing a new character, and leave it up to my imagination.

From: Maggie
Age: 23
Los Angeles, CA
Which episode of Di Gi Charat (anime) is your favorite?
I like all the episodes; it's hilarious. But if I had to choose one, I would pick the one with "De Pu Ra Ge Bou Pyo." (From "Di Gi Charat Summer Special 2001"). It was really, really funny. The part where Takeshi and Yoshimi are singing (talking) made me laugh so hard I started to cry.

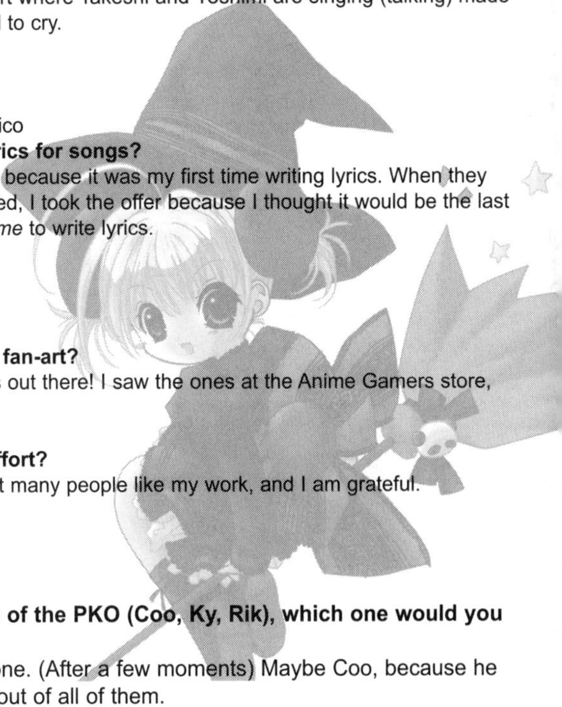

From: Cat Clan
Age: 21
Guadalajara, Jalisco, Mexico
Did you enjoy writing lyrics for songs?
Actually, it was really hard because it was my first time writing lyrics. When they asked me if I was interested, I took the offer because I thought it would be the last time someone would ask *me* to write lyrics.

From: Jesse Lampert
Age: 18
Richmond, VA
What is your opinion on fan-art?
There are really cute ones out there! I saw the ones at the Anime Gamers store, and I liked them a lot.

Do you appreciate the effort?
Yes, I do. It shows me that many people like my work, and I am grateful.

From: Kilt Boy
Age: 14
Manila, Philippines
If you were to date one of the PKO (Coo, Ky, Rik), which one would you choose?
Oh. ...Uh, that's a hard one. (After a few moments) Maybe Coo, because he seems the most normal out of all of them.

A History of Di Gi Charat

July 1998	A cat-eared character is featured as a small illustration in *From Gamers*, the monthly informational magazine passed out at Gamers.
August 1998	The character is featured in a 4-panel comic called "Gema Gema," and reveals herself as the "hybrid-cat-eared girl Di Gi Charat."
December 1998	Di Gi Charat is featured on the Broccoli New Year's card and officially becomes the mascot character of Gamers.
February 1999	Di Gi Charat gets her own section, "Dejiko's Room," on the Broccoli website.
	First CD "Welcome!" is released. (Sung by Hiroko Kato)
March 1999	An open audition is held to decide the voice actor for Di Gi Charat.
May 1999	Di Gi Charat voice audition finals are held in Roppongi Velfarre, and Asami Sanada is chosen.
June 1999	Rabi~en~Rose makes her first appearance in the "Gema Gema" comics.
July 1999	Petit Charat makes her first appearance in the "Gema Gema" comics.
	Di Gi Charat anime is announced at Tokyo Character Show.
October 1999	Di Gi Charat 1st Concert is held at the Roppongi Velfarre.
	Di Gi Charat radio show "Dejiko's Room" first airs.
	First album "Party Night" released.

The first incarnation of Di Gi Charat.

144

November 1999	"Di Gi Charat" anime is a featured animation in the "Wonderful" program (Tokyo Broadcasting Station).
	Various Di Gi Charat manga, including "Dejiko's Adventure" is serialized in magazines.
	Majin Gappa makes first appearance in the "Gema Gema" comics.
December 1999	CHOCOLA, the first Di Gi Charat art book, is released. It sells out in one week.
January 2000	Hokke Mirin makes her first appearance in the "Gema Gema" comics.
February 2000	Di Gi Charat Second Concert, "Valentine Concert," is held at the Roppongi Velfarre.
March 2000	Di Gi Charat DVD volume one released.
April 2000	Di Gi Charat Drama CD Box Gold Version is released, new character appears within the drama.
June 2000	Di Gi Charat Third Concert, "Dejiko's Party," is held at the Roppongi Velfarre.
	New character featured in Drama CD Box is named as "Pyocola Analogue III."
July 2000	Manga "Leave it to Piyoko!" is serialized.
August 2000	Di Gi Charat Festival is held at Ikebukuro Sunshine City.
September 2000	Di Gi Charat CD Box Black Version released, three new characters are announced within the drama.

October 2000	Di Gi Charat Fourth Concert held at the Roppongi Velfarre.
November 2000	Di Gi Charat Concert Tour held in a total of five major cities in Japan.
December 2000	Di Gi Charat art book CHOCOLA 2000 released.
Januray 2001	Di Gi Charat Festival held at Ikebukuro Sunshine.
March 2001	Di Gi Charat Concert in Yokohama Arena held.
May 2001	Di Gi Charat Festival in Tokyo Big Sight held.
July 2001	Audition held at Anime Expo 2001, where Karen Hsin is selected to sing the English version of "Welcome."
August 2001	Di Gi Charat Concert Climax held at the Roppongi Velfarre.
September 2001	Di Gi Charat Concert Tour 2001 is held in a total of five major cities in Japan.
	Anime Gamers, the USA branch of Gamers, opens in Los Angeles, California.
December 2001	Di Gi Charat Cruise & Dinner Show held in Symphony Cruise in Tokyo Bay.
	Di Gi Charat art book CHOCOLA 2001 released.
	"Di Gi Charat the Movie" released in theaters in Japan.
January 2002	"Panyo Panyo Di Gi Charat" airs as part of the program "Gamers Express."

February 2002	Di Gi Charat "Happy!" Valentine Concert held at the Roppongi Velfarre.
May 2002	Broccoli Carnival, a Di Gi Charat & Galaxy Angel joint concert, is held at the Roppongi Velfarre.
July 2002	Original concept and design artist Koge-Donbo visits the Anime Gamers store for an autograph session.
October 2002	Broccoli the Live, a Di Gi Charat & Galaxy Angel joint concert, is held at the Yokohama Arena.
December 2002	Di Gi Charat art book CHOCOLA 2002 released.
February 2003	Di Gi Charat "Smile" Valentine Concert held at the Roppongi Velfarre.
March 2003	Broccoli announces a new Di Gi Charat series, "Di Gi Charat Nyo" at Tokyo Big Sight.
April 2003	Synch-Point announces USA release of "Di Gi Charat the Movie" and "Leave it to Piyoko!"
June 2003	Di Gi Charat Concert "Welcome-nyo!" held at the Roppongi Velfarre.
July 2003	Di Gi Charat celebrates her fifth anniversary.
	Broccoli Books announces "Di Gi Charat Theater" English manga release.

A Close Look at Dejiko

Dejiko Brain
Klutzy, yet cunning (at least as much as a 10 year old can be). Always thinking about how to become an actress.

Dejiko Ears
Has the ability to not hear things that she doesn't want to hear. She is particularly quick to hear praise about herself.

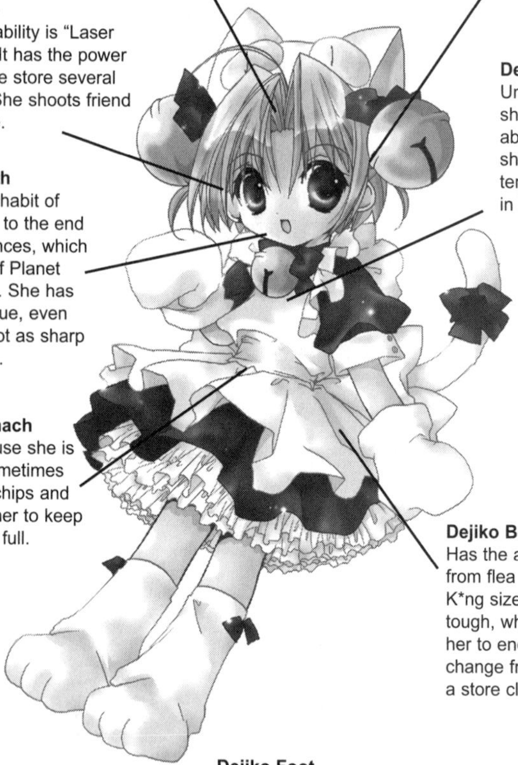

Dejiko Eyes
Her special ability is "Laser Eye Beam." It has the power to destroy the store several times over. She shoots friend and foe alike.

Dejiko Heart
Unique & confident, she rarely worries about others, but shows moments of tenderness. Madly in love with Iori.

Dejiko Mouth
She has the habit of adding "nyo" to the end of her sentences, which is a dialect of Planet Di Gi Charat. She has a sharp tongue, even though it's not as sharp as Puchiko's.

Dejiko Stomach
Black. Because she is poor, she sometimes eats potato chips and soda for dinner to keep her stomach full.

Dejiko Body
Has the ability to change from flea size to King K*ng size. She's also very tough, which has allowed her to endure the big change from a princess to a store clerk.

Dejiko Foot
Has a powerful kick. Judging by her choice of hiking to go on a picnic, she does like to exercise.

A Close Look at Rabi~en~Rose

Rabi Brain
Basically the straight-man among Dejiko and gang. She likes to hide the fact that she is poor, and is embarrassed about her real name. She is an honor student at school.

Rabi Eyes
Near-sighted. She usually wears black-rimmed glasses. When she transforms into Rabi-en-Rose, she wears contacts.

Rabi Ears
She can fly by turning the bunny ears really fast and making them into a helicopter. In the anime, she has the ability to move her ears at will.

Rabi Mouth
She is very polite to customers, using formal language. When she talks to Dejiko, she shows her real emotions.

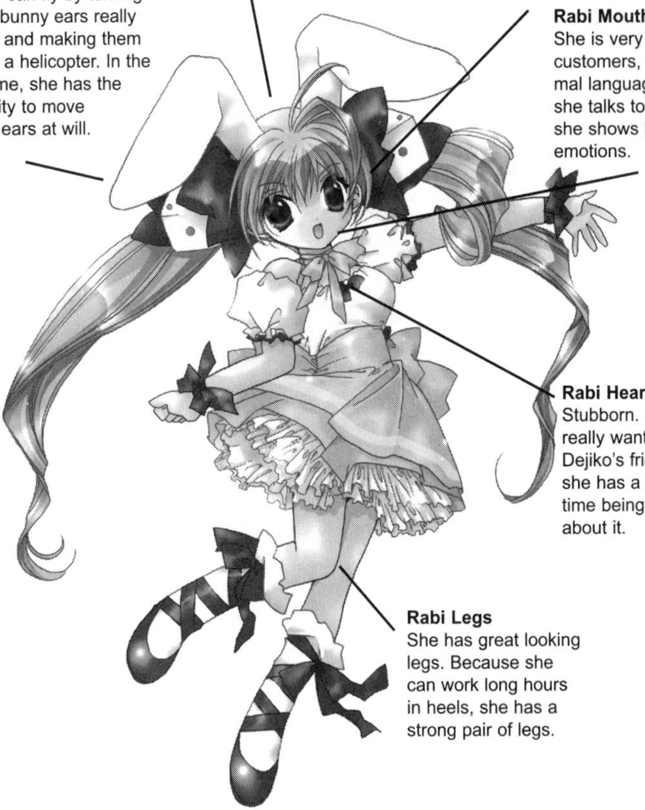

Rabi Heart
Stubborn. She really wants to be Dejiko's friend, but she has a hard time being honest about it.

Rabi Legs
She has great looking legs. Because she can work long hours in heels, she has a strong pair of legs.

A Close Look at Puchiko

Puchiko Brain
She looks like she isn't thinking much, but based on her sharp wit and tongue, her head is constantly churning out thoughts.

Puchiko Eyes
Currently practicing "Laser Eye Beam." But all that comes out is water, smoke, and unidentifiable objects. But every once in a while, she succeeds.

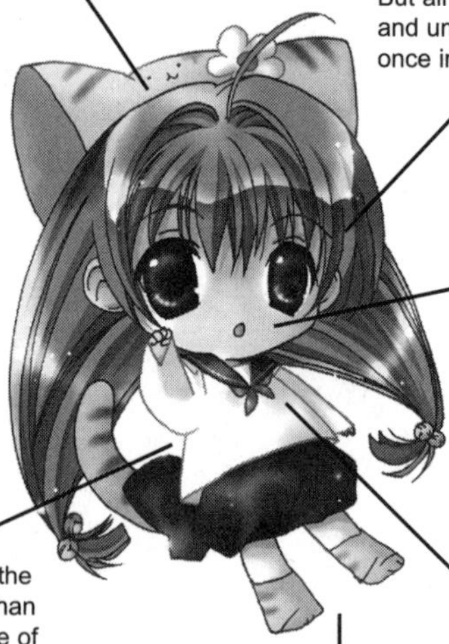

Puchiko Mouth
Sharp tongue. She doesn't talk much, but when she speaks, she causes big damage. She ends her sentences with "nyu."

Puchiko Body
Like Dejiko, she has the ability to grow taller than a building. In the case of Puchiko, her size increases when she's sleepy.

Puchiko Heart
She is unhappy that others don't trust her to do things on her own due to her size. She does not want to be treated as a child.

Puchiko Feet
She is not very fast when walking or running. She doesn't seem to like to stand, and is always sitting on Gema.

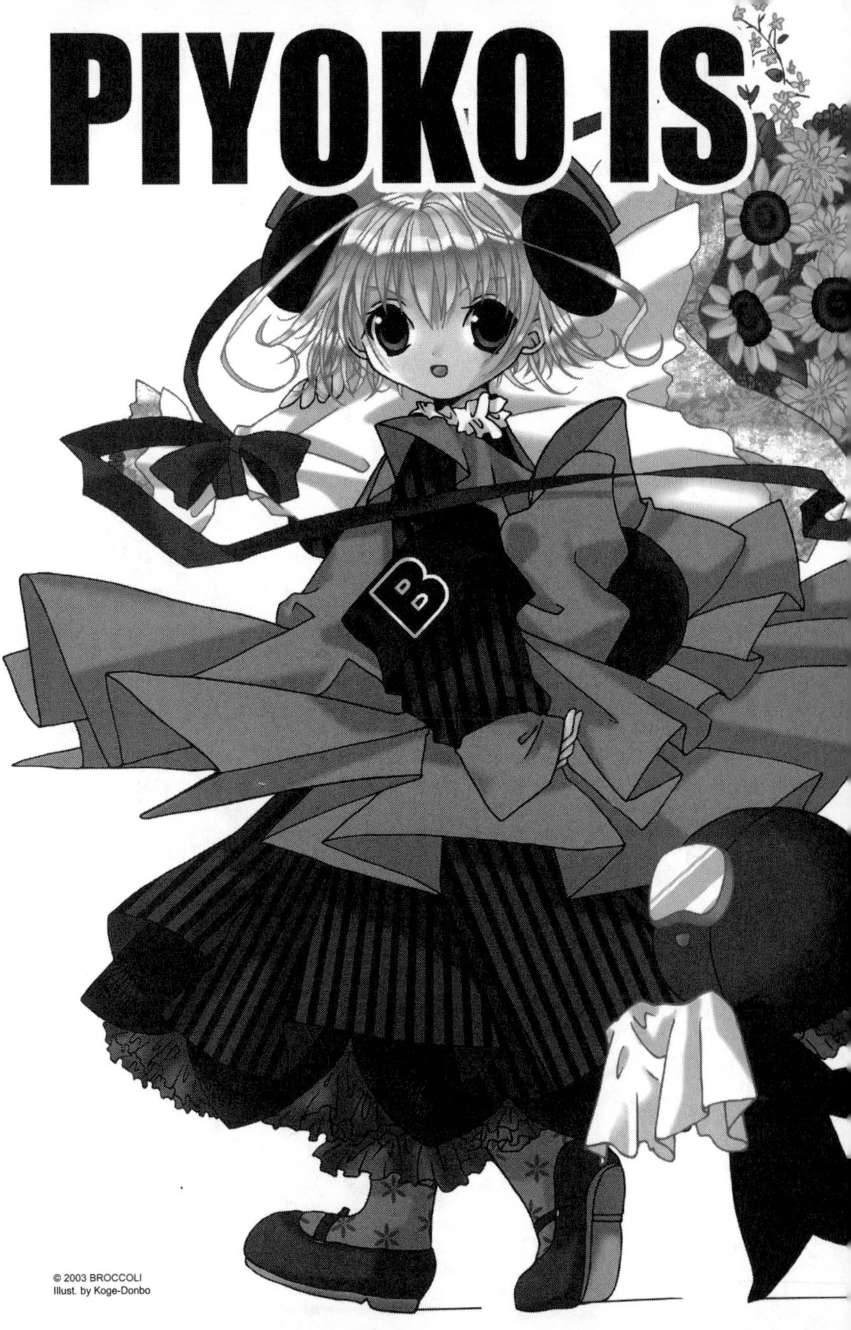
PIYOKO-IS

Get Ready for Adventure!

Only Dejiko and her friends can save the Gamers store!

Di Gi Charat Theater
Dejiko's Adventure

by Yuki Kiriga

brought to you by
BROCCOLI BOOKS

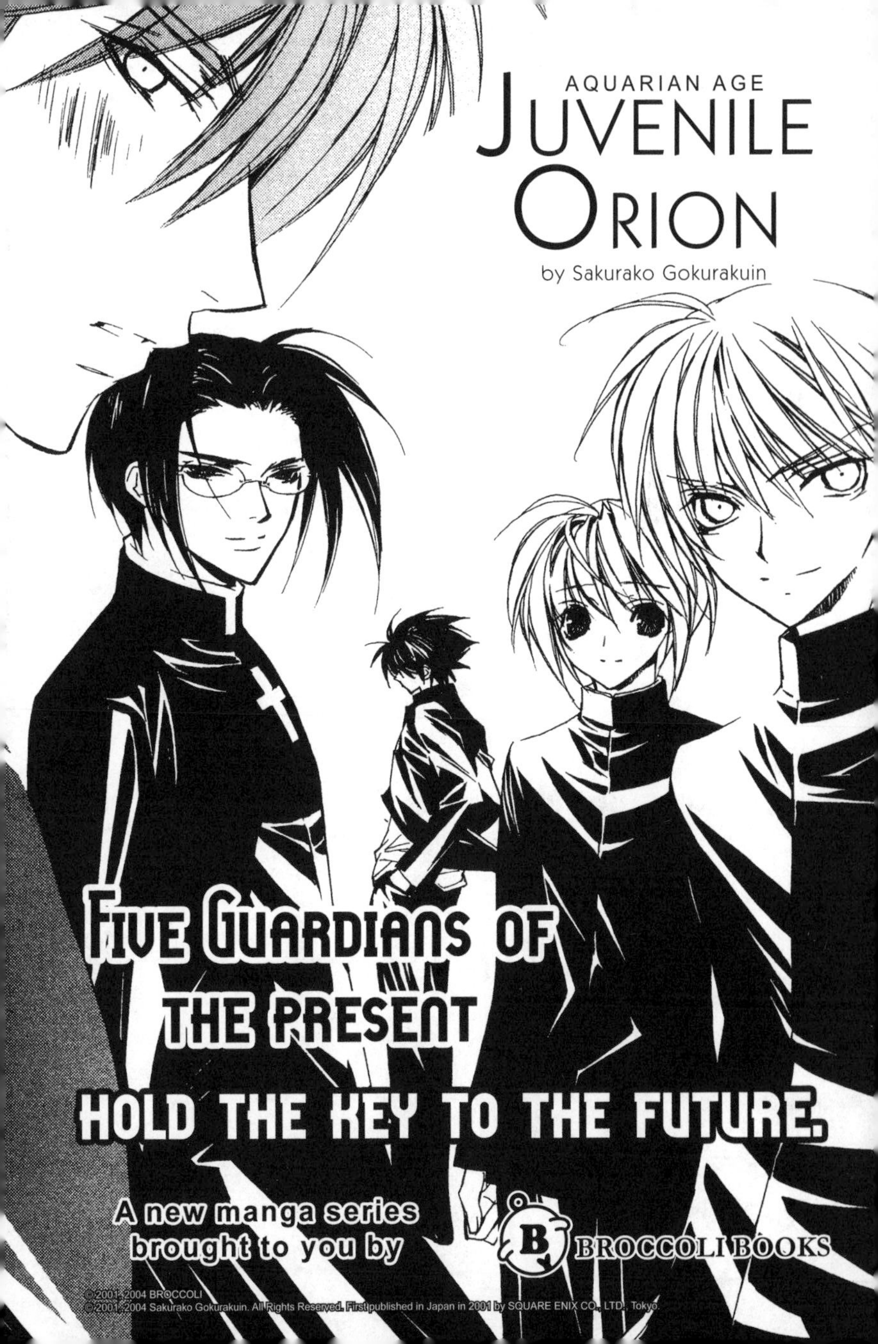
AQUARIAN AGE
JUVENILE ORION
by Sakurako Gokurakuin
FIVE GUARDIANS OF THE PRESENT
HOLD THE KEY TO THE FUTURE.
A new manga series brought to you by
BROCCOLI BOOKS
© 2001, 2004 BROCCOLI
© 2001, 2004 Sakurako Gokurakuin. All Rights Reserved. First published in Japan in 2001 by SQUARE ENIX CO., LTD., Tokyo.

FIVE ANGELS

AT YOUR SERVICE!

When the going gets tough...
the tough get Angels!

Galaxy Angel
by Kanan

It's up to five lovely females, each
possessing a unique specialty, to
protect the young Prince Shiva and
save the universe!

A new manga series
brought to you by

BROCCOLI BOOKS

READ :: POINT :: CLICK .:

broccolibooks.com

After reading some Broccoli Books manga, why not look for more on the web?
Discuss with other fans in the forums, check the production staff blog and MORE!

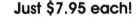

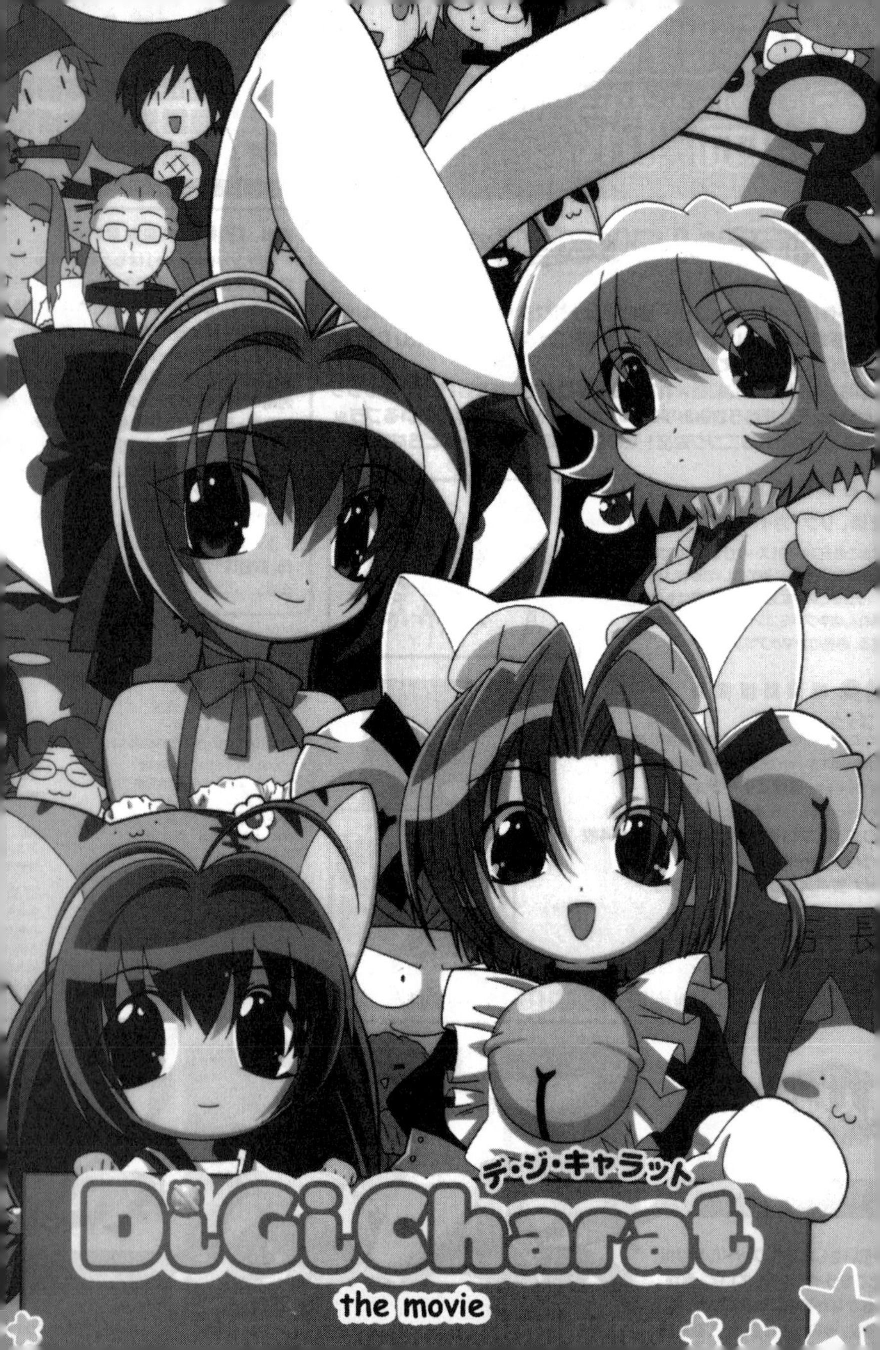
デ・ジ・キャラット
DiGiCharat
the movie

A grand adventure
of epic proportions!
(sort of)

In this animated movie, Dejiko decides to go back home to see her father and mother. But the trip back home will be a long one, especially with the Black Gema Gema Gang getting in the way! Will Dejiko, Puchiko, and Rabi~en~Rose make it safely to Planet Di Gi Charat?

Directed by the original director Hiroaki Sakurai. Screenplay by Mamiko Ikeda. Animated by MADHOUSE.

Bonus features include:
  - Informational booklet with translation notes and more!
  - A bonus episode featuring the Black Gema Gema Gang!
  - More Gema Gema comics!
  - ...and much, much more!!!

COMING SOON TO DVD!!

Brought to you by

Synch-Point

www.synch-point.com

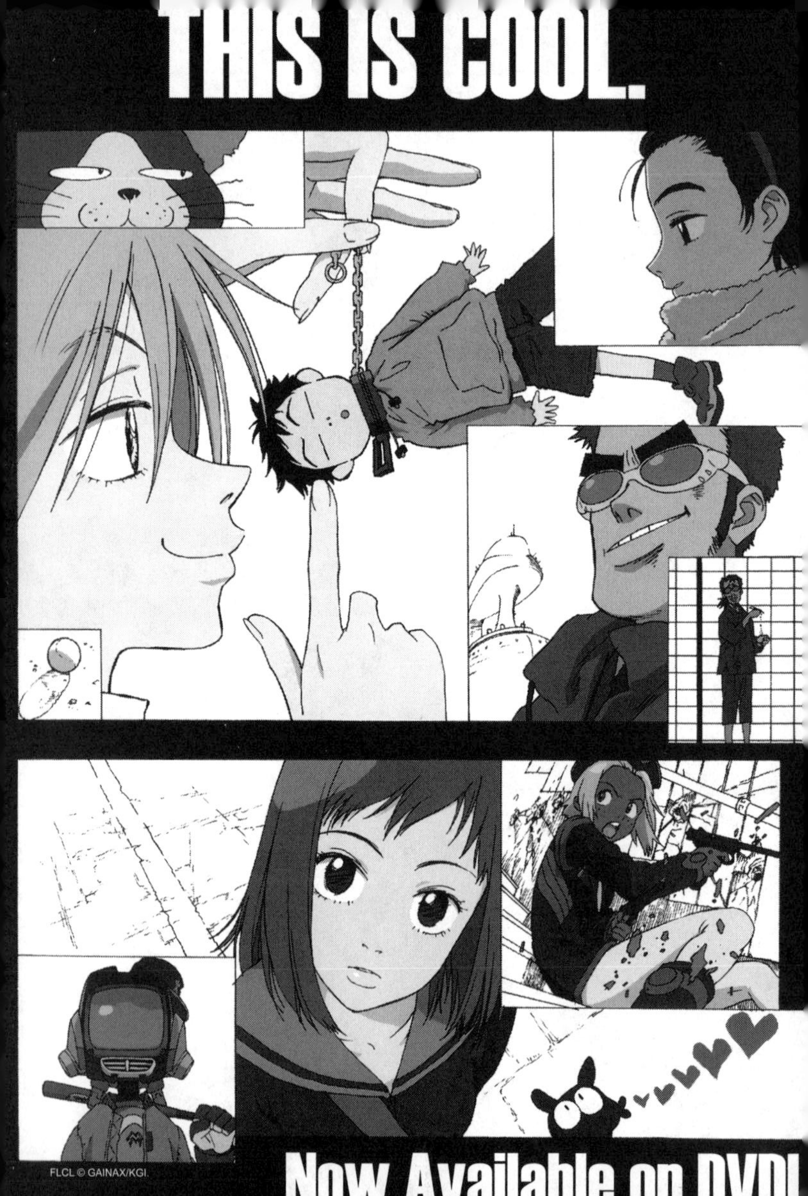
THIS IS COOL.
FLCL © GAINAX/KGI.
Now Available on DVD!

YOU'RE READING THE WRONG WAY!

This is the end of the book! In Japan, manga is generally read from right to left. All reading starts on the upper right corner, and ends on the lower left. American comics are generally read from left to right, starting on the upper left of each page. In order to preserve the true nature of the work, we printed this book in a right to left fashion. Those who are unfamiliar with manga may find this confusing at first, but once you start getting into the story, you will wonder how you ever read manga any other way!